*The*

# NECESSARY
# JOURNEY

*The*

# NECESSARY JOURNEY

## MAKING REAL PROGRESS ON EQUITY AND INCLUSION

## ELLA F. WASHINGTON

Harvard Business Review Press

Boston, Massachusetts

The web addresses referenced in this book were live and correct at the time of the book's publication but may be subject to change.

Library of Congress Cataloging-in-Publication Data

Names: Washington, Ella F., author.
Title: The necessary journey : making real progress on equity and inclusion / Ella F. Washington.
Description: Boston, Massachusetts : Harvard Business School Press, [2022] | Includes index. |
Identifiers: LCCN 2022021837 (print) | LCCN 2022021838 (ebook) | ISBN 9781647821289 (hardcover) |
    ISBN 9781647821296 (epub)
Subjects: LCSH: Diversity in the workplace—Case studies. | Social justice—Case studies. |
    Organizational learning—Case studies. | Equality—Case studies. | Industrial management—
    Case studies.
Classification: LCC HF5549.5.M5 W375 2022 (print) | LCC HF5549.5.M5 (ebook) | DDC 658.3008—
    dc23/eng/20220801
LC record available at https://lccn.loc.gov/2022021837
LC ebook record available at https://lccn.loc.gov/2022021838
ISBN: 978-1-64782-128-9
eISBN: 978-1-64782-129-6

The paper used in this publication meets the requirements of the American National Standard for Permanence of Paper for Publications and Documents in Libraries and Archives Z39.48-1992.

# CONTENTS

Contents

*The*

# NECESSARY
# JOURNEY

# Hope through Stories

The rumbling of helicopters swarming through the night, every night for almost a week, is a sound that I will never forget. On one of those nights, I was sitting at my desk grading papers, but I gave up, unable to concentrate because of the chopping and whipping sound of the copters' rotors. Police presence had increased everywhere. Restaurants were boarded up. Curfew was 7 p.m. And all this was just piled on top of the alternative reality we'd been living through because of the pandemic. I'd spent months tracking toilet paper deliveries to stores that ran out in minutes, seeing empty aisles at the grocery stores, being physically isolated from my family and friends in an effort to remain safe. I vividly remember asking myself, "Where am I?" I was not in a war-torn country experiencing a civil war, or was I? Technically, I was at home in Washington, DC. The nation's capital and the country as a whole were on edge. George Floyd had been murdered. Silence was not an option for so many Black Americans and our allies globally.

To be honest, though, I was curious and a little bewildered by the unmistakable shift I saw happening in the deeply unsettling moment. I noticed how companies were responding to Floyd's murder. They were making bold statements, denouncing White supremacy, and pledging millions of dollars to racial justice.

I was confused by what I was witnessing, because I had been doing the work of diversity, equity, and inclusion (DEI) for my entire career, and there had been many previous moments of tragedy for people of historically marginalized identities. These incidents included the murder of seventeen-year-old Trayvon Martin, a Black child, in 2012; the Pulse nightclub shooting (an attack on the LGBTQ+ community in Orlando, Florida) in 2016; and the White supremacist rally in Charlottesville, Virginia, in 2017. Sadly, the list goes on. Yet, this summer, this murder became different from the rest. For the first time, businesses were being vocal about social injustices in a way that those of us working in the DEI space had never seen before. On the Friday after Floyd's murder, I got a text from my longtime mentor and friend Laura Morgan Roberts telling me that it was time for us to speak out. She asked me if I wanted to write an article with her, on a forty-eight-hour turnaround time. I emphatically agreed, and together we penned a plea to businesses in an HBR piece published on June 1, 2020: "U.S. Businesses Must Take Meaningful Action Against Racism." We did not want this occasion to be another moment that would be quickly forgotten in the next news cycle. Instead, we saw it as an opportunity for businesses to finally get serious about DEI.

At the time, there was an extreme lack of transparency about DEI across organizations. Only 4 percent of public companies disclosed basic diversity information from their EEO-1 reports (US Equal Employment Opportunity Commission reports, requiring, among other information, a company's demographic workforce data on "race/ethnicity, sex and job categories").[1] Even fewer companies made their annual diversity reports publicly available. But I could tell that something was changing in this moment.

I spoke with countless CEOs and chief human resource officers in the months that followed the Floyd tragedy, and the conversations fell into a predictable pattern. First, the leader would express deep concern and talk about the programs the company had in place. Almost always they would fixate on the programs. Are they the right ones? What other programs could they institute? Everything was focused on execution. Programs are not a bad thing, but there's more to DEI than programs. I would explain to these leaders that DEI is a journey. It includes creating programs, yes, but also making cultural changes, finding new ways to influence people, making difficult decisions, and more.

Over the years, many have used the concept of a journey to describe DEI efforts, yet it was often used as a catchall phrase: "DEI is a journey." Quite frankly, most people struggled to define what the journey actually means.

Think of standing on a ledge above an expansive stretch of land, full of thick forests, rushing rivers, open fields, hills. On the other side is your destination. You can't even tell how far it is. You're going to journey across. You figure out where you are starting from in relation to where you want to go. There will be obstacles, mistakes, places where things slow you down. People may give up along the way. You will have to change paths. Weather will affect your journey. But if you are committed to your destination, you navigate, persist, and keep going until you get there.

This is what DEI is like. You don't just deploy a program and call it a day. You look out, find a starting point that aims at your destination, set out on a journey, deal with what comes at you, and adjust along the way.

Most leaders were receptive to this idea as I explained it and, as leaders do, still wanted to define what the DEI journey meant to them. There were two questions that every leader nervously asked me by the end of our first conversation:

- Where are we on this DEI journey?

- How do we compare with other companies on the journey?

It became abundantly clear that each organization I talked to was struggling to visualize its DEI journey. Yes, a few organizations had been sharing their journey for years, but they were often seen as anomalies or organizations with unlimited resources, so other leaders had a hard time seeing themselves imitating or borrowing on the wisdom from those journeys.

What's more, the harder reality to share with these leaders was that there is no one-size-fits-all solution for DEI; each organization needed to take an intentional, nuanced approach to defining its path forward. This observation often left them even more frustrated about where to start if there was no one way that everyone should start. They're up on that ledge looking at the expanse they need to cross, and they are not even sure of how they should enter. Or even more terrifying, they worry that when they do enter, they might never reach their goal.

I asked myself, "How could organizations make progress on DEI if they could not see a clear path forward?" And that's what motivated me to write *The Necessary Journey*. To help leaders, I decided to write a book that would profile organizations that are on their journey. I wanted to demystify what DEI is about and bring the journey to life—the struggles, the mistakes, the successes. I wanted to include big companies and small, tech, health care, and even a small distillery. While every story here will help leaders see and understand what companies do on their necessary journeys, each story is meant to highlight a particular aspect of the journey that's different from the others. You'll see themes across these stories, but each one brings something unique.

In the end, this book is my effort to answer those two questions for leaders: Where are we on the journey, and how do we compare with others? And I aim to do it in a way that will resonate with people: through stories.

## A Story-Driven Approach

*I'm writing my story so that others might see fragments of themselves.*

—Lena Waithe, screenwriter and producer

I have written this book deliberately as a series of narratives because I believe in their power to inspire and teach. Stories are a compelling tool, perhaps the most powerful one, to connect the human experience. They allow us to feel, learn, shift perspectives, and, in the best cases, spur action. But I'm not relying on stories alone. Though each chapter is a narrative, my approach marries what we know from forty-plus years of academic research on DEI with the practical lessons I have learned in my work helping hundreds of companies on their DEI journeys. I hope that you will see yourselves in the stories presented here and that these stories will enlighten organizations on their own journeys.

I also hope that this story-driven approach brings a unique perspective on DEI and will complement the many excellent books that take a framework-driven or how-to approach to the topic. Those books are invaluable, but so too is a story-driven book, especially because leaders need to visualize themselves taking this journey. There's no better way to create that positive image than to see others doing it.

Each chapter in this book explores a different company's DEI journey, including where the company started, where it struggled, and where its journey is going. I researched each company to understand the eternal perspective of their journey, but the core of this book comes from the intimate personal interviews I conducted with each leader via video chat. The quotes you will read are from these candid and courageous interviews. I hope that by sharing these stories, I will inspire you and help you navigate your own journey.

## My Own Necessary Journey

Every company and leader featured in this book is taking their own path on their necessary journey. My own nontraditional professional journey has taught me the power of understanding the individual paths that lead us to where we are today and help us to get to where we want to be. Early during my PhD program in organizational behavior at Northwestern University, I realized I did not fit in with my peers. It was not because I was a Black woman in a predominantly White and male academy. That was a challenge, of course, but my exclusion was driven by my knowledge early on that I wanted to actually help organizations on the front line with their DEI challenges instead of only researching and writing about it from the ivory tower.

In one of my first-year seminar classes, I remember reading an in-depth experimental paper that used a sample of undergraduates as its subjects. I asked the professor how that sample was relevant to the way managers in organizations actually lead. I will never forget his answer: "We do not care much about that; we care about the research." As a student in a business school and with my background in finance, I was deeply confused by this answer and wondered if I had made a mistake by enrolling. Still, I was discouraged from telling anyone that I did not want to become a tenure-track professor and instead wanted to work in the industry. I was told by one professor that if I ever wanted to graduate with a PhD, I must pretend to be like everyone else until the very moment I earned my degree; then I could go off and get whatever job I wanted.

Every day at school, I felt a deep sense of cognitive dissonance. Why, as business school scholars, didn't we make more of an effort to connect with what was happening in the business world? Why was it *discouraged*?

I pledged to spend my career closing that gap between academic and practitioner worlds in any way I could. My journey didn't come without difficulty. I felt ostracized from the academy when I took a job consulting with EY.

Yet now, after more than a decade, I feel some vindication. I've closed the gap and married the valuable academic discipline with real-world application, having consulted with hundreds of global firms, developed a global DEI practice at the Gallup organization, and now running my own DEI consulting firm. The research informs the practice, and vice versa.

And I am glad to report that things have changed in the academy. Years after those first uncomfortable moments at Northwestern, my journey came full circle as my practical experience was deeply valued and I was welcomed on the faculty of Georgetown University's Mc-Donough School of Business as a professor of the practice, where I enjoy teaching scholars and practitioners today.

My own journey mirrors the themes of the organizations highlighted in this book. It has not been a straight path. It has not looked like anyone else's. It has been filled with doubt, frustration, and success and has been wonderfully gratifying and worth the ups and downs. It wasn't easy, but I never, ever considered it optional. It was always necessary.

# DEI in Context

Before I tell the stories, it will help you, the reader, to understand the history of DEI as a concept and discipline. I'll keep this brief, but knowing the roots of the ideas will help set the context for the stories told here, some of which started back in the 1980s or 1990s.

Although the wave of attention to DEI in 2020 was new to many, the reality is that *diversity management* (as it was originally termed in the 1980s) has been studied for more than forty years. Foundations were laid during the civil rights movement of the 1950s and 1960s. President John F. Kennedy's 1961 Executive Order 10925 required federal contractors to take "affirmative action" to end discrimination. Affirmative action is defined as "any measure, beyond simple termination of a discriminatory practice, adopted to correct or compensate for past or present discrimination or to prevent discrimination from recurring in the future."[2]

Title II of the Civil Rights Act of 1964 made it illegal for employers with more than fifteen employees to discriminate in hiring, termination, promotion, compensation, job training, or any other term, condition, or privilege of employment on the basis of race, color, religion, sex, or national origin.[3] The act also created the US Equal Employment Opportunity Commission (EEOC) to enforce the law and eliminate unlawful employment discrimination.[4] Since its enactment, Title II has been expanded to outlaw discrimination based on pregnancy, and in June 2020 the Supreme Court extended protections to include sexual orientation and gender identity.[5]

Affirmative action was met with required compliance but also opposition. The policy was historically criticized as constituting reverse discrimination, giving preferential treatment, stigmatizing beneficiaries, and undermining principles of merit.[6] Not everyone opposed it, however. Some employers began to identify the ethical, moral, and business cases for affirmative action and led aggressive plans in support of it. Xerox, for example, embraced affirmative action. In a groundbreaking effort in 1968, Chairman Joseph C. Wilson wrote a letter to all Xerox managers, calling for increased hiring of African Americans.[7] That same year, the company formed the first employee resource groups (ERGs).

In the 1980s President Ronald Reagan curtailed enforcement of affirmative action and publicly expressed his opposition.[8] Nevertheless, many prominent employers said that they would continue their EEO/affirmative action programs, regardless of whether government policy changed. A 1985 study of *Fortune* 500 companies, prompted by the proposed changes to affirmative action requirements and Executive Order 11246, found that more than 95 percent intended to "continue to use numerical objectives to track the progress of women and minorities in their corporations, regardless of government requirements."[9] A year later, a similar *Fortune* 500 survey found that 88 percent of the companies planned to make no changes to their affirmative action plans and 12 percent planned to increase their affirmative action efforts in 1987.[10]

To follow through on affirmative action meant companies needed structure, and it came in the form of what was then called *diversity management*. This structure sprang to life after a 1987 study commissioned by the secretary of labor, William Brock. The study was designed to understand the labor and economic trends that would shape the last years of the twentieth century and keep America competitive in the global marketplace moving into the twenty-first century.[11] The Hudson Institute developed the report, Workforce 2000, by conducting the biggest corporate study on record, surveying 645 companies.[12] It forecast a decline in the labor share of White men and predicted that 85 percent of all new job entrants by the year 2000 would be minorities and women.

The report also made it clear that the US workforce of the future would become increasingly diverse and would need to grapple with multiple dimensions of diversity. These issues would include an aging workforce, the needs of women to work and care for families, and the full integration of Black and Hispanic workers into the workforce. Other concerns were how to improve worker education and skills to offset the decline of manufacturing jobs and to meet the increased need for technical and professional workers.[13] In an official statement, President Reagan addressed these future workforce issues: "The Department of Labor's Workforce 2000 study indicates a continuing vital need for job skills training. . . . This situation may afford unique opportunities for people from groups that historically have not entered the labor market."[14]

It was a shocking finding at the time. Workforce 2000 is credited with creating a major shift in how businesses thought about the future workforce composition and the need for workforce diversity initiatives.[15] Before the study, diversity was a compliance exercise; many programs focused on helping women and minorities assimilate into White male workforce cultures.[16] But after the report, policy and compliance suddenly didn't matter as much to companies. Instead, they needed diversity management to deal with what looked like a demographic reality. Diversity efforts were wrapped up in business survival, as Roosevelt Thomas Jr., a pioneer of diversity in the workplace, said in a 1990 essay in *Harvard Business Review*:

> Affirmative action had an essential role to play and played it very well. In many companies and communities, it still plays that role. But affirmative action is an artificial, transitional intervention intended to give managers a chance to correct an imbalance, an injustice, a mistake. Once the numbers mistake has been corrected, I don't think affirmative action alone can

cope with the remaining long-term task of creating a work setting geared to the upward mobility of all kinds of people, including white males. . . .

And that is precisely why we have to learn to manage diversity—to move beyond affirmative action, not to repudiate it.[17]

Thus diversity management was born. It spawned academic research on the outcomes of diverse teams (results included increased creativity and better problem-solving) and the psychological aspects required for diverse teams to truly maximize their potential.

By the beginning of the twenty-first century, there was a perception that the position of marginalized groups in the workplace had vastly improved. For example, in the first decade of this new century, talk focused on the US entrance into a post-racial era with the election of the first Black president, Barack Obama, in 2008. There was also a sense that women's equality had been achieved with greater numbers of women advancing to leadership positions. In 2010 women held 14.4 percent of executive officer positions at *Fortune* 500 companies and 7.6 percent of top earner positions, and more than two-thirds of companies had at least one female executive officer.[18]

Yet there's often a mismatch between media rhetoric and the realities of the lived experiences of marginalized groups. Despite the overall gains, the reality of the early twenty-first century was similar to what it is today: White men, who make up 35 percent of the US population, continue to be overrepresented as the dominant group in the corporate world. In 2000 some 96.4 percent of *Fortune* 500 CEO positions were White men; twenty years later, they held 85.8 percent.[19] Diversity management efforts early in this century seemed to have increased diversity at the bottom of organizations in entry-level positions, but the number of women and minorities drastically dwindled as you looked at the higher levels of the organizational chart. Sadly, that distribution still holds today.

Diversity management initiatives had largely focused on increasing demographic diversity but neglected to focus on the cultural elements needed to support a diverse environment. Further, many of the early corporate efforts focused on sensitivity training and failed to integrate diversity in other business processes and activities.[20]

The term *inclusion* gained popularity beginning around 2000 to signal the importance of creating environments where everyone could thrive, not just survive, in a culture that wasn't theirs. Organizations began to rename their diversity efforts as *diversity and inclusion*, or D&I. In the 2010s some organizations started adding *equity* to their lexicon to acknowledge that systemic changes to processes and policies were also needed to create an equitable environment for all. By the end of 2020, many companies had shifted to, or were at least considering, adding equity to their diversity efforts. D&I was becoming DEI.

Today, the most common terminology is *diversity, equity,* and *inclusion*—DEI. However, other terms, such as *belonging, justice, engagement,* and *racial equity,* have been integrated into the dialogue, and many companies have chosen to rename their DEI efforts with some configuration of these terms. Many are still parsing the difference between DEI and DEJ (diversity, equity, and justice) efforts, for example. Yet words must mean something. An organization adds little to its cause if it changes its terminology without attaching specific meaning and action to the words. From a practitioner perspective, I encourage companies to use the terminology that will speak most to their internal and external stakeholders. In this book, I use either DEI or whatever term the company itself uses. But no matter which words are used, leaders must be clear on the expected behaviors, activities, and outcomes these terms reflect. I too must be clear. So, in this book, I use the following general definitions:

> *Diversity:* people's real or perceived differences that affect their interactions and relationships. This definition encompasses all types of diversity, not just demographic diversity.

> *Equity:* the quality of being fair and impartial with the understanding that all members of society are not starting from the same place of equality and that, consequently, there must be systematic changes that create opportunities for everyone to succeed.

> *Inclusion:* the active creation of environments where everyone can succeed *and* where people experience the emotional outcome of feeling valued, welcomed, respected, and supported. Both factors, the doing and the feeling, the act and the outcome, are crucial to creating real inclusion.

In the preceding history of DEI, I largely focused on corporate efforts in the United States. However, DEI is global, and the lens by which it is approached largely depends on the history, statutes, and cultural contexts of each country. For example, in the United States, DEI arose from the civil rights movement and thus has largely focused on race and gender. In other countries, such as India, issues of social hierarchy through the caste system have been at the forefront of DEI.[21] In Europe, citizenship and immigration status have been at the center; for example, many studies of organizational performance in Europe have focused on the impact of immigrant team members.[22] In places like Saudi Arabia, issues of women's rights under the male guardianship system are core to DEI efforts.[23]

Global companies have struggled with having a cohesive DEI strategy that incorporates local nuance. Further, employees looking to connect with their global team members often lack the cultural competence and historical understanding to tackle issues that, like race, can show up vastly differently in each country. For example, when I facilitated conversations about the Black experience in the workplace during the summer of 2020, some UK team members struggled to understand how the experience of their Black colleagues in the United Kingdom was not necessarily the same as that of their Black American colleagues.

While the United States has been a leader in formalized corporate DEI efforts, the future of the workplace is global. Thus, all DEI efforts should consider the global lens. In this book, I highlight companies that, like Sodexo and Infosys, have taken on DEI from a global perspective. The history, language, norms, and workplace inclusion challenges can differ vastly by culture and geography, yet even if your company is not multinational, DEI is about elevating humanity in the workplace.

This worthy goal applies to every organization and every individual in the organization.

# The DEI Maturity Model

Every story in this book uses one simple framework that helps describe where a company finds itself on the necessary journey. This framework helps answer the two questions leaders inevitably have when considering the topic: Where are we on the journey, and how do we compare with others?

A person's or a company's progress on the necessary DEI journey occurs in five stages (see figure I-1). An understanding of these stages now will help you as you read the stories in this book and think about your own journey.

### *Stage 1: Awareness*

At this first stage, an organization is grappling with what DEI is and why it matters to the organization. A company must usually undergo an awakening of some sort before it realizes that it has not been intentional about DEI. The Workplace 2000 data precipitated one such awakening. So did George Floyd's murder.

Companies and leaders at this stage may find themselves asking, "What is the point of DEI?" I also see this question come up in newly formed organizations—startups especially—that are moving fast and innovating. They're often unintentional about their human capital

**FIGURE I-1**

### The five stages of the necessary diversity, equity, and inclusion (DEI) journey

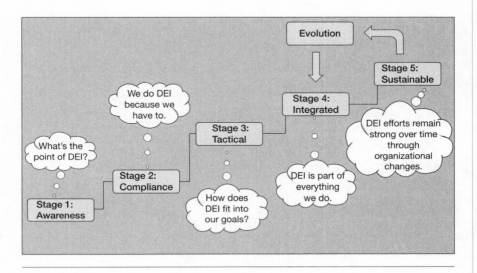

structures and practices in that early-stage survival mode. Many companies I have talked with at this stage recognize the difference between having good intentions and being intentional. Leaders at this stage say, "We have always had strong values, but we never were intentional about DEI efforts until now." At the awareness stage, the core question you need to answer is, "What is DEI, and what does it mean for us?"

## *Stage 2: Compliance*

Aware companies then need to meet industry or government requirements, for which there are many. Maintaining legal standards, such as

EEOC laws in the United States, and avoiding discrimination lawsuits, is not the most fun part of DEI, but it's an important part. Different industries and countries will have different compliance rules as well.

The general thinking at this stage is often, "We do DEI because we have to." In the 2010s I would share the DEI maturity model and ask leaders to rate honestly where they thought their company was on the journey. Generally, leaders would indicate that they were not much further along than this second stage, compliance. To test just how widespread this self-assessment was, I began to track responses to the question from more than a thousand executives and MBA students, and 62 percent of them indicated they were at the compliance stage.

Some companies see stage 2 as the end point, the checking of the proverbial box, and they get stuck here. "As long as we're meeting the law, we're fine" is the thinking. There is a historical basis for why many companies get stuck at this stage. Although diversity initiatives had been adopted by 70 percent of *Fortune* 50 companies by the 1990s, this era also saw some of the biggest EEOC lawsuits and settlements, including these:

- $81.5 million, Publix Super Markets, June 1995

- $172 million, Texaco, November 1996

- $192.5 million, Coca-Cola, November 2000[24]

What scared people was that many of the companies that were subject to discrimination suits—Coca-Cola, Texaco, Microsoft, Xerox (yes, even the pioneers that made diversity a priority in 1969 were still on their journey), Johnson & Johnson, and others—had in place diversity policies and programs they thought would protect them.[25] But policies and programs were not enough. Many companies were afraid to explore the possibilities of diversity management because they feared the ramifications of getting it wrong. They got stuck in the compliance stage and failed to mature their DEI approach over time.

Compliance is not inherently bad for DEI; many companies had to start at the foundational levels of awareness and compliance. However, in the thirty-plus years since the birth of diversity management, most companies have made little to no progress, and some have even gone backward. For example, McKinsey & Company studied more than one thousand large companies in fifteen countries from 2014 to 2019. It found that the number of companies that showed material progress on increasing gender or ethnic diversity on their executive teams increased by only one percentage point for women and two percentage points for ethnic diversity.[26] At a DEI conference in 2018, the number one frustration that human resource executives shared with me was this: they had the organizational resources committed to DEI but had been unable to make any real progress in the last two decades.

Even today, though discrimination lawsuits are less prevalent, the majority of organizations are still in the compliance stage. In a study of more than ten thousand workers conducted in partnership with Slack's Future Forum in November 2021, some 31.6 percent of employees said their companies were at the compliance stage more than any other stage (see figure I-2).[27] This result is not surprising, because many organizations have not done the soul-searching work to make real changes to their internal cultures.

FIGURE I-2

## Majority of organizations still in stage 2 (compliance) of diversity, equity, and inclusion (DEI) efforts

*Which of the following options best describes your company's approach to diversity, equity, and inclusion (DEI)?*

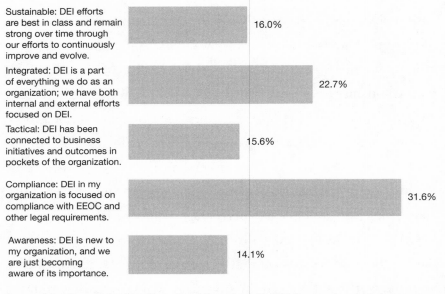

Sustainable: DEI efforts are best in class and remain strong over time through our efforts to continuously improve and evolve. — 16.0%

Integrated: DEI is a part of everything we do as an organization; we have both internal and external efforts focused on DEI. — 22.7%

Tactical: DEI has been connected to business initiatives and outcomes in pockets of the organization. — 15.6%

Compliance: DEI in my organization is focused on compliance with EEOC and other legal requirements. — 31.6%

Awareness: DEI is new to my organization, and we are just becoming aware of its importance. — 14.1%

*Source:* Future Forum Pulse, Wave 5, conducted November 1–12, 2021. Number of completed responses = 10,279.

## *Stage 3: Tactical*

In stage 3, organizations shift from "Have we met the rules?" to "How does DEI fit into our goals?" They may be thinking about how DEI can help them strategically attract consumers and may link DEI initiatives to a specific business outcome. Or they may simply believe being a DEI leader will create a positive public perception, especially when DEI is prevalent in the news cycles and companies are looking to stand out. These DEI efforts are laudable and usually well-intentioned.

Yet at this stage, companies typically still lack a strategic DEI approach that drives the entire business. Instead, their efforts are disjointed. They may be individually successful, but the result is that DEI is found in pockets of the organization instead of at its core. This fragmented result becomes problematic when one area of the organization is committed to DEI while others are not. For companies at this stage, two people in the same company can experience very different realities of DEI.

One classic example of a company at the tactical stage is Nike, a megacorporation historically at the forefront of supporting social justice issues. Nike's DEI story began in 1988 with its first "Just Do It" campaign to address systematic racial, gender, and sports biases. The company's first major television campaign focused on inspirational messages and included commercials for sports and active lifestyles for all customers regardless of age, gender, or physical fitness level. One of the first ads featured Walt Stack, an eighty-year-old marathon runner who defied ageist expectations of fitness.[28] "Just do it" became Nike's signature slogan and accompanied continued socially conscious branding through the years, such as the 1995 ad featuring Ric Muñoz, an openly gay HIV-positive runner during the height of the AIDS epidemic, or the same year's "If you let me play" ad, which addressed the benefits of organized sports for girls.[29] In 2007 Nike featured Matt Scott of the National Wheelchair Basketball Association in an ad. In 2017 Nike released "What will they say about you?," which featured five women from Arabic countries pushing social norms to succeed in sports like boxing and skateboarding. In 2018 Nike made a bold statement in support of racial justice, featuring Colin Kaepernick after he brought a lawsuit accusing National Football League owners of colluding to keep him out of the league after his protests against racial inequality and police brutality.[30] Notably, Nike was one of the first companies to publicly speak out in 2020, four days after the murder of George Floyd, with its "For Once, Don't Do It" campaign that advocated not ignoring the existence of racism in the United States.[31] A few days after it released the campaign, Nike also made a $40 million commitment to supporting the Black community.[32]

That's an impressive track record for one company. And despite the genius and timely external marketing around inclusion through the years, Nike has struggled to match its external advocacy with its internal realities. In 1991 American labor activist Jeffrey Ballinger published a report on Nike's factory practices in Indonesia, exposing below-minimum wages, child labor, and appalling sweatshop-like working conditions.[33] In 2003 Nike settled a racial discrimination lawsuit filed by four hundred employees for $7.6 million for claims that Nike managers used racial slurs in addressing Black customers and employees, accused Black workers of theft, and prohibited them from advancing professionally.[34] As recently as 2018, Nike faced a gender discrimination lawsuit alleging unequal pay for women and fostering a work environment that allowed sexual harassment.[35] Just weeks after its support of George Floyd, the #blackatnike Instagram account surfaced and began positing messages from anonymous current and former employees sharing experiences with racism.[36] In June 2020 CEO John Donahoe sent a company memo acknowledging these disparities: "While we strive to help shape a better society, our most important priority is to get our own house in order," Donahoe wrote. "Nike needs to be better than society as a whole. . . . While we have made some progress over the past couple of years, we have a long way to go."[37]

The company provides a clear example of how disjointed DEI efforts in the tactical stage can lead a company to an identity crisis. In some ways, Nike was excelling, particularly in customer-facing units. In other ways, it was woefully inadequate. To get past this tactical part of the journey, organizations must create alignment between their DEI efforts internally and externally, and it must come from the top down and emerge from the bottom up.

## *Stage 4: Integrated*

If the organization can do that—align internal and external efforts and drive change top down and bottom up—then it can reach the integrated stage of its journey. At this stage, the company has DEI informing its entire sphere of influence and can truly say, "DEI is part of everything we do." The organization has clearly defined its DEI strategy and has taken a close look at how DEI has an impact across its internal and external stakeholders, including employees, customers, partners, suppliers, shareholders, competitors, and the communities it touches. Humility is the most common attribute of companies at the integrated stage because for most established organizations, getting there takes time and a fair amount of experimentation on what works and what doesn't. Companies with long-standing, sometimes-celebrated DEI programs must be humble enough to change course when they realize parts of their strategy are not working or are absent. You will meet some companies like this in the coming pages.

A company's entire sphere of influence being connected to DEI is what differentiates it at the integrated stage (see figures I-3 and I-4). The sphere for each company is different. Some companies are large global

FIGURE I-3

## Spheres of influence model

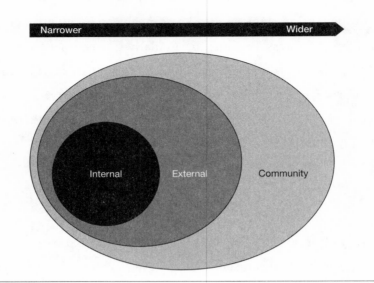

FIGURE I-4

## Spheres of influence of DEI

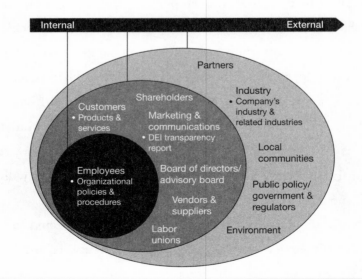

entities with hundreds of thousands of employees. Others are smaller businesses whose outer reaches are the local community. That's okay. Integrated companies are making a difference in all their spheres of influence. In the age of increased calls for corporate social responsibility for all companies, it's not enough to only consider the impact of DEI internally. It's a great place to start, but as companies mature, they must consider their ability to have a larger impact and to make sure that their espoused values and actions agree internally and externally.

Companies at the integrated stage have not reached perfect DEI, and they're humble enough to know it. However, these companies are thoughtful about their DEI efforts and have a strategic plan in place to make continued progress, connect DEI to their business imperatives, and commit to long-term accountability.

## Stage 5: Sustainable

In stage 5, the organization can focus on creating systems and structures that remain sustainable through the naturally occurring changes in business cycles, strategy, and, crucially, leadership. Companies with successful DEI efforts are often linked to the passion and commitment of one leader or to a company's superior financial performance, which enables the firm to devote significant resources to DEI. Take the former CEO of Intel, Brian Krzanich, who in 2015 announced a $300 million five-year plan to bring the company's workforce to "full representation" by 2020. Krzanich said, "It's time to step up and do more. It's not just good enough to say we value diversity, and then have our workplaces and our industry not reflect the full availability and talent pool of women and underrepresented minorities."[38]

Krzanich initiated a multipronged effort to increase hiring of under-represented groups, including a $4,000 employee referral bonus and a $5 million partnership to develop a high school computer science curriculum for the Oakland Unified School District. That same year, the company published a fifteen-page report on the impact of its efforts. The report showed that the number of women and minority hires had surpassed the initial 40 percent goal for the year in just six months.[39] After the 2017 White supremacy violence in Charlottesville, Virginia, Krzanich announced that Intel would accelerate its efforts to fulfill its diversity goals two years ahead of the original 2020 goal.[40] Under his leadership, hires from underrepresented communities increased by 31 percent. The company also increased its female workforce by almost 43 percent. Intel's DEI work considered its sphere of influence and went beyond internal operations into community partnerships. For example, the company invested $5 million with Georgia Tech to boost a more diverse pipeline in the technology industry.[41]

In 2018 Krzanich resigned. For some companies, this change in leadership would have meant the end to the DEI era brought about by a particular leader. However, Intel exemplifies a company with sustainable DEI efforts, as its next CEO, Robert (Bob) Swan, continued to set ambitious DEI goals. In 2020 Intel pledged to increase the number of women in technical roles to 40 percent and double the number of women and underrepresented minorities in senior roles by 2030.[42]

Intel is a strong example of sustainable DEI efforts. However, sustainability takes more than strong leadership. It takes commitment to stay with an effort, even when times are hard for the business. In early 2020 DEI-related job openings declined by 60 percent, which was twice the rate of overall job openings.[43] DEI-related jobs are typically with human resource departments, which are usually hit hard during recessions. But it was striking how quickly companies were willing to abandon their DEI efforts compared with other functions when they anticipated tough times ahead. Even more disconcerting was the 50 percent surge in DEI-related job openings in June 2020 and the 2.6-fold increase in vacant DEI executive and leadership positions such as chief diversity officer by July of that year, during the worst of the pandemic.[44] An organization is not truly committed to DEI if its efforts are expendable, being based on the economy or the prominence of inequality and injustice issues in the news cycle. The goal is for companies to see DEI as a core business imperative that is connected to the purpose and mission of the organization. Thus, as they do for any other core business strategy, organizations at the sustainable stage are committed to DEI efforts through organizational changes. DEI is integral to their culture.

· · ·

The preceding stages outline the necessary journey and some of the milestones you will find along the way. Once an organization moves through all five stages of the DEI journey, its work is still not done. True commitment to DEI requires continuous improvement by a reassessment of strategies and initiatives as the organization grows over time and as the world changes. If you open your first-ever office in India, you have new DEI challenges. If some event in the world shines a bright light on inequity that we didn't know was there, then there is more work to be done.

Even the organizations that are further along in their DEI journey must continually evolve. The center of DEI is humanity, and the challenges of bringing humanity into the workplace will always be changing. Different generations enter and others leave, technology changes the realities of work, and society continues to set new expectations for businesses and their role in our lives. The global pandemic has dramatically changed what the workplace looks like and how it will look in the future. Whether employees are working from home, are essential workers, or are parents or caregivers, we now know what we have always felt but often denied: that we cannot check our identities at the door when we begin our workday. The workplace must acknowledge and center our humanity, and DEI is a part of that process.

# Hope

In a world that now demands that businesses take DEI seriously, I know you might feel a bit at sea. You want to make a difference, you recognize inequity, you see injustice. But you don't feel equipped to make a difference. Or you simply don't know where to start.

I am here to give you hope through stories. Stories of organizations that are passing through every stage of their journey and that continually work to create environments and structures that allow for everyone to thrive. Human stories that include mistakes and successes. Missteps and triumphs. I hope you find them inspiring.

But I expect you will also find these tales instructive and practical. Even though I'm telling stories here, my goal as a research practitioner is to leave you with ideas on how you can create change in your organization no matter where you sit. The stories are full of tactical steps, frameworks, and strategies that have helped companies on their DEI journey and that may help jump-start yours, too.

Finally, you will notice that I end each story in this book the same way. I ask the leaders who so generously gave their time and honest answers to tell me what a workplace utopia would look like for them. I like to ask this question because I think it's important to visualize success and a better possible future. I don't ask it because we are striving for unicorns and butterflies or some impossible state of being. I ask this question because so much of our lives is spent working that it is our human right to authentically thrive in those work spaces, and I want leaders to dream about what will make those spaces better. It's what I did back in graduate school, when I realized my workplace utopia wasn't like others'. Mine was not in deep academia but rather in a place few could imagine at the time, one where practice and research worked together to improve DEI. I was on that ledge, looking over that landscape, and I saw a way across—a way that most others didn't see. It wasn't easy, but I stuck with it through the ups and downs. I made the necessary journey and continue on it today. I know what my workplace utopia is. My hope is that as a reader of this book, you ask yourself what yours is. And I hope that you start to dream big about what a diverse, equitable, and inclusive workplace can look like and that you are spurred to action to make those dreams a reality.

# 1

# A Good Mission Is Not Enough for DEI at Iora Health

**COMPANY:** Iora Health

**STAGE:** Awareness

**BEST PRACTICES:** Setting a vision, DEI audit, alignment with business impact

**KEY QUOTE:** "We made a choice that we are going to serve diverse patient populations. I love that because of the diversity, our employees and patients get to learn from each other. It makes us better." —Rushika Fernandopulle, MD, cofounder and CEO, Iora Health

Iora Health was founded in 2010 with the intent to be disruptive. The founders wanted to transform the broken health-care system by building a different kind of primary care. Instead of a system that capitalized on sick patients, Iora Health invested in technology and put patients at its core, using a value-based approach in which the company gets paid for keeping people healthy. The proven model has cut hospital-izations by more than 40 percent while improving patient engagement and overall health outcomes.[1]

Iora's president, Alexander (Zander) Packard, had been with the company since its inception, alongside cofounder and CEO Rushika Fernandopulle. They were serious about their mission—"We're restoring humanity to health care"—and it was working. The Boston-based startup had grown since its founding. In 2017 Iora spent $75 million to expand its primary care clinics, paving the way for bringing better health care to more people.[2] More believers have come on board, as have investors in Iora's innovative approach. In February 2020 the company closed another $126 million in funding to continue its mission-based work. By July of that year, Iora Health was recognized for leading in the transformation of primary care and was operating forty-eight practices in ten states, serving tens of thousands of Medicare beneficiaries.

## "All These Other Rooms I Didn't Even Know Were There"

Both Fernandopulle and Packard had put their heart and soul into building a company where everyone is committed to helping people live their happiest, healthiest lives. Despite the success and positive impact, Packard could not shake the feeling that Iora—that he—had missed the mark on creating an internal company culture that was intentional about DEI. The point was brought home to him, painfully, at the end of the day on Friday, May 29, 2020. The country was in an uproar after the murder of George Floyd, a Black man killed by police in Minneapolis. He learned that day, to his surprise, how the current events were affecting his teams. He felt ill equipped to address the emotional storm happening at work and did not know how to support his colleagues in this moment of pain and frustration. Packard found himself at a crossroads—what he describes as an intensive self-searching process. He asked himself, "What is the role of an organization in addressing the wrongs of the world around us?"

He wouldn't let himself be paralyzed by his uncertainty. So, with all these thoughts running through his head, a huge amount of self-admitted anxiety about saying the wrong things, and much uncertainty about what he might uncover when he talked to people, Packard set out to talk with four of the Black leaders on teams across the organization. He had always thought of himself as a leader who built close relationships, so it was a moment of pain when he realized that there were critical conversations with his teams that he had never had. Packard described the moment: "I've been living in a house, and I opened the door. And there were all these other rooms I didn't even know were there. And I felt naive, I felt irresponsible, I felt uncaring. But it was good. It was a formative experience for me. It was important to be vulnerable; it was important to talk about what I didn't know, and just to sit with that discomfort was really powerful."

What he learned through these emotional one-on-one conversations, and later shared with his CEO, would change the course of Iora Health forever. It was the first time Packard realized that a noble mission didn't excuse you from the hard work of DEI. The mission alone, as strong as it was, didn't connect to DEI strongly enough. The company had not paid enough attention to DEI for its employees. It was through these pivotal conversations that Iora decided to embark on its DEI journey.

## Beginning the Necessary Journey: "We Need Expertise"

As an organization that had been mission-focused on improving the world for its patients, Iora had thrived, but the racial reckoning in the United States and beyond had made it clear that they had not done enough for DEI. Packard and Fernandopulle were analytical thinkers, so their reaction to this realization was to make a plan to fix it. They knew the first step toward a change was to gain an understanding of where they were on the DEI journey.

They were self-aware enough to know they needed help, which isn't always the case. Some companies don't want to bring in outsiders, either for fear that a consultant will shine too bright a light or because they think that they can fix problems on their own. Fernandopulle held no such illusions. "We said, 'Look, we need expertise here. We think we're well intentioned. We pay attention. But this is not what we do for a living.'"

They hired my DEI strategy firm to conduct a full-scale audit, including stakeholder interviews of the entire executive team, employee focus groups, and a review of the organizational infrastructure, internal policies, processes, and communications. This audit process is intensive but invaluable.

Organizations going through a DEI audit often feel particularly vulnerable. They are asking someone from the outside to objectively assess them and search for pain points. Even with a CEO deeply committed to the work, it is not uncommon for other leaders to question the need to spend time and resources on such an effort. Even with companies like Iora, which had detailed demographic metrics of its patients and employees (kept completely confidential, of course), the company was missing a read on how its employees were experiencing inclusion and equity every day on the job. Leaders who do not understand that DEI is about more than metrics can be particularly difficult to get on board. Another point of resistance to these types of first-time audits is that team members may be hesitant to talk about DEI openly if the company does not have a previous culture of these conversations. Rightfully so, employees worry about how the information they share in focus groups and surveys may be used against them. It's vital to the success of audits that the leadership team be on board and promote the audit. The practitioner must also establish unquestioned trust that the information they find will only be presented in the aggregate and not attributed to individuals and that action will be taken based on the information shared.[3] Unfortunately, many organizations that conducted listening sessions during the summer of 2020 did not follow up with meaningful actions. Employees felt like they were sharing their pain just to make the organization feel better, but they saw no promise of action. One of the golden rules of employee engagement is to never ask employees to share how they are feeling if you are not committed to acting on what you learn. Yet a recent survey showed 80 percent of employees believed leaders would not act on challenges brought forward by an employee engagement survey.[4] When employees share their authentic experiences through surveys, focus groups, one-on-one conversations, or other mechanisms where they are explicitly asked to open up, there is an implicit promise that the organization is going to do something with the answers. When that promise is not upheld, it can lead employees to regret sharing in the first place and become much less likely to participate in future assessments of culture and engagement.

The audit my team conducted clearly showed that Iora Health had a unique employee culture where most employees genuinely enjoyed working there. This finding made sense to me. As a value-based company, Iora Health focuses on its employees just as much as it does its patients. For example, when the company celebrated ten years, it published a report that allowed employees to share their experiences working for the organization such as their motivators, their biggest lessons learned, and how the pandemic affected them personally and professionally. Iora's culture of care for its employees consistently showed.[5] The employees' sense of pride in their work is captured in data and interviews from the Iora Health community. For example, employees were asked to share their favorite company value out of the following five values:

- We act with passion.

- We serve with humility.

- We feel empathy.

- We bring creativity.

- We demonstrate courage.

Interestingly, "We serve with humility" and "We feel empathy" tied for the most popular responses, a true testament to the culture that the company has created and reinforced.

But my audit showed that the same niceness that employees valued was also what was holding the organization back from having meaningful conversations about DEI, particularly race. I also learned that although Iora had made initial investments in tracking the demographics of its employees and patients, it had not specifically tried to build a diverse pipeline of talent, examine group opportunities for a diversity of employees, or consider the DEI challenges of many of its frontline employees. Again, the culture was good. The mission was noble. But there was no structure around DEI, and it wasn't until Packard engaged in honest, deep conversations with those four employees that Iora leaders realized they needed to step up.

. . .

With the audit complete, I worked with Iora on a four-step plan to launch the company on its necessary journey. These steps could be a good model for your organization or could at least inspire you in your efforts to get started.

## Step 1: Set the Vision

Before Iora could fully embark upon its DEI journey, the company had to first set a clear vision for how it wanted to show up in the DEI world.[6]

In June 2020, when Iora set out on its journey, almost every US company was feeling peer pressure to speak out against racial inequality and to share a plan of action for eradicating racial and other inequalities. Many companies made bold and impressive statements. For example, longtime social justice advocates Ben & Jerry's boldly stated, "We must dismantle White Supremacy."[7]

While these statements were laudable and impressive, they were equally intimidating for companies like Iora, which had never made public statements on social justice topics and was not quite sure where it fit into the landscape of DEI more broadly. The reality is that each organization must decide on its unique approach to DEI. We cannot all be Ben and Jerry's, and that's okay. It would be inauthentic to try to emulate another company's culture. But this doesn't serve as an excuse for inaction. You can't just say, "Our company isn't the kind that makes statements like Ben & Jerry's." You have to dig into what you believe and discover the best way to express it. Each organization can be thoughtful about its own vision and how it wants to prioritize DEI efforts.

As I had done with many other organizations, I began my work with Iora by scheduling one-on-one time with all the members of the executive team to understand each person's perspective. For true cultural change to take place, you need to know both the culture of the company and the views of the individuals. And as my conversations clearly indicated, the leadership team at Iora Health was deeply committed to the organization's mission and trusted Fernandopulle's leadership wholeheartedly. Most of the leadership team agreed that the organization was at the awareness stage of its DEI journey. Nevertheless, and unsurprisingly, I heard ten different perspectives on the ideal way for

Iora to go about demonstrating its DEI commitment. Each leader is simultaneously on their own individual DEI journey and navigating what is best for the organization. Therefore, for a team of leaders to embark on a collective DEI journey, they must set aside time to agree on a united vision.[8]

Here are some guiding questions I asked the Iora leaders. If you are at the awareness stage, you will want to ask these questions to help your team develop a collective vision:

1. How do we want to be known by our stakeholders for our DEI efforts?

2. What are our priorities in terms of the following goals?

   a. Having a diversity of team members

   b. Evaluating and achieving equity in our processes

   c. Developing a culture of belonging and inclusion

3. What has so far held us back from achieving these goals as an organization?

These conversations about a DEI vision are often the very first time the leaders are discussing their perspectives out loud with one another. Allow enough time and space for follow-up dialogue, as the participants often need multiple conversations to align on a strong DEI vision.

The Iora leadership team had a two-part conversation on its DEI vision. During the first part, the team members spoke candidly about the experiences each leader had with race and shared what DEI meant to each of them. Some leaders discussed being largely unaware of issues of race and privilege in the past, whereas others shared deeply personal experiences with race when they were growing up and during their careers. In the session, Fernandopulle noted his surprise that although he had been working with most of the team for almost a decade, they had never had these conversations. Packard also commented that he had often wondered about the ethnic background of a colleague but had never been confident enough to ask about it. These conversations are powerful ways for leaders to let their guards down with one another and bring in the human aspect of themselves. If leaders are uncomfortable being open with their peers, it is almost impossible for them to show vulnerability in DEI conversations with their teams. Furthermore, because each person has an internal working definition of DEI, leadership teams should collectively define what DEI will mean for the broader organization.

The second part of the conversation about a vision continued the momentum. The leaders defined what DEI would look like at Iora and explicitly discussed the trade-offs that would have to be made to bring the vision to life. For example, they discussed the trade-offs between serving all patients under their duty of care and protecting employees from racist patient interactions. The leadership team questioned where they would need to draw the line to keep their employees psychologically safe while also serving as many patients as they could, despite the patient's personal beliefs. When given the Ben & Jerry's example of how some companies prioritize DEI, Fernandopulle shared that as a health-care company, Iora was held to a higher standard: "Maybe Ben & Jerry's does not care if racist people don't buy their ice cream. We do care. Our duty is to serve all patients."

Another challenge Fernandopulle raised was the desire to be seen as a preferred place to work and receive care by underrepresented communities but also to be financially successful as a small company. "We are not in a position to donate profits," he said. "Can we create DEI goals that also help drive performance?" There was powerful brainstorming during this discussion. Another leader provided a different perspective: "We may not be able to donate profits, but maybe we can donate our PTO [paid time off] or some other resources that have not been considered." Though each leader's view of the business was based on their own role there, the discussion made it clear that the team wanted to align the DEI efforts with the business imperatives of the organization, including employee support and patient care.[9] Each leader left the session sharing personal commitments that connected this vision with things they would do to make it come to life from the top down and from the bottom up.

Once the leadership team has decided on the vision of the future and DEI priorities, the real work toward achieving that vision can begin.

## Step 2: Evaluate Your Current State

Once you have a clear vision, the next step on your journey should be to evaluate the current state of your organization. The aim is to have a baseline to measure progress against.

Many organizations rush to set metrics for future success without first evaluating their present status. Omitting this step diminishes the effectiveness of the DEI journey in a couple of ways. First, and most obviously, without an evaluation, the baselines are loose or poorly understood. As Maya Angelou reportedly said, "If you don't know where you've come from, you don't know where you're going." How will you know what progress looks like if you don't know what the current state looks like? Second, evaluating the current state answers questions about why your status quo looks like it does. By understanding the reasons for your organization's culture, you will be better able to do something about it, rather than tossing around generic goals that may or may not address the underlying situation.

For example, Iora's Fernandopulle noted that gathering data was a reality check at this stage and required all of leadership to question their assumptions about the current state. "Let's do an audit," Fernandopulle said. "We think we're pretty good at hiring people without being biased, but are we really? And do we think there is some stuff we are not doing?"

An effective current state assessment requires a thoughtful approach that allows for analysis of both formal and informal processes, procedures, and behaviors in the organization. I advocate for some type of external resource such as a trained DEI professional who can be an objective evaluator. However, if you decide to conduct the assessment in-house, the working group must have a clear mandate to be impartial and honest about the findings. It's often hard for us to look within ourselves and be honest about biases that may exist or systems of inequality that we have unknowingly perpetuated. But that is exactly what we must do to understand the current state of the company and to move forward to achieve the desired vision.

Use the following questions as guidelines principles for evaluating your organization's current state:

- What are our formal DEI policies, procedures, and processes?

- What are the informal ways things get done in our culture?

- Do the current approaches meet our DEI goals?

- How do employees experience our organizational culture?

- How do customers and other external stakeholders experience our organization?

For the leaders at Iora, answering these five questions yielded several areas where DEI efforts could be improved:

- Hiring and recruitment

- Onboarding and training

- Internal opportunities for advancement

- Interfacing with patients

The team made many recommendations around these areas. For example, the group recommended that the organization should explore nontraditional pathways for sourcing a more diverse applicant pool, given the perception that Iora team members in the corporate office were from similar Ivy League networks and the perceived lack of transparency when leadership roles became open.

Another area of opportunity was communicating clear career pathways for the health coaches, as there was a perceived career ceiling for certain roles. Still another recommendation was to provide managers with training and other tools to encourage employees to be their full selves at work.

In all, my consulting team generated twenty-seven recommendations. The Iora leadership team immediately set out to prioritize the recommendations and develop a strategy that would demonstrate how committed the company was to change.

# Step 3: Set a Strategy

You have a vision, and you know where things stand. Your strategy is squarely focused on closing the gap between this vision and your present status. Notice how this approach makes the strategy specific to your situation. You're not just picking some general DEI metrics to hit. You're closing a documented gap.

To this point, you've been in the tactical stage of your DEI journey. Now is when, by setting your strategy and executing it, you have the greatest opportunity to move beyond the tactical stage into more of the integrated stage. When a DEI strategy is successfully implemented, there are positive implications for its broader sphere of influence. At Iora, for example, the successful implementation of its internal strategy would lead to DEI improvements with patients, partner facilities, and, eventually, the health-care industry at large.

Your DEI strategy, like any other strategy, should have well-defined changes in policy, behaviors, and outcomes and should include clear pathways to measure and otherwise evaluate progress in these elements. It can be tempting to try to boil the ocean during these strategic alignment sessions, but companies that are most successful in implementing their new strategy home in on a short list of priorities that can be connected to short- and long-term goals. Because a thorough assessment will likely yield a long list of recommendations, prioritization from HR leaders or the overall senior leadership team is needed to drill down into a specific strategy that is best suited to meet the organization's needs. Even with outside expertise, creating an impactful DEI strategy requires internal stakeholder alignment.

Once I got to know the leadership team better, I realized that supporting the Iora care team members was an immediate need for the organization. The leaders had learned that the care team members were experiencing uncomfortable patient interactions, such as when a patient would make a racist or sexist comment. Such incidents were a struggle for the employee and took an emotional toll. Notice how specific this priority is to Iora. Many companies would never have such a situation arise. But in this case, considering how Iora wanted to be a supportive employer of its team while also honoring its mission to serve patients with the highest level of care, this difficult interaction between staff and patient was a DEI challenge unique to the company. Addressing this challenge required a clear vision of what was most important to Iora.

And it is a uniquely difficult challenge, as Packard learned when the company gathered information from frontline employees. They have to provide care, of course, but how do you do that to the best of your ability in the face of abusive language or actions? And how does a company that explicitly puts patients at the core of its business accept the idea that in some cases, the customer (or patient, in this case) isn't always right and that the employee shouldn't have to endure certain customer behaviors? Packard described the quandary:

Delivering health care doesn't give you the right to be the judge of someone's character. And yet, we also don't want to create an environment where we perpetuate and make it okay for patients to come in and betray that trust or to be dismissive, violent, rude, aggressive. We had to figure out "Where's that line?" And are we drawing that line in a different place than other organizations, because of the culture we want to build, because of the pride we take in our team? Because of the priority we want to place on team members feeling really empowered and confident and trusted?

And I think we're still working through that. I think we've said, "Look, we will always treat patients who have a variety of different views, even if those views differ from our own. But what we won't stand for is this disrespectful, dangerous, violent, aggressive behavior toward team members." And we have a pretty low tolerance for that. That is our organizational commitment.

The following sequence of steps summarizes the previous discussion on strategy development:

1. Define the vision.

2. Evaluate your organization's current state.

3. Determine your strategic priorities.

4. Set short-term and long-term goals for each priority.

5. Define metrics and accountability for these goals.

6. Determine how the strategy will be implemented from the top down and from the bottom up.

## Step 4: Execute the Strategy

Everything's in place, but success is hardly guaranteed. Even the best-laid strategies will fall short if there is no clear direction on who will bring the strategy to life in the organization. While some firms have well-resourced DEI functions, the vast majority of organizations will need both grassroots employee involvement and leadership engagement to create lasting cultural and behavioral changes.[10]

Iora lacked the DEI infrastructure of some of the other companies you've read about. It still isn't a large organization. So it created an internal working group of leaders, a three-person talent and culture team, and developed an on-the-ground team to carry forth the strategic priorities and create a strong employee feedback loop on the effectiveness of the changes being made. This team reports back to the executive team quarterly on progress toward goals in order to maintain accountability. Quarterly reports from the talent and culture team on progress toward DEI goals were implemented to maintain accountability. Regardless of how you execute the strategy, it needs champions, leaders, accountability, and continuous feedback on what's working and what's not.

## Diverse Customers, Diverse Company

Iora was at the early stages of an intentional DEI strategy, but some of the previous cultural elements they had in place already showed promise for its long-term journey. For example, the culture survey launched in 2020 was slated to be an annual opportunity for employees to provide feedback. Along with the immediate push to support employees who faced racist patient interactions, the company devoted more resources to focus on diverse-slate hiring by making sure each position that was going to be filled had an applicant pool that included women and underrepresented minorities.

Despite this early progress, as happens with many companies, the realities of the business landscape had an impact on Iora's DEI journey. In 2021 it was acquired by One Medical for $2.1 billion.[11] In the acquisition, Fernandopulle became One Medical's chief innovation officer. Iora had to merge its current strategy with the existing strategy at One Medical, which had developed its own DEI strategy and priority areas for investment. For some companies, such a merger could have been a major disruption to the progress they had made in recent years, but the team at Iora Health, along with the DEI team at One Medical, remains committed not only to merging the company cultures but also to making the new organization a place where everyone feels welcome and truly comfortable being themselves.[12]

When I asked Fernandopulle what a workplace utopia looks like, the answer unsurprisingly focused on how diversity is necessary because the company's customers are diverse.[13] People find a workplace utopia when the diversity of their customers is matched by a diversity of employees and leaders and when there is open, honest discussion of the difficult aspects of the DEI journey.

"We're not a concierge practice serving rich White people," Fernandopulle said. "We are in neighborhoods where people often don't get good health care. We can have an interesting business model where we can do this concierge-level care for free to people. It's hard. It's not easy. But we made a choice that we are going to serve diverse patient populations. I love that because of the diversity, our employees and patients get to learn from each other. It makes us better."

When I interviewed Fernandopulle, the company was facing one of its biggest DEI challenges for patients: encouraging its patient population to get the Covid-19 vaccine. Yet Fernandopulle described this challenge as a way to get closer to a workplace utopia: "We're about to embark upon giving Covid vaccinations to our patients. And as you know, there is a whole history of why particularly minority communities are skeptical, and rightfully should be, of the medical system. This is why you have to have a diverse workforce. If we didn't have a diverse workforce, we could never engage in that conversation with our patients. We wouldn't understand that point of view." But now, the company can have the conversation and can help people become more comfortable with vaccination through empathy and understanding. Through conversation. "I think the utopia is that we keep doing that," Fernandopulle said, "and getting better at it."

FIGURE 1-1

## Iora Health works to restore humanity to health care, aiming to deliver robust, dynamic primary care that transforms patients' lives.

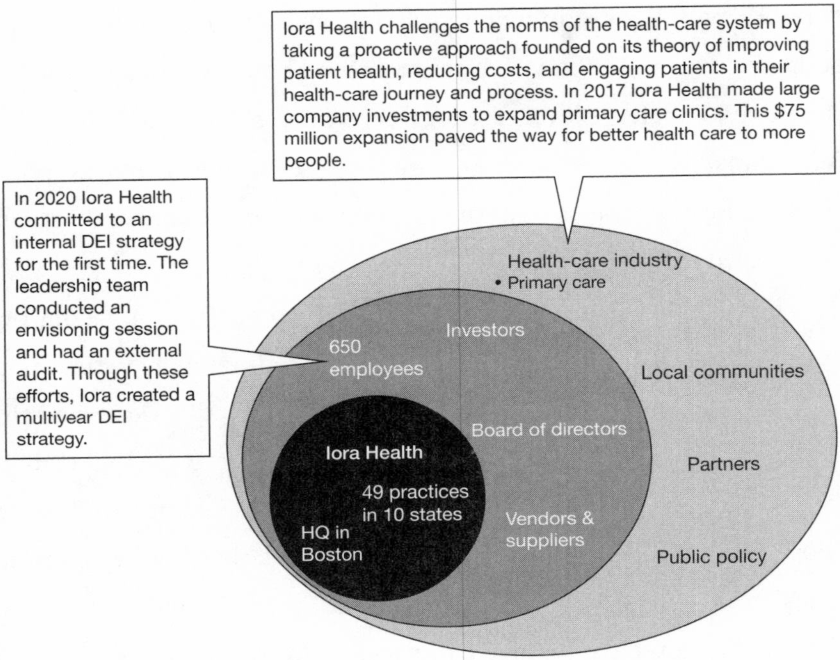

Iora Health challenges the norms of the health-care system by taking a proactive approach founded on its theory of improving patient health, reducing costs, and engaging patients in their health-care journey and process. In 2017 Iora Health made large company investments to expand primary care clinics. This $75 million expansion paved the way for better health care to more people.

In 2020 Iora Health committed to an internal DEI strategy for the first time. The leadership team conducted an envisioning session and had an external audit. Through these efforts, Iora created a multiyear DEI strategy.

Health-care industry
• Primary care

Investors

650 employees

Local communities

Board of directors

Iora Health

49 practices in 10 states

Partners

HQ in Boston

Vendors & suppliers

Public policy

# 2

# Tapping the Power of Decentralization to Foster Inclusion at Slack

---

**COMPANY:** Slack

**STAGE:** Tactical

**BEST PRACTICES:** Companywide acceptance of responsibility for DEI; top-down and bottom-up initiatives; incorporating external DEI efforts into companywide strategy; mental health employee benefits

**KEY QUOTE:** "We want to make sure that leaders are supporting DEB [diversity, equity, and belonging] so it's not just living in one group. I want our leaders to be able to say, 'I am doing this because I believe in it,' as opposed to 'This is something that's being pushed down on me from the top.'" —Jeunée Simon, senior program manager, diversity and inclusion, Slack

---

Dr. Rachel Westerfield, Slack's global manager of experience specialists, described feeling the weight that many Black Americans felt in the weeks following the murder of George Floyd in May 2020, where the world seemed to be just waking up to the four hundred years of pain of being Black in America. "There was one particular week," said Westerfield, who holds a PhD in industrial and organizational psychology, "when I could barely get out of bed. I reached out to some other Black colleagues and some direct reports, and I said, 'Is it just me or is it particularly hard to breathe today?' People were in tears. Everyone I talked to was like, 'Yes! I can't think, I can't join my calls.'"

The murder and its aftermath were debilitating, and yet most Black employees during this time were expected to soldier on at work as if it were business as usual. Slack was different. After CEO Stewart Butterfield made an internal statement that called out to BIPOC employees (employees who are Black, Indigenous, or other people of color), saying that he was heartbroken by the current events, he demonstrated his compassion through actions by making counseling available and encouraging employees to take advantage of a unique company benefit.

Westerfield and other Slack employees had the opportunity to take advantage of Slack's "emotional time off" benefit—paid time off that gave employees the latitude to acknowledge their humanity during tough moments. Westerfield remembered how important this benefit was. "The fact that I could even make recommendations to my team members to take the emotional time off or ask tough questions out loud and not feel like there would be some kind of strange repercussion or worry about being labeled as someone who is too emotional and can't do their job was a huge deal to me," she said.

But she did more, remarkably making a candid, public response to CEO Butterfield's message and efforts:

Stewart, this is one of the reasons why I am here. You know I have been in tears and off camera on Zoom all week. And I can guarantee that the people who are reading this right now, who have been in meetings with me, didn't even think to ask, why I was off camera or if I'm okay.

And I'm not saying these people are bad people, I'm saying that they didn't think about it. I'm saying that they were able to mute their TVs and not have to deal with it for a second, because as long it's muted it's not happening, right? You can interpret that however you want, but I can't mute it.

Westerfield's in-depth response sparked many internal Slack conversations, and she was grateful that her CEO would open that door for dialogue on the public platform. Butterfield continued to welcome thoughts from employees on how Slack could do better on issues of racial equity.

"The idea that he would get out in front of this and publicly condemn what is happening both internally and externally, it just felt like it created so much more of a safe space for people to be themselves and to really feel," said Westerfield. "And I think that when you allow yourself to really experience what's happening real-time, you also get closer to healing or at least get closer to figuring out what your next step needs to be versus repressing it and feeling like you have to deal with it later."

Westerfield had joined Slack two years prior after more than ten years at a Big Four consulting firm. She has seen DEI efforts of all kinds, some better than others, during her career. She decided to leave the world of consulting for a startup partly because of the authenticity she saw in the company.

"One of the things that drew me to Slack," she said, "was I felt like I could really be my authentic self all the time. So, whether I'm in front of my team, whether I'm in front of leadership, or whether I'm in front of a customer, I'm always Rachel every day, all day, and that is what I love. When things hit the fan in 2020, that was not an exception. I never had to hide how I was feeling about anything."

The experience Westerfield and other employees had during this time—their ability to have direct, unfettered public dialogue with the CEO—is a relatively unique experience. While Westerfield was feeling comfortable directly communicating with the CEO and other colleagues about what she was feeling, I was consulting with many other companies that had different approaches. These CEOs were looking for help crafting perfect messages; they wanted something to say to employees as a kind of final word, as a way to avoid responses and dialogue. For example, many companies had companywide town hall conversations during the summer of 2020 but were nervous about the types of questions they would get from the audience. As a result, I witnessed some of these companies opt to not allow for questions from the audience in order to stick to a crafted script. In these instances, employees left the town hall, which further frustrated by their organization's seemingly performative actions did not allow for meaningful dialogue or authentic questions.

Slack was different, and that is largely because of its decentralized approach to DEI. Westerfield's positive experience was an artifact of the culture that Slack's leaders have been working to create all along.

# Young and Decentralized

Butterfield and Slack have enjoyed a couple of advantages in their journey. One is the mere fact that Slack, a younger company, was founded in 2014, during a decade in which DEI programs, and cultural shifts, were already underway. Companies with decades or centuries of legacy cultures face different challenges than those faced by a relative newcomer. A newer company can shape equity and inclusion into its culture from the start, and Butterfield aimed to do just that with Slack. Jeunée Simon, senior manager of DEB, described the beginning of Slack's journey. She said the CEO looked around and realized he was surrounded by mostly White men in an industry whose workplace culture and hiring practices seemed to reinforce a cycle of hiring and promoting mostly White men. As someone who was about to lead a company, Butterfield realized he had a choice. He could perpetuate the cycle or disrupt it. He wanted to do the latter. Butterfield knew that if he was going to try, he would need help. So even as he launched his company, he engaged a DEI strategy firm to get started.

Notably, Slack has no chief diversity officer or similar single person serving as the executive diversity leader like most of its industry peers. Instead, there is a committee-like structure where Simon, the senior program manager of diversity and inclusion, works along with the chief people officer and the vice president of people, along with a larger group of leaders from the recruitment, legal, and communications teams, to tackle DEI. This strategy reflects both how diversity and inclusion were woven into the company's core strategy early on so that they were part of everyone's job and Slack's decentralized—often from the ground up—approach to DEI. Simon said the benefit of this strategy is that there is shared accountability for DEI across multiple channels in the organization. "Since there is not a CDO [chief diversity officer]," she said, "we are able to keep each other honest as we need to come to a decision. When I think about decentralization, I think about, 'How can we make sure that leaders have some skin in the game?' We consider, 'What are the goals that we have for our leaders? How can we make DEB aligned to those goals?' Maybe they're actual numeric goals, but maybe they are development goals. If we have a centralized program, we still need people throughout the organization to support it and not feel like it's something that's being pushed down from the top."

Simon acknowledged that the current team structure is ever evolving and may change in the future, depending on the needs of the organization. Giving themselves the permission to pivot after deciding what is working and what is not is exactly what more organizations should be doing. Although the decentralized process is working well today, the organization may consider hiring a CDO. More organizations should consider whether the CDO role is the best course for them in light of their current needs, their culture, and how they make decisions. In fact, organizations that do not thoughtfully consider if a CDO is right for them before hiring are in danger of undermining their efforts and may face backlash if the new officer is not seen as supported by the C-suite. The DEI journey is about growth and evolution, not being married to past structures, metrics, or decisions that are no longer working for the organization.

The second advantage in Slack's DEI journey is that its own product is a foundational tool in its strategy; this tool has shaped the company's decentralized approach to community and inclusion. Slack uses its group chat and productivity platform for grassroots employee resource groups, or ERGs.

"One of the really interesting things about Slack is that the platform lends itself to community," said Simon. "And so, you can find a community. There is a Mahogany community for people who are Black from the African diaspora. Because there are these pockets of community, identity becomes so important and [so is] finding space for being heard. But then also you have an easier way to amplify asks from communities and connect across them. [ERGs] have been central to the company from its founding."

## Four Steps to Connect ERGs to the Business

Right now, Slack hosts seven ERGs, all started by employees from the ground up:

- Ability (for employees who identify as having a disability)

- Earthtones (for employees who identify as people of color)

- Fuego (for employees who identify as Latinx or Hispanic)

- Mahogany (for employees who identify as Black or part of the African diaspora)

- Out (for employees who identify as LGBTQ+)

- Veterans (for employees who are military veterans of any country)

- Women (for employees who identify as women or nonbinary)

Creating these spaces in the company is good in and of itself, but research demonstrates that the most successful ERGs are those that connect back to the business.[1] As ERGs are the main vehicle for promoting diversity, equity, and inclusion at Slack, the company has made a concerted effort to connect them to the business's strategy. Simon shared the four steps Slack has used to make that connection.

## *Align Leadership*

Without leadership, Simon said, nothing else will go. "[If leaders are not on board,] then you're doing work for nothing and I'd rather people save their labor and their energy." Alignment, she said, explaining benefits of ERGs, comes through communication. Companies need to encourage their creation and use, explain the benefits and how they foster community, and then try not to control them in a way that the groups don't want to be controlled. The grassroots nature must be allowed to thrive.

## *Create Feedback Loops*

Leadership meets with the leads of the ERGs every month. This practice has bidirectional benefits. The leaders get to hear what's going on and uncover employee concerns and other issues rising to the top. The ERGs gain early insight into the direction of the company and how to influence it. ERGs can also test new ideas. "If we had a feedback process that we revamped," Simon said, "we would roll it out to them first to get their feedback and make sure that we're incorporating any of that." Further, these types of feedback loops can help a company consider possible unintended consequences of new internal or external efforts. When companies make culturally insensitive missteps, people often wonder, "Why didn't someone catch this?" or "Who was in the room when that decision was made?" Take Pepsi's 2017 commercial, for example, which depicted Kendall Jenner resolving a protest by handing a police officer a can of Pepsi. The commercial received backlash accusing the company of trivializing the Black Lives Matter movement and was taken down after only a day.[2] Lack of diversity among the creative team who developed the ad was one of the major criticisms Pepsi received.[3] Creating feedback loops with groups like ERGs could help uncover potential company missteps before they are public.

## Add Senior Leadership Sponsorship

As the crucial link between leadership and the ERGs, sponsors help Slack shape the ERGs' goals. Simon explained that sponsors create buy-in: "They help you to reach your goals in the lightest way possible and leverage your sponsor on your behalf anytime you have blockers." I advise my clients that having senior leader sponsors as a formal part of an ERG structure is vital for the success of the ERG because it allows their work to get greater exposure across the organization and creates shared responsibility for success between the ERG and senior leadership team.

## Keep It Simple

Slack's ERGs are highly effective and evolved, but they got there by not trying to be perfect from the start. "Have one goal," Simon said. "Have a clear understanding of why you are coming together as a community and what would best serve that community. And then focus on one thing to help show the impact of the ERG within that community." For example, Alex King, a previous leader of the Mahogany ERG, explained the group's origins:

> The ERG started as a private Slack channel that we organized around our shared identity and allowed us to come together and push for whatever we needed—whether that was something official like senior leadership support or just getting to know people. I remember one of the senior engineering leaders seeing me in the hallway on my first week in headquarters asking me, "Do you want to be added to the Black employee channel?" And I was like, "Hell yeah!" It became a conduit for us to have conversations, to ask advice, and to create community together before we even became an ERG. We continued that purpose of connection as Mahogany.

## ERGs and Hiring

While remaining decentralized, ERGs, with the support of sponsors and leadership, can incorporate inclusive practices into basic business processes like hiring. For example, the decentralized hiring process at Slack looks different from the practice at most of its Silicon Valley competitors. Slack proactively recruits through all-women coding camps and programs that focus on training Black and Latin programmers—much different channels from the more traditional pipelines like Stanford and MIT. In 2015 the company worked with Textio to ensure that job descriptions were as inclusive as possible. Recruiters were also specifically trained to look at skills beyond a candidate's academic credentials. The interview process itself was also designed to mitigate bias.[4] It used a blind review of coding rather than the "whiteboard review" that has traditionally been a part of software hiring processes. Instead of having to solve a coding problem in real time, candidates are given a problem to complete at home. All personal identifiers are removed before the assignment is evaluated against a rigorous rubric.

Nonetheless, in 2017 it became clear that even this approach created challenges for candidates who did not have time for homework because of caretaking responsibilities or other reasons. So Slack began to offer the option to complete the assignment in the office for those who preferred that approach.

Still, the company had to put guardrails on the decentralized nature of hiring. While decentralization brought great benefits to Slack's diversity, it also meant that not every group was hiring with the same criteria, leading to potential inequities. The company is now trying to create some unity across groups.

"We asked ourselves, 'How can we look at our hiring processes to make sure they are equitable?'" Simon said. "We launched new inclusive hiring guidelines, which we had not done before, in order to start putting DEB into the actual foundation of the language that we use," no matter where these guidelines were being applied in the company. "We are still in this decentralization foundational process," she added, "which I think is where we need to move from in order to make sure that it's embedded across each department. Each department ladder should have inclusive behaviors embedded into their feedback process, which is not something we have yet."

In this case, reining in the decentralization benefited diversity. After Slack standardized behavioral interview questions for each role to ensure each candidate is asked the same set of questions, regardless of the interviewer, the number of women in technical roles grew by almost 5 percent in a year.[5]

## ERGs and Transparency

If the work of the DEI strategy is largely decentralized, coming as it does from employees in ERGs, they must be kept in the loop. Slack realized this need for employee engagement early on and has created vehicles of constant communication about how the company is doing on DEI. To that end, Slack publishes a quarterly newsletter with representation numbers in its departments. Externally, the company publishes a yearly report to hold the company publicly accountable.

The internal newsletter is crucial if there's going to be a public report. "We wanted to make sure that those numbers weren't the first time that our employees were seeing that information," Simon said.

Slack continues to push, from employees up, which data is reported. By 2017, its diversity report included information on the percentage of employees who identify themselves as having a disability, information that is not widely included in other companies' similar reports. In 2018

Slack publicly released its EEO-1 report for the first time and committed to do so in the following years for even greater transparency. That year, it also confirmed equal pay and promotion rates across genders for the third year running.[6] In 2019 Slack became a public company and grew to more than two thousand employees. Its most recent data, published in April 2021, shows the following statistics:[7]

- Globally, women constitute 44.5 percent of Slack's workforce, including the following:

  - 34.0 percent of people in technical roles

  - 45.2 percent of managers

  - 33.3 percent of director-level and higher positions

- In the United States, 13.5 percent of Slack's workforce is composed of people from one or more underrepresented racial or ethnic backgrounds, including these:

  - 14.2 percent of technical roles

  - 11.9 percent of US managers

  - 10.2 percent of US director-level and higher positions

- 6.1 percent of Slack's US workforce, including 6 percent of managers, identify as LGBTQ+.

- 1.5 percent of Slack's US workforce identify as having a disability.

- 1.6 percent of Slack's US workforce identify as veterans.

## ERGs and the Work Burden

Especially in a decentralized approach to DEI like Slack's, the work of DEI often falls on the shoulders of the very people who need the support of such efforts. The responsibility can place an undue burden on those who need support and who are also working for it.

"I think it's important to be very humble in this work," Simon said, "because, you know, we have our employee resource groups that center on women, people of color, veterans, abilities, LGBTQ+, and I looked around the room once, and these were the people that were driving these programs. And so that was a humbling moment to be part of that, but that made me realize that, even more so, we need to focus on how we recognize those individuals."

Simon explained that because of the heavy load that many people carry to ensure DEI, she has pushed leadership hard to recognize those doing the work as much as possible. "I say to all of our employee resource group leaders that we encourage them to put any of the work that they do into their performance reviews. For example, if you bring someone into the company to have a conversation around equity or to have a conversation that centers around women or people of color, that is something that is pushing us forward to better understand each other and to better connect our communities."

More leaders should be this explicit on the question of who is carrying the burden of DEI and how organizations can lift those people up. Through Simon's DEI efforts, Slack has created more support and recognition in several ways. For example, it assigns two leaders for each

ERG, and each leader gets *coaching and sponsorship opportunities*. In addition to these once-a-month coaching sessions, Slack has a community incubator program to develop new ERGs. It also has a Women in Leadership community to support the career growth of women leaders. Another effort is a six-month formal sponsorship program called Rising Tides, created for emerging leaders who have historically lacked access to career development coaching and other similar resources. Program participants receive executive coaching and one-on-one sponsorship with a Slack executive team member, with a focus on building a supportive community of peers. The 2020 cohort focused on people of color in the United States, particularly senior-level underrepresented women and nonbinary employees who were on the verge of entering leadership roles.[8]

Slack and Simon also push *feedback*, both regularly scheduled and spontaneous sessions, to ensure that the ERG leaders are aware that their hard work is being recognized. It's also an opportunity for the leaders themselves to speak up if they feel frustrated, overwhelmed, or unsupported.

The ERG teams, not just the leaders, also need support and recognition of their hard work and the burden of being the creators of the DEI culture. Here, Slack relies on straight-up *rewards* in the form of gift cards with notes of appreciation and spot bonuses that ERG leaders are empowered to distribute to their communities.

Finally, Slack works to increase the *visibility* of the ERG members doing the heavy lifting. Simon explained, "We made sure to start [group messages] with sponsors and individuals [who were on an ERG team] along with a manager, and Stewart, our CEO. We recognize the overall leaders through coaching, but we also think about how we can drive any visibility to their work [to people at the top of the organization]."

## Amplifying DEI Outside of Slack

Part of any company's DEI journey is its decision to go beyond the representation efforts in its own business to focus on the community and broader systemic issues that create inequity. To that end, Slack moved quickly to show itself as a leader beyond just what's good for Slack. It started Slack for Good, an initiative that aims to increase the number of people from historically underrepresented communities in the technology industry. One Slack for Good program, called Next Chapter, helps formerly incarcerated people find long-term employment in tech and combats stigma and bias surrounding these reentering individuals. To date, all three apprentices from Next Chapter are now full-time engineers at Slack, and the company has shared a blueprint for other firms to build similar initiatives.[9]

The ability and willingness to share what's working with others is a crucial step in the journey. Companies too often treat nearly everything about their business as proprietary, lest they let a competitive advantage slip away.

And even this public-facing function is decentralized at Slack. "Before Next Chapter was launched," Simon explained, "I hadn't seen a lot of those conversations about these biases happening." She noted that the ERGs are what pushed the conversation further and got the company to start the program supporting a historically stigmatized group. "I'm focused really internally to make sure that we are holding ourselves accountable to our employees," she said. But the ERGs are the ones getting the company to move forward with something like Next Chapter.

One of Slack's most innovative DEI efforts was to launch a nonprofit arm, Future Forum.[10] The forum aimed to help leaders across industries reimagine work through data and dialogue, to create a people-centric and digital-first future of work. Since its launch, the foum has conducted a quarterly Future Forum Pulse survey of more than ten thousand knowledge workers around the globe and consults with subject matter experts to produce publicly available playbooks to help decision-makers with real-world challenges.

I have had the pleasure of being one of the subject matter experts helping the team understand the DEI trends from the workforce data. The data collected offers groundbreaking insights, particularly on what elements make a work environment more inclusive across industries, company sizes, and stages of the DEI journey. Some of the early findings include these:[11]

- White employees reported 25 percent higher sense-of-belonging scores than did Black employees, 21 percent higher scores for level of access than did Latinx counterparts, and double their Asian American colleagues' scores for managing stress and anxiety.

- As of June 2021, 80 percent of Black, 78 percent of Hispanic, and 77 percent of Asian American respondents want a flexible working experience, through either a hybrid or a remote-only model, all higher rates than that of White employees.

- Black employees, in particular, have shown gains in feelings of belonging while working remotely and expressed a strong preference for flexible work.

  - Of Black respondents, 81 percent say they want flexibility in where they work, compared with 75 percent of White respondents.

  - With respect to when they work, 66 percent of Black respondents want a fully or mostly flexible schedule, compared with 59 percent of White respondents.

While the data has continuously shown that flexible work arrangements improve the employee experience across the board, the positive, cumulative effects of remote work are especially evident for Black knowledge workers, whose employee experience scores significantly rose between August 2020 and August 2021. Black men made the biggest gains in employee experience out of all demographic groups in the United States. The significant upswing in the percentage of Black respondents who agreed with the following statements in August 2021, compared with August 2020, is striking:

- "I value the relationship I have with my coworkers": 76 percent, up from 48 percent

- "I am treated fairly at work": 73 percent, up from 47 percent

- "Management is supportive": 75 percent, up from 43 percent

Simon discussed the importance of work like this being done more broadly: "Future Forum is looking at what is the future of work. A lot of the research that they're doing showcases how inclusion, first and foremost, is necessary for people to do their best work to feel safe, to feel heard, and to have that sense of belonging, then also to make use of that diversity. Making sure that you have a diverse workforce, making sure that in that workforce, people feel as though they belong and have a sense of purpose—that will help your bottom line."

## Can Decentralization Scale?

You might think that Slack has it all figured out. It has accomplished notable steps in its DEI journey through its ground-up, decentralized approach. You could argue that the company is aiming toward the integrated stage, as it has clearly thought about the power of its sphere of influence throughout the community and industry. Yet like many companies, Slack has struggled to further develop its efforts in a way that moves it out of the tactical stage and fully into the integrated stage, where all its DEI efforts work in concert and the company can truly say "DEI is a part of everything that we do."

In a way, Slack's present situation is what happens when a decentralized approach sets the right tone but a company needs to scale it. Scaling is difficult without some centralized coordination. As Simon explained, Slack has the right message and the right sentiment and was lucky it could build these into the company culture from the very beginning, but "we can't scale sentiment. We can't scale good behaviors. So how can we build them into systems and processes?"

Slack finds itself right in a moment of tension between decentralization and scale. Can the company preserve what helped it make such big leaps in DEI while also scaling these efforts as the company and its focus on DEI continue to grow? Can it continue without a CDO? Should it have more companywide policies? How can it get to the next step of its journey?

Simon, while not a CDO, does have a team to support her leadership, but she has been very clear with Slack's senior leadership team that success is not going to come unless everyone, especially managers, takes accountability. In a decentralized DEI strategy, managers play the most critical role in helping DEI goals come to life. Many companies struggle to activate their manager population, even when there is strong centralized leadership from the top.[12] Engaging the managers is even more difficult in a decentralized setting. Still, Simon believes it can be done. Her vision is that inclusive behaviors and values are goals for managers to hit. "Within each department, leaders should have inclusive behaviors," she said. "We've embedded that in our feedback process to make sure that we highlight cultural contributions. But we want to know, how is your manager hitting those values? How are they not hitting those values?"

A centralized function is probably the best way to measure and respond to those questions. Without it, the pressure Slack's leaders feel to keep diversity constantly circulating in the groups, constantly providing feedback and guidance, mounts. Decentralization, Rachel Westerfield said, is "nice because it doesn't make it feel like it's any one person's responsibility to say, you know, 'One, two, three, be diverse now.' But it also puts the onus on individuals like myself to be conscious at all times to keep pushing it and keep promoting it, because there's no system in place for us to just follow the prompts and do the thing."

As Slack's global manager of experience specialists, Westerfield continues to grapple with the balance between the decentralized approach and the need for more centralization as the company scales. "Each leader has to take responsibility within their teams," she said, "because I don't feel that there's necessarily a formal effort. When I do hear top-down communications, it feels like we're asking for a concerted effort on diversity, and we are defining diversity as diverse skills and not necessarily diversity in the sense of wanting to join a Zoom and see a great reflection of racial and ethnic diversity in the meeting."

What Westerfield and probably other managers are feeling seems to be how informal a decentralized approach can feel. And decentralization makes sense in a startup environment. It's an agile mentality. But just like any other operational aspect of a business, growth and scale require more formal processes and order.

As a leader of these efforts, Simon thinks that if Slack is to hold on to its decentralized approach to DEI and continue to forgo a CDO, then the leaders need to have real stakes in the game. They need a structure to follow and the freedom to feel that DEI is not a top-down mandate. So, give managers goals—whether they're actual numeric goals or just goals aligned to development opportunities and what you're doing with them in your group. Ask the managers if they can spell out what diversity means in their group. Then make sure their responses fall within the bounds of the company's goals and strategies.

Even then, Simon imagines that some centralized program will help the diverse group of managers and bottom-up efforts better align as the business scales. As Slack continues to push its individual efforts, it looks toward the future, where these efforts will create a more integrated ecosystem.

In the meantime, Simon shared some best practices for making sure a decentralized approach to DEI manages to hang together across the organization. "I'd say start small," she recommended. "Say, companywide, we're going to focus on X. For example, we're going to focus on development and retention of employees, and this is how it's going to look." And then appeal to each decentralized group: "This is what it's going to look like in our sales team. This is what it's going to look like in our engineering team. Have that companywide goal, and start with that."

From there, she added the next steps: "Capture what you learn in each outpost, because you will learn so much. Rolling the same thing out into sales and marketing and then engineering will show you how the same goal will be approached in different ways. You'll learn how to communicate with the individuals within the roles, rather than have one message for everyone."

It's unclear if Slack will eventually opt for a more centralized approach, with a CDO and a full D&I office. In the meantime, Simon serves as the linchpin between the bottom-up culture that has driven Slack's DEI efforts to date and the emerging need to wrangle an ever bigger, more culturally diverse organization.

Simon knows that more change will be needed, and she is prepared to adapt. She recognizes how no one really masters DEI; they just work hard to stay on the journey and reach that strategic phase when some of the tactical issues are worked out and you can look at the bigger picture:

> You have to approach things with a sense of humility. I will
> always have blind spots. There will always be people who

are not being included. And so, from my perspective, it's, "How can I make sure that we're focusing on accountability and not perfection?" And to build trust, you need to actually listen to people, and they need to see the impact of their feedback.

My biggest thing is, "How can I make sure that I'm building trust and listening? How can I make sure people don't think we're gaslighting them, allowing them to think that we've got it all handled?" I need to keep letting them know that we're continuing on in this journey and will continue to work toward something that feels inclusive and more equitable.

We're not where we want to be. I don't think we'll ever be where we want to be, because there will always be something that is better than where we are. It takes time to break down the structures or to change to have a larger impact, particularly since we're in a for-profit world. So how do we disrupt the status quo? That will take time, and so I think that the humility [is] saying, like, "This is where we are, this is what we're doing within that feedback loop, this is what we tried. This didn't work and we will continue to try something else." And I think that is a forward momentum and accountability. It's so important to have external accountability, even if it is only like a moment to check yourself and say, "Okay, we still have more to go."

When I asked Rachel Westerfield to share what a workplace utopia looks like for her at Slack, she paused for a long time before painting a beautiful picture:

I pause because I think that work is such a reflection of life, and if you think about it, organizations are really just microcosms of the world. I think that the reason why I pause is because I don't know how we could create a true utopia inside when there's so much wrong outside. I could talk about these ideas of equality and harmony, and I would love to see the faces on my Zoom calls or in meetings at all levels reflect what the world looks like. I would like for us to all shoulder the same emotional intellectual attachments to equality. As the folks who are Black and Brown feel every day, I would like to not have non-Black or non-Brown employees feel like they have to be allies versus just human beings who want to see other human beings treated like human beings.

I want to see less nepotism. I want to see us stop requiring twenty years of management experience when we know that the institution is not built to create opportunities for Black and Brown people to be in management for twenty years.

I want to see people have smarter and more strategic conversations that set people up for success without having to be tied back to the institution that's been oppressing them for longer than not. And I feel like we always talk about leadership responsibility. I want to see Stewart's actions, I want to see our CEO's actions be reflected in all of his direct reports and all of their direct reports and all of their direct reports. I really want to see that cascade, and I want each individual employee to feel empowered to have those conversations.

And I want all that to be just as important as the work itself. I know that at the end of the day, we're a business that thinks about our top and bottom lines. I really do want that to be a part of our fabric, so that people who do have those prejudices, people who secretly allow or even desire some level of oppression, won't even feel comfortable working at the company. I want them to feel pushed out, and I want it to be so obvious that if someone asked why they left, they wouldn't even feel comfortable answering the question.

FIGURE 2-1

**Slack's mission is to make people's working lives simpler, more pleasant, and more productive. Slack is a channel-based messaging platform where people communicate, collaborate, and get work done.**

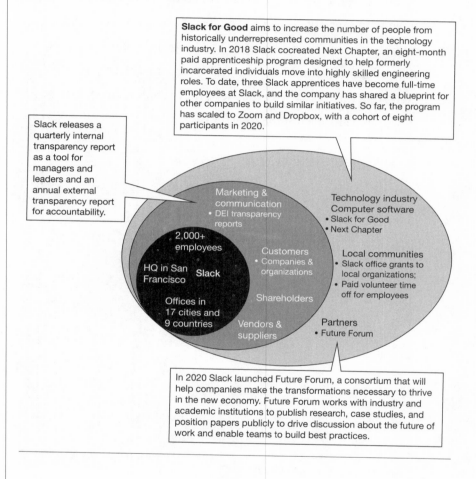

**Slack for Good** aims to increase the number of people from historically underrepresented communities in the technology industry. In 2018 Slack cocreated Next Chapter, an eight-month paid apprenticeship program designed to help formerly incarcerated individuals move into highly skilled engineering roles. To date, three Slack apprentices have become full-time employees at Slack, and the company has shared a blueprint for other companies to build similar initiatives. So far, the program has scaled to Zoom and Dropbox, with a cohort of eight participants in 2020.

Slack releases a quarterly internal transparency report as a tool for managers and leaders and an annual external transparency report for accountability.

Marketing & communication
• DEI transparency reports

Technology industry
Computer software
• Slack for Good
• Next Chapter

2,000+ employees

Customers
• Companies & organizations

Local communities
• Slack office grants to local organizations;
• Paid volunteer time off for employees

HQ in San Francisco  **Slack**

Offices in 17 cities and 9 countries

Shareholders

Vendors & suppliers

Partners
• Future Forum

In 2020 Slack launched Future Forum, a consortium that will help companies make the transformations necessary to thrive in the new economy. Future Forum works with industry and academic institutions to publish research, case studies, and position papers publicly to drive discussion about the future of work and enable teams to build best practices.

# 3

# Questioning the Status Quo on DEI at PwC

**COMPANY:** PwC

**STAGE:** Sustainable

**BEST PRACTICES:** Acceptance of, and even embracing, mistakes, which are inevitable; transparency; calling people in, not out; addressing hard questions about fairness

**KEY QUOTE:** "At a human level, we are trying to get to an environment where every person can feel like they are on equal footing to realize their full potential. For me, utopia is where every person gives 100 percent of what they are capable of, and when they do, they get great opportunities." —Tim Ryan, US chair and senior partner, PwC

On Friday, July 8, 2016, Tim Ryan was five days into his new role as the PwC US chair, senior partner, and CEO. He woke up energized and ready to activate his shiny, new hundred-day plan for revenue growth, changing PwC's business model, improving the firm's technology, and establishing many other well-thought-out plans.[1] Yet when he rose to face the day, the nation was reeling from a week of racial unrest stemming from the police killings of Alton Sterling in Baton Rouge, Louisiana, on July 5 and Philando Castile in Falcon Heights, Minnesota, the next day.[2] The week culminated on July 7 with the killing of five police officers by a Black US Army veteran angry over the police violence against Black men.[3]

On that day, Ryan decided to send an email to the firm's fifty-five thousand US employees, an email he himself described as unremarkable. The theme was to be brave. "We know these events are on your mind," he told the workers, "and we must be brave and press on."

However unremarkable he thought the email was, the response to it was anything but. The leadership team received hundreds of emails in response to Ryan's firm-wide note. One employee wrote: "Tim thanks for the email, the firm has long stood for diversity and inclusion but for me, when I came to work this morning, the silence was deafening." This email represented the feelings of many employees who felt PwC had not done enough to speak out against the injustices being felt all over the country.

## *The* Pivotal Moment

The responses to Ryan's letter created a pivotal moment—*the* pivotal moment—for Ryan and his hundred-day plan. He changed the trajectory of how PwC approached DEI forever. "The hundred-day plan went out the window," he recalled. "I realized that as a very young CEO at the time, here I am with a very ambitious business plan, and I had 100 percent physical attendance. But I didn't have 100 percent mental and heart attendance. For me, this was the real turning point. In order to really achieve success, you need people who are really engaged with their hearts and minds, and we did not have that."

The firm was already two decades into its DEI journey, but now Ryan was quickly learning that it had missed a foundational element in its approach: the ability to be comfortable talking about race. PwC had made significant progress on its DEI strategy—perhaps much more than other companies had achieved—yet in the end, people still avoided talking about race if they could manage to. Ryan shared how a good number of leaders, including himself, would admit to being uncomfortable with conversations about race: "I would ask a group of leaders in 2016, primarily White men, 'How many of you are uncomfortable knowing if you should use the word *Black* or *African American?*' More than half the room would raise their hands. And I was in that group. Here I am leading it as [the] US firm's chairman, trying to do the right thing, but was so unsure on that basic question."

The needed conversation was about being brave enough to have the uncomfortable but necessary conversation about race. Ryan said, "We had to objectively look in the mirror. We could have been defensive and said, 'Wait a minute. We have been rated number one by DiversityInc and gotten numerous awards.' But instead, we looked in the mirror and said, 'We are not nearly as good as we think we are.' We did not let ourselves be defensive. Instead, we set out with a number of very clear, deliberate goals."

Ryan decided to pause and plan a firm-wide conversation. Twelve days later, PwC hosted a daylong discussion about race, a remarkable thing for a firm of PwC's size and an even more remarkable commit-ment for a client-serving organization to dedicate an entire day—effectively overriding millions of dollars in billable hours—for this effort.

Though many *Fortune* 500 companies have DEI efforts, PwC's long-standing commitment to DEI has led by example in questioning the status quo and in being the first of its peers to act. From boldly talking about race in 2016, when even saying the word *Black* was taboo in most workplaces, to leading the industry in publishing its first "Diversity and Inclusion Transparency" report in October 2020, PwC had made great progress, recognizing that DEI efforts are an integral component and priority of business strategy.

## PwC's Head Start

PwC has been leading the charge for DEI in the workplace since the 1990s, before many other companies had started being intentional about such efforts. In the early phases of its journey, the firm focused on gender equity. PwC experimented with a new approach that al-lowed employees to work part-time without derailing their path to partnership. The program showed signs of success in 1993, when two part-time women employees were admitted to the partnership. PwC's DEI efforts led it be named one of the top hundred best companies for working mothers. PwC carried this momentum into supporting the LGBTQ+ community as well. In 1999—well before law dictated it in 2013—PwC was among the first companies to offer benefits to same-sex domestic partnerships, a transformative decision that will resonate in US history for generations to come.[4]

So even in the 1990s, PwC had built a track record of not only talking the talk but also walking the walk. The company had taken actionable steps toward lifting up and supporting employees who faced both underrepresentation and societal discrimination.

PwC's commitment to these efforts continued into the first decade of the twenty-first century at the same pace. In 2001 the first woman partner was elected to the board of directors and the first CDO was named and then elevated to the executive leadership team in 2003. The importance of this representation has helped PwC create a globally consistent approach to DEI and continue to drive its DEI strategy. Some other key initiatives that were birthed at the time include these:

- **LGBTQ+ Partner Advisory Board (2004):** an initiative to raise the visibility of successful gay role models.[5] Board members led the Out Professional Employee Networks (OPEN) in their local markets with a focus on networking, career development, allyship, and community service activities. The program is now called Shine.

- **Vanguard (2010):** a yearlong leadership development program for the firm's Black new hires. This program evolved to the current program, Thrive, an innovative two-year experience for Black and Latinx new hires at the entry level. Thrive helped lay the foundation for a successful career through culture workshops, networking, connectivity, and leadership engagement.

- **Start Internship (2004):** PwC's diversity summer internship program uniquely designed for high-performing college sophomores and rising juniors who self-identify as members of traditionally racially or ethnically diverse groups in the professional services industry (Black, Latinx, American Indian or Alaska Native, Native Hawaiian or Other Pacific Islander, or two or more races), protected veterans, and individuals with disabilities.[6]

By 2015, PwC was a shining example of DEI. That year, the company also received a 100 percent on the Disability Equality Index.[7] The next year, it had the most diverse leadership team in the firm's history.

But despite all these achievements and accolades and the continued significant DEI efforts of the firm, before 2016, when Tim Ryan became the US firm's chair and senior partner, PwC was still at the tactical phase of its DEI journey, having moved through the awareness and compliance stages. While the company had many DEI programs deployed in specific situations and places, it was missing the bigger picture of the work needed to change the experience of *all* its employees. As a firm in which most employees were White (59.9 percent), male (51 percent), and straight (58 percent), PwC's efforts had not fully addressed the deeper issues many of its employees were experiencing day to day.[8] Further, the organization was also at the tactical stage because it had not yet fully considered the potential of its sphere of influence to have an impact on DEI outside of PwC's workforce. A broader, external outlook is a critical element of the integrated and sustainable stages of DEI. In 2016, when Ryan sent the provoking memo, there was a turning point. The firm realized that while its metrics and programs were good, those alone were not enough. Chief purpose and inclusion officer, Shannon Schuyler, recounted that the company's main stance was that training at intentional moments throughout the career path, especially for racially and ethnically diverse communities, would help everyone get along. But it had become clear that some elements were still missing from the DEI strategy, Schuyler explained:

> I look at what we've done for the past two decades, and we've had a significant commitment around D&I. But I think we, like many organizations, thought diversity and inclusion were about programs. It was saying we need to send especially our diverse employees to training to help them succeed. You can only get so far in building a culture of belonging if you take the people who are not in the majority to educate them but you don't educate the majority. We were knowledge-oriented in our training, but we didn't get the emotional side. That was the pivotal change for us. We realized this is about getting into the deep dialogue about why we make the decisions that we do emotionally and how that impacts not only people's work but also their lives.

## Beyond Programs and Training

The need to tap into the actual employee experience at PwC is what spurred the firm-wide conversation, which itself begot a further series of firm-wide candid conversations about race in 2016. For Ryan and the rest of the leadership team, it was an eye-opening experience that left no doubt PwC needed more than programs and training. They learned about the complexities of the Black professional work experience. For example, the leaders heard from employees who explained how they must teach their kids that they may get pulled over by police for no reason other than the color of their skin and how to deal with such a fraught situation. The employees explained how they carry their PwC business card with them in case they get pulled over, to prove to police that they can afford the car they're driving. This is an experience that people of color can relate to. As a Black woman, I myself have often made sure to have my Georgetown faculty ID with me when traveling alone at night, in case I get pulled over by police.

Some of the Black PwC professionals in New York shared stories of walking the hallways of the Manhattan office feeling as if they were being watched and constantly feeling as if they did not belong. Ryan described these stories as heartbreaking. He was embarrassed that he hadn't known about them. He walked away from this first firm-wide conversation with a strong conviction: "If we don't make it safe for [employees] to talk about what's really on their minds, we'll never be the business we want and serve our clients the way we want to."[9]

Although the 2016 candid conversation on race was a proud moment for the firm, Ryan had to face the reality that PwC was not truly using its sphere of influence to make the greatest impact possible for DEI:

> After our daylong discussion on race, I was leaving the office.
> It was eight o'clock at night. It was an exhausting day, one
> that started in Atlanta and ended in New York. One of our

Black professionals, a senior manager, stopped me in the office and he said thank you. But—and there was a but—he said, "What's PwC's role outside of the firm?"

I will admit, at first I was like, "Can I just get a break?" Like we just did this momentous thing. Can I take a breather? But that night I tossed and I turned, and he was right. We were sitting on a major brand at PwC. We have thousands of clients. We do have a bigger role. After listening to him and then talking to dozens of CEOs, we landed on the idea of creating a new coalition. We asked them to voluntarily work with us to make commitments that will make the business community better.

The new coalition that was cofounded by PwC and eight other CEOs is called CEO Action for Diversity & Inclusion. Its goal is to collectively take measurable action in advancing D&I in the workplace. Recognizing that change starts at the executive level, CEO Action went after the commitments of CEOs of the world's leading companies and business organizations. It is the largest CEO-driven business commitment to D&I in the workplace. CEOs and presidents are pledging to act on supporting a more inclusive workplace for employees, communities, and society at large. For PwC, the coalition's founding was a significant step past the tactical phase and into the integrated and sustainable phases of its journey.

Still, even with the powerhouse brand of PwC, Ryan shared with me how challenging it was to get CEOs to commit to the coalition during its early stages. "We asked CEOs to recognize a topic they are uncomfortable with or would like to improve in and work voluntarily to make D&I commitments," he said. The coalition started with 112 CEOs in 2017. Although membership steadily grew in the first few years, a major uplift in support came in 2020, with 400-plus companies joining in the last six months of the year. With the onslaught of a global pandemic, the murder of George Floyd, and the ensuing protests demanding change, companies felt pressure to do something. Some of them opted to address issues of racism head-on, put in systemic changes, and created financial pipelines for disenfranchised communities. This was a new landscape for many CEOs, Schuyler explained. "These CEOs who are currently in their role focused on share price and never thought they would have to deal with or speak out on social issues or lead in a time where there are no sidelines. CEOs cannot opt out today, because if they opt out, then the narrative will be written for them."

Still, many companies faced backlash from opting in and making bold DEI commitments in 2020 when they had not previously done so. They were accused of performative allyship or activism to increase their social capital rather than actual devotion to the cause. Though Ryan acknowledged the reactive nature of many of these companies, he is less concerned that these actions are performative and more excited that the companies have finally joined the conversation. "The good part," he said, "is companies are stepping up and they are listening to their communities, their people, and other stakeholders like investors, boards, and policy makers. Frankly, only time will tell how many hang in there as we progress. But one of the things that I love about CEO Action, its strategy, is to get people in the boat. And once we all get in the boat, we pull each other along where it is a healthy competition."

environmental sustainability. As a part of the strategy, PwC renewed its Access Your Potential initiative, committing $125 million to this initiative that aims to close the opportunity gap and support a more equitable future for twenty-five thousand Black and Latinx college students as they prepare for and begin in-demand careers. PwC aspires to hire ten thousand Black and Latinx students at the firm by 2026.[13]

Looking toward the future, PwC has launched a new global strategy called the New Equation, which doubles down on its commitment to DEI; operating responsibly in sustainable ways; and driving a human-led, tech-powered approach. Ryan described the strategy: "We have evolved into a community of solvers coming together in unexpected ways. We are bringing the strength of our people, capabilities, and technology together to support our clients in building trust and delivering outcomes for their businesses."[14]

## Why Not?

When we look at PwC's journey, we know it's not over. It continues, and the progress has been largely continuous and positive for three decades now. The company has been able to move forward by challenging the status quo. With many of PwC's breakthrough moments, the company was deciding to do things that simply weren't done or things for which there was an easy business reason not to do it. Providing a path to partnership for part-time women who were having children was simply not something companies did or thought they needed to at the time. Benefits for domestic partners were exceedingly rare before

Questioning the Status Quo on DEI at PwC

data on the racial and ethnic makeup of their workforce.[11] Many organizations are fearful of sharing their demographic data, even internally. As a DEI consultant, I once had a chief human resource officer tell me, "Once we share our data, then we have to answer the tough questions about why our numbers are this way, and we are just not ready for that conversation."

But that is exactly the point. How can you challenge the status quo if you refuse to face it? The conversation is your destination, not an obstacle to be avoided.

PwC's ability and decision to release its "Diversity and Inclusion Transparency" report itself is a huge demonstration of commitment and a willingness to be held accountable, to have the hard conversations. How did it do what other companies are afraid of? Part of the answer has to do with PwC's head start on DEI efforts. Even if it was not as far along in its journey as the firm thought it was before 2016, its two decades of work, combined with world events that were forcing it to confront the topics, gave PwC the ability to embrace the moment. Schuyler described what led the firm to this decision: "We have been invested for two decades, with chief diversity officers for eighteen years. It was really important for us to make sure that people knew that we weren't hiding anything. We wanted to show the things we have been getting right and not just talking about, such as recruiting and pay equity. But then other areas, frankly, we were not doing as well as we thought, and we have to own that."

PwC released an updated "Purpose and Inclusion Transparency" report in 2021 with eighteen measures of D&I.[12] The firm also announced a new plan to focus on recruitment, training, technology, and

In forming the CEO Action for Racial Equity fellowship, the CEO Action coalition again challenged the status quo of corporate America staying out of government and policy decisions. The coalition launched the fellowship by uniting the talent and resources from more than a hundred signatory companies in 2020. The goal was to provide the opportunity for CEO Action signatories to advance racial equity through public policy. Using CEO Action as a platform, the fellowship will mobilize the business community collectively across industries and regions to enact legislative and regulatory change.[10]

In 2020 PwC continued to question the status quo by going public with its own progress on DEI. In an industry first, it published its D&I data and strategy in its "Diversity and Inclusion Transparency" report, led by Shannon Schuyler. The report shared the organization's demographics by employment level as well as the company's detailed strategy for making progress in representation and equity at all levels. This data included fourteen data points deemed relevant to PwC's business: the US employee workforce; new joiners; partners and principals; US boards of partners and principals; US leadership teams; interns, including those from the Start program; promotions; new partners; global engagement partners of *Fortune* 500 accounts; suppliers; LGBTQ+ communities; veterans; and people with disabilities.

The significance of this report can't be understated. In July 2020 only 4 percent of public companies shared their DEI data. This low disclosure rate is starting to change. By January 2021, the numbers had increased to 6.3 percent of America's largest corporations disclosing diversity data that could be derived from an EEO-1 report. Despite the progress, 68 percent of companies in the Russell 1000 still release no

Because of PwC's vision and leadership, CEO Action for Diversity & Inclusion has accelerated its growth, increasing its membership by more than 40 percent in a single year (2021) to over two thousand CEOs and university presidents and more than seventeen hundred actions shared in 2021. The coalition represents more than eighty-five industries and more than thirteen million employees. It is a trailblazer on looking beyond your immediate environment and considering your larger impact in the world. It's advanced stuff.

## "What More Can We Do?"

In 2020 Tim Ryan was again confronted with the question of what more could be done, just as he had been in 2016, but this time from his CEO peers:

Prior to George Floyd's murder, CEO Action was all focused on what we can do better inside our four walls. What George Floyd's killing did was bring light to the public policy chal-lenges that we have in this country. And what I'm proud to tell you is, I heard from a couple hundred CEOs after George Floyd's killing who said, "I'm glad we're doing what we're doing with CEO Action, but what more can we do?" That led to a week's discussion and debate and ultimately led to PwC deciding to address public policy. We started a fellowship, CEO Action for Racial Equity, where for the first time, we're advancing racial equity through public policy at scale.

the twenty-first century. There were financial and business reasons not to take a full day of business off to discuss equity and inclusion. Businesses typically took a neutral posture to world events and, to some extent, to public policy. But in each of these cases, PwC simply didn't adhere to the status quo.

That's the very first best practice that emerges from PwC's journey: Question the status quo. Break it. Ask why not? What follows are other lessons learned from the journey.

## *Not Everyone Will Agree*

DEI has not always been the popular thing for organizations to do. In fact, many organizations have traditionally faced significant resistance to DEI efforts, and some still do today. Ryan is no stranger to resistance to the change he wanted to bring to PwC. He recalled the resistance he encountered:

> A leader's job is to listen and be humble but, at the end of the day, to make decisions. I learned very early on that if I'm worried about what everyone else is thinking, my head would be swiveling around all the time. I had several very close friends of mine inside the firm reach out to me and say, "Tim, we didn't elect you for this; you're focusing on the wrong things." That hurt, but I listened and came to appreciate where they were coming from. But it didn't deter me from what I needed to do. I needed the thick skin to know not to get angry at them but instead to spend time with them and bring them

along. But also not to let those opinions take away from doing what I knew was right.

As a leader, Ryan has prioritized welcoming diverse perspectives. He makes it a personal mission to respond to employees who reach out to him. One experience he shared was that of a senior manager struggling with the societal injustice messaging she was seeing in the firm from her vantage point:

> She wrote to me and said, "Tim, I'm all in on what this firm is doing. I thank you. I appreciate it. But I want to share my perspective. My husband is a Minneapolis police officer; he works the night shift. We have two children, and I put them to bed and kiss him good night not knowing if he is going to come back, given all the violence we are having in our city right now. I carry that stress and hide it from my kids. He does not condone what happened to George Floyd; he knows it was wrong. But I need your help, Tim, to make sure everyone knows not all police are bad."

Ryan described listening to her point of view and others, saying these conversations have made him a better leader and helped him adjust his messaging:

> I listen and do not get defensive when people give me feedback on how to better communicate. It's without a doubt made me a better leader, whether it be people who have said we're going

too far or others who have said, "Tim, your messaging might be construed as you're condemning an entire group." I've had to listen every time, and it makes me better at what I do.

## *Embrace Mistakes*

Missteps are always going to happen, so use your mistakes to move forward. Think of Ryan's firm-wide email. Once feedback started pouring in, showing that people felt unheard and unaddressed, Ryan could have dug in. He could have simply said, "I've done what I can," and moved forward with the growth plan he was so excited to execute. Instead, he acknowledged that the memo wasn't enough, and he opened a broader dialogue, which was the pivotal moment that opened his eyes to what PwC had missed in its DEI efforts.

As a leader, Ryan has learned the fallacy of reaching toward perfection instead of continuous improvement. "We have moved PwC very fast, and I'm very willing to say we got it 80 percent right, 20 percent wrong. But don't get defensive. Fix your issue, and move forward. I believe that's how successful organizations move."

Embracing and learning from mistakes, Schuyler said, builds trust with employees, clients, and other stakeholders who know you've made a mistake whether you acknowledge or embrace it. Now more than ever, when trust is both harder to earn and easier to lose, companies must be able to build it. This focus on trust is the underpinning of PwC's move-forward strategy, the New Equation. Ryan said, "Our new strategy is one that is relentlessly focused on our clients and other stakeholders, helping them build trust and deliver outcomes for their businesses."[15] As part of the new strategy, the PwC Trust Leadership Institute (launched in 2021) will equip more than ten thousand business leaders with the skills to help build trust around tomorrow's challenges and realities. The institute is designed for today's and tomorrow's C-suite—executives and board members who will lead and advise society's most trusted organizations.[16]

## *Transparency Is Necessary for Change*

Disclosure of where you are in your DEI efforts and where you want to go is a way to create accountability and in turn build more trust with stakeholders. Transparency takes tremendous courage (and challenges the status quo, too; companies tend not to disclose internal information if they don't have to). "It makes a lot of leaders, even people within the diversity inclusion group, say, 'Oh, please don't do it,'" said Schuyler. "Because they'll see that we haven't made progress. So, the first thing you have to do is say what it is. The numbers are there."

Of course, there is always the possibility that the numbers you publish won't show progress or will show that you're falling short of your goals. That's okay. The disclosure simply signals that it's time to evaluate what's going wrong and to adjust. But lack of transparency removes accountability. "If we let ourselves not share numbers for the next five years," Schuyler said, "we won't be able to make progress on the numbers."

Further, perfection is not the goal on the journey, as perfection is not possible. Rather, it's important for organizations to always remain humble and willing to keep putting in the work.

## *Call People In, Not Out*

Schuyler said it best about the tenor of DEI discussions like the one PwC had: "This isn't a blame game, and it's not an apology tour." One of the traps some companies fall into when tackling DEI is letting the conversations become only about why they are falling short, what's gone wrong, and who's at fault for a lack of progress. In the countless town halls across organizations led and observed in 2020, leaders often shied away from open questions from team members for fear they themselves would be put on the spot about their DEI shortcomings. Dodging open dialogue did not eliminate the blame game from employees. They instead still shared these sentiments with their smaller groups and teams. The common result was the employees' continued belief that their organizations were not truly committed to DEI.

Instead of shying away from the tough conversations, you as a leader need to acknowledge any shortcomings and then invite all your people in to participate in improving the situation and, crucially, give them the tools they need to participate and move the needle. "Yes, we want you to be accountable," Schuyler observed, "but we also need you to be part of this."

Calling people in, not out, extends outside the organization as well. Ryan has seen how making it a mission to be a leader in DEI has affected others:

> Our goal is to help inspire the business community to be the
> best it can, and we will be spending more and more time
> to both share our mistakes, share our learnings, share our

financial assets, and our human capital assets, to try to make the business community a better, more inclusive environment for all.

One of my most satisfying moments is when I'll be talking to another CEO about a piece of business and they'll say, "Look, I want to thank you for pushing us and the leadership that you're providing the business community." I expect more from us now, and as CEOs we should expect more from each other.

### Address the Elephant in the Room: "What about Me?"

Inevitably, when DEI programs begin to show progress, some people believe that progress comes at their own expense.[17] There's a real tension between doing the right thing for *everyone* and what that might mean to *someone*. Schuyler explained: "I spend a lot of time talking to our White male partners who have done the right thing for the past fifteen years as they worked for that next big job. And now . . . it's going to be a woman or a Black or other underrepresented] partner getting it because they're ready and equally qualified for it. And the White males are very upset and believe it's unfair." PwC is not alone in facing the challenge of some members of the majority feeling they will be left out or disenfranchised in some way, given a higher focus on DEI.[18] Yet many leaders shy away from the issue instead of addressing the elephant in the room and having the uncomfortable conversation. Schuyler's approach is one of candor about the commitment the firm has made moving forward: "I can open up that data and say, 'Are you telling me we've been around for 160 years and 9 percent of our partners are Black and 64 percent are White men? So which part is not fair?' So have a conversation, acknowledge that it's happening on their watch, but also help them to realize it isn't about making anyone feel inferior. We are actually trying to get to a place of parity. That's still emotionally hard for a lot of people."

The conversation is a tough one because cultivating equity from traditionally inequitable structures will likely make people who have traditionally benefited from those structures uncomfortable. Yet these conversations create some necessary growing pains on the journey. Schuyler encourages connecting these decisions to the overall impact of the organization, for example, that having diversity will make the firm stronger and ultimately more profitable. She explained that the message should highlight the abundant opportunities (instead of a deficit mindset, where only one person can benefit) and courageously set a standard of inclusion: "Maybe you don't get that role, but you will end up with another role. There are opportunities that are here; we just have to look at it differently. We want to help the majority become allies, and that means you are a part of this. I think we are to the point where we obviously want to keep all our people who want to do the right thing. But if there's somebody out there who's just saying, 'No, I'm out, and I'm not willing to reflect on or change my behavior,' we don't need them here." Schuyler strongly believes that the more companies collectively stand by their DEI values in their decision-making, the less likely that people will have exclusionary mindsets.

# A Devastating Moment

Tim Ryan's initial daylong conversation about race and the ensuing candid conversations during the year were critical to PwC's continued work on creating a culture of care, belonging, and trust with employees. But Ryan couldn't have known at the time how important this work would become.

Two years later, Botham Jean, a PwC employee in Dallas, was sitting on his couch, watching football in his apartment. An off-duty police officer mistook Jean's apartment for her own and, thinking she had found an intruder in the house, shot and killed him.[19]

It was a visceral, devastating moment. In 2016 it had become clear that PwC wasn't having the conversations it needed to. This time, the firm's culture faced up to tragedy by embracing conversation, acknowledging the injustice, and working through the detrimental impact of the tragedy on the workplace. Ryan sent a companywide email about the tragedy, writing, "Emotions are raw not only in Dallas but across the firm. It is important that we all take time to understand the experiences our underrepresented minorities—and especially, in this situation, our black colleagues—experience in everyday life so that we can all be better co-workers, friends and allies." PwC also spearheaded a Day of Understanding for more than 150 companies touching more than 600,000 participants.

Ryan could see real progress in the firm's culture. "What made me proud is the fact that we knew what to do," he said. "In the face of tragedy—not just a name on the news or a name on social media, but one of our own—we knew what to do. All across the country, the silence was not deafening."[20] The firm later honored Jean's legacy with a portrait and room named after him in the Dallas office as well as establishing a scholarship in his name at his alma mater, Harding University.[21]

Looking toward the future, PwC will continue to evolve and question what DEI should be in the workplace and in society as a whole. Shannon Schuyler hopes to foster even more deliberate time spent on diversity and inclusion, which she believes will spill out well beyond the firm's culture to foster more conversation among families, friends, and communities. She described her vision:

> Behavior change is what you need. I want people to be able to live in the moment and stop themselves before making the biased decision. People who are empathetic enough to slow the busy world down to be in the moment and realize the decisions that they are making. They still might decide the best person for a role is a White student that I knew from Notre Dame, and that's fine. But I am amazed when people are able to take the time to consider what would actually make the team better, how they can bring different voices to the table. To me, [utopia] is having fifty-five thousand people reflect on their individual decisions throughout the day. That would be not only a change within us, but that would be a huge start to societal changes when we think about how that rolls over to their personal life, their friends. And if we're doing this, it's going to cascade.

Leadership is obviously crucial to a company's necessary journey toward a more equitable culture. How do we enable the leadership of the future to continue to push DEI forward? Ryan elevates the importance of systemic DEI education. "One of my dreams," he said, "is to have a universal course on DEI taught in every college and university that covers four elements: demographics, which helps us understand where we are as a society but also important business factors like talent strategies and customer segmentation strategies; measurement, such as return on investment or calculating pay gaps; leadership, which is critical in the business world; and the value of public and private partnerships."

PwC was fortunate to have Ryan at the moment when it needed a leader like him. But what drove him to continue PwC's decades of work to new levels? When I asked him what I ask all leaders, "What does a workplace utopia look like to you?" he shared this story:

> I was nineteen years old. I was shucking lettuce in the back room at the supermarket that I worked at while I was paying for college. And there was a boy who had a disability who worked at the supermarket, and me and my friends were making fun of him. I was the leader of the group making fun of this boy, behind his back, of course.
>
> The store manager was a guy named Richie, who has since passed. He walked by and he heard me. And he pointed at me and he said, "Knock it off!" He said, "He's giving you 100 percent of what he's capable of giving you. What more do you want?"
>
> I learned more in that experience than I did in any other one moment in my life. My job is to create an environment where everybody can give 100 percent what they're capable of. And when they do, they get great opportunities, and for me that's utopia.

FIGURE 3-1

## PwC is a global network of firms delivering world-class assurance, tax, and consulting services. The firm's purpose is to build trust in society and solve important problems.

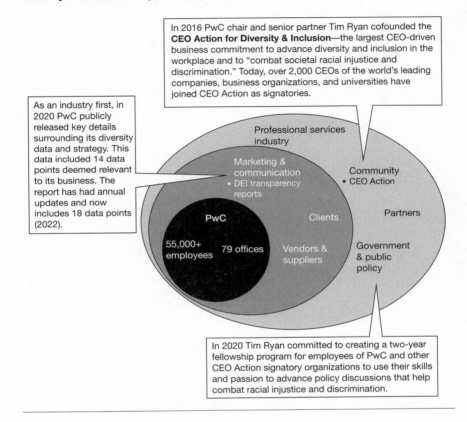

In 2016 PwC chair and senior partner Tim Ryan cofounded the **CEO Action for Diversity & Inclusion**—the largest CEO-driven business commitment to advance diversity and inclusion in the workplace and to "combat societal racial injustice and discrimination." Today, over 2,000 CEOs of the world's leading companies, business organizations, and universities have joined CEO Action as signatories.

As an industry first, in 2020 PwC publicly released key details surrounding its diversity data and strategy. This data included 14 data points deemed relevant to its business. The report has had annual updates and now includes 18 data points (2022).

Professional services industry

Marketing & communication
• DEI transparency reports

Community
• CEO Action

PwC

Clients

Partners

55,000+ employees

79 offices

Vendors & suppliers

Government & public policy

In 2020 Tim Ryan committed to creating a two-year fellowship program for employees of PwC and other CEO Action signatory organizations to use their skills and passion to advance policy discussions that help combat racial injustice and discrimination.

# 4

# Harnessing the Power
# of Diversity of Thought
# at Uncle Nearest

---

**COMPANY:** Uncle Nearest

**STAGE:** Integrated

**BEST PRACTICES:** Clear values, culture of diversity of thought, creating industry change (sphere of influence), acknowledging trade-offs

**KEY QUOTE:** "When you set this as your intention from the start, then you are able to build a culture where DEI is so innate that people will question when something is not aligned with that value." —Fawn Weaver, CEO and founder, Uncle Nearest

---

Nathan "Nearest" Green, known to many as Uncle Nearest, was an enslaved man living in Lynchburg, Tennessee, in the 1850s. He made whiskey using a special charcoal-filtering technique he learned when cleaning water back home in West Africa. His method of filtering whiskey through charcoal made from sugar maple trees became known as the famous Lincoln method, named for the Tennessee county where the technique proliferated. The method is still used today.[1]

One person Green taught the Lincoln method to was a young Jasper Daniel, a natural entrepreneur who saw genius in Green's method and product. Daniel so believed in this whiskey that he started selling it as far and wide as he could. When the Civil War ended, Daniel bought a distillery and named it after himself, subbing in the first name Jack.

Jack Daniel's first master distiller was Green, Uncle Nearest, now a free man and a mentor and close friend of Daniel's. Green worked at the distillery for many years until he retired, but his story, and the credit for one of the most recognizable brands in the United States, evaporated and was lost for decades.

Lynchburg locals remembered Uncle Nearest, but the rest of the country didn't until Clay Risen highlighted Green's legacy in a 2016 *New York Times* article, "Jack Daniel's Embraces a Hidden Ingredient: Help from a Slave."[2] Risen's article was revelatory to most, but he also thought it was incomplete. He shared the challenges of getting the true, detailed story with so little archival material. Having cobbled the narrative together mostly from oral history, Risen believed there was still more to the story to uncover.[3]

## An Undaunted Spirit

Fawn Weaver was inspired by the story and wanted to uncover more. "For me, as an African American, it was mind-boggling," she said in a podcast interview. "We know that African Americans have been involved in so many brands over the centuries, but we've never been able to point to one and say: this person actually had a name and this person had a significant role."[4] Weaver planned a trip to Lynchburg to interview as many people as she could about the story, with plans to write a book and movie to honor Nearest Green's legacy.

In interviews with Weaver, Green's family told her the one thing that would truly honor their ancestor was to give him his own bottle of whiskey. Weaver was so inspired she invested $1 million of her own money in 2017 to found a distillery. In a few short years, Uncle Nearest has become the fastest-growing whiskey brand in the country.[5] In the company's first four years, Weaver raised $60 million, and today, Uncle Nearest is the bestselling African American–owned and African American–founded spirit brand of all time, from a company that employs fewer than a hundred. Available in all fifty US states, twelve countries, and more than twenty-five thousand restaurants, stores, and bars, the brand has seen 100 percent growth each quarter to date.[6] Its three ultra-premium whiskeys have garnered more than 150 awards. Uncle Nearest has earned 25 Best in Class honors, and more than 370 awards, including being named one of the top five whiskeys in the world by *Cigar & Spirits* magazine.[7]

In the $70 billion wine and spirits industry, where less than 1 percent of wineries and distilleries are Black-owned and where there is a lack of BIPOC leadership, Weaver knew that as a Black woman, she would be fighting an uphill battle from the start.[8] But Weaver was undaunted. She sought not only to make history as an inclusive brand breaking barriers as the first spirit to commemorate an African

American and the first to have a Black master distiller on record but also to create a top-performing organization. Her strategy for making it happen was to embrace diversity in all forms, including diversity of thought.

## The Tricky Topic of Diversity of Thought

As a researcher and consultant, I'm wary of the term *diversity of thought*. In principle, it's good. Having many ideas from many people who think in many ways will improve performance.

However, the concept is often used as a weak substitute for doing the work. It's a way to avoid difficult DEI conversations around race, gender, gender identity, sexual orientation, disability, and so on. I have heard countless leaders suggest that since they have diversity of thought on their teams, they don't need to be focused on demographic inequity or changes to the makeup of teams. Even if their leadership teams comprise mostly men, mostly White, from mostly from the same colleges and socioeconomic backgrounds, these leaders use diversity of thought as their excuse not to work on those other necessary DEI tasks.

True, DEI progress requires both demographic and attitudinal diversity, and diversity of thought isn't always found where you'd expect it to be. "People often focus on demographic diversity like race and gender, but the reality is, that is not the totality of diversity to me," Weaver said, noting that you can't project how people will think simply from their demographics. She shared one of her favorite examples of this observation:

My husband's parents moved to Nashville from California, and they had a neighbor who, if you saw him in a movie, you would automatically paint him as a [White, uneducated, poor person]. Big, jacked-up truck and the White guy with the long beard and the tattoos and the bald head. I saw him outside one day, and my mother-in-law said, "He doesn't like Black people." I asked if he told her that, and she said, "No, just whenever we are out there, he never says hello. He never even bothers looking at us." Pop chimed in. "Oh, yeah, he doesn't like Black people."

So the next morning, I see him outside washing his truck. I go out the back door, and I start walking over there just to say hello, to test out whether this assumption was their projection onto him or if this was accurate. As I'm walking over, I got about halfway down the yard, and I started hearing "No diggity, no doubt, play on player," from the hip-hop song ["No Diggity," by Blackstreet]. I walk over, and when I tell you, I talked to this man for about fifteen minutes, his whole playlist was Black old school, 90s R&B music. Talk about a person who had a hard exterior! Yet the moment I said hello with a smile, it was like pouring water on a desert.

A lot of times, we project our views onto other people based on what we think they will think about us, and it can be a missed opportunity for true diversity of thought.

Simply having demographic diversity doesn't ensure diversity of thought, and Weaver was going to be sure that Uncle Nearest had both.

# Intentionality as a Virtue

A common mistaken assumption of people I encounter in my work is that minority-owned businesses don't need to put as much effort into DEI. After all, they have more diverse leadership out of the gate, which seems like sort of a head start.

This assumption couldn't be faultier, for many reasons. First, DEI goes beyond representation alone. Every organization, no matter its demographic makeup, must be intentional about the equitable nature of its systemic structures such as hiring and promotion, in addition to focusing on making the culture diverse, equitable, and inclusive.

Further, many organizations intent on DEI get so caught up in the demographic numbers they forget about focusing on the larger organizational mission. When I ask clients, "How does your DEI strategy connect with your vision?" they often struggle to make the connection.

So while Weaver is a Black woman, she knew that she would need to intentionally tie her DEI efforts to her very clear mission: to put the Uncle Nearest brand on par with the best-known whiskey brands in the world. It started with hiring a team, from an industry with a deep lack of demographic diversity. One way she could have approached this challenge would have been to prioritize hiring minorities to start her company. There is a popular cultural notion of Black excellence—a way for Black communities to be self-reliant and prosper in spite of the systemic inequalities they have faced.[9] Psychologists have demonstrated the underpinnings of this idea. It is an identity protection mechanism that emerges in historically marginalized groups and is manifest in people's desire to cluster within their own demographic groups to buffer against discriminatory experiences such as racism and to affirm their identity.[10] This is why historically Black colleges and institutions such as my alma mater, Spelman College, have been places where Black students have a stable and nurturing environment and, later in life, are more likely to report they are thriving than their Black peers who graduated from predominately White institutions.[11] Yet, if we are seeking diversity in the workplace, we need to recognize the downsides of demographic clustering. Homophily, or the tendency of individuals to associate with similar others, is well documented in workplace research as people tend to find themselves socializing and networking with others who are like them.[12] Further, research has shown that many people fall victim to the similar-to-me cognitive bias during hiring and promotion processes that can lead to disparate impacts for underrepresented groups.[13]

So, it would not be surprising for an entrepreneur like Weaver, from an underrepresented background, to aim to hire other underrepresented employees when given the opportunity. It would be a mechanism to provide opportunities that are not readily available for them. Indeed, Black employers are more likely than White employers to hire Black employees.[14]

Yet Weaver wasn't thinking that way. She was adamant that minority-owned businesses that seek to grow to the highest levels of success must prioritize diversity in hiring, even when their counterparts do not, and that the notion of Black-only excellence, for example, would ultimately be a disservice to the business and the communities that would benefit from the business.

"I think you have to look at what a business's motivation is," she said. "If your motivation is making a whole lot of money, we as African Americans as a whole, we spend a much greater amount than is our percentage of the population. If you're just trying to make money, then do that, all day long, and you'll be fine." Because African Americans spend disproportionately, she was saying, then a product "by Black people and for Black people" would do well if the goal was purely to make money.[15] But as she explained, Weaver had bigger ambitions:

> Money was not my motivation. That is the difference. I am looking at who I want to position Uncle Nearest with, which is Jim Beam, Jack Daniel's, and Johnnie Walker, brands that have [been] sustained for 150 years. You cannot do that by limiting your diversity. So, I'm going to ask the reverse question: If Black excellence is good enough for us, why is it not good enough for everybody? The idea that we have to just take a sliver of the pie, and take our Black excellence, and only showcase it to those like us, it's like preaching to the choir. There is no diversity in that. Why would we do that? We are creating a product that is excellent. We are bringing together a team that is excellent. And we are going to make sure that everybody knows it.

To be clear, Weaver would seek demographic diversity on her team; she was not forgoing that part of her DEI journey. She was only saying that she was not interested in demographic issues alone. Diversity of thought, which would come from multiple types of people—and, often, unexpected people—would make Uncle Nearest a brand beyond its diverse roots, competing with august incumbents.

## The Four DEI Pitfalls of Startups

The first stage of the DEI maturity model, awareness, describes organizations that are just beginning to understand the necessity of intentional DEI efforts. While you might wonder how any company today could be just coming to this conclusion, I have seen, before and after the events of 2020, countless organizations that are just entering the awareness stage and are standing at the very beginning of their journey.

Companies at the awareness stage have generally fallen into two camps. One group is the older, successful company that has never needed to prioritize DEI. For example, I worked with a hundred-year-old family-owned business in the Midwest. It had prided itself on being run by family values, and it struggled greatly to change its culture when a new CEO who was passionate about DEI joined in the mid-2010s. During initial conversations with the executive team, the new leader found that the most common thought on DEI was along the lines of, "I am not sure why we really need this; people love working here. If there were a problem, we would know." The organization did have an impressively low rate of attrition, which did suggest that employees valued working there. However, focus groups with employees and a cultural climate survey revealed issues the leaders never knew were present. The culture was rife with exclusionary practices, and leaders had no idea how to talk about topics such as gender and racial stereotypes that often surfaced on teams and interfered with employees' ability to get work done. Ignorance is not bliss when it comes to DEI, and companies that have failed to openly discuss the need for DEI almost always have internal employee implications, even if the employees have been quiet about those challenges in the past.

The second type of company at the awareness stage is the startup so focused on survival that it neglects to create strong human capital practices, including DEI practices. Startup companies are often founded by a single entrepreneur or a few founders who come together to bring a business vision to life. The phrase *startup culture* is used to describe highly mission-oriented places where people wear many hats, have autonomy, and are encouraged to share their most creative ideas. Startup culture rejects layers of bureaucracy, rigid processes, slow decision-making, and lack of employee voice.[16] And still, these companies often whiff on DEI because of a lack of role clarity, including who is responsible for the human capital work. Startup founders often think their mission is the same thing as their culture, and while the two inform each other, culture must be deliberately built in to be sustainable. I have seen many startups realize they are only at the DEI awareness stage because they did not focus on it from the beginning, even with the best intentions from founders to create a workplace where people want to be. Even companies with philanthropic and community-serving missions still have to be intentional about their internal DEI efforts (as Iora Health found out; see chapter 1).

Under Weaver's leadership, Uncle Nearest learned from the mistakes of previous startups and largely avoided what I consider the four major DEI pitfalls that startup companies face. The whiskey maker has intentionally tried to avoid these DEI missteps by fostering diversity of thought in potential candidates, even before they start working there.

## *Lacking Cultural Clarity*

Weaver was crystal clear on the organizational culture and values she wanted Uncle Nearest to operate by, and her determination shows. When you visit the Uncle Nearest website to inquire about job opportunities, a statement immediately grabs your attention:[17]

> Prior to submitting your resume, however, please review our guiding principles. Every Uncle Nearest team member keeps the following as our company's north star, and that is an expectation our founders have of every person who joins this remarkable group of individuals.
>
> Our guiding principles are:

1. We do it with excellence or we don't do it at all.

2. Every day, we pound the rock.

3. We accept each other's differences.

4. All team member opinions are welcome.

5. We are creating a culture of radical candor.

6. We are building a brand to outlive us.

7. The more we know, the more we have yet to learn.

8. We do all things best when we do them with honor.

9. We speak life, we speak light.

10. Even in business, family comes first . . . and rest is extolled.

Weaver intentionally crafted this part of the company website. Notice how it encourages diversity of thought along with the more traditional view of what diversity is. "We are super clear about our company principles," Weaver said. "A person can't even apply to work here without seeing our ten principles, and diversity is one of those."

Almost every organization has a list of values on its company website. What makes Uncle Nearest unique is the way these values come to life in the company culture and the expectations of all employees. Weaver is clear about the expectations; she knows that the company will not be for everyone, and that's okay. It means that Uncle Nearest is more likely to hire someone who fits in from the start and who brings that diversity of thought that Weaver considers so crucial:

> We have built a culture of confidence here. We want people
> who are going to challenge us, who are going to challenge
> our thoughts and our decision-making in the company. I don't
> care if you are an executive assistant or if you're a senior vice
> president: you have the same power in terms of opinion and
> thought and things that you're bringing to the table. If you're
> not a confident person, you won't survive in my company. So
> don't bother applying. What this means is, if you're not com-
> fortable being your truest self, your freest self, who you are

when you're at home and being that way when you're around the team, then it just doesn't work. And so, for example, we don't have people in our company who are in the closet, because that's counter to our culture.

## *Failing to Intentionally Create a Diverse Team from the Start*

Most companies today, even those identified as doing the best with DEI, are playing catch-up on their diversity demographics. Weaver set out to create a team that would embody diversity of thought and reflect the world around her. Yes, this approach would help her create the internal culture she desired, but equally crucial, the team would be a significant competitive advantage in the wine and spirits marketplace, she said:

> From the beginning, I insisted that the right people be in the right jobs. I'm African American; the first two people that I brought in alongside me were White. I was looking for energy, not color. That being said, understanding that as I'm looking for the energy and as I'm looking for the diversity of thought, it was imperative that my company looked like America. Today, if you look at my team, it is almost identical to the statistics of America. We are 50 percent women. If anything, we try to overindex on Black, Latinx, and LGBTQ+ populations, but the goal is to mirror America. I think one of the reasons why we've been so successful [is that] we're doing something that other spirit brands haven't figured out how to

do, which is to market to everyone. And we can do that because we literally look like the people we are marketing to.

## *Overlooking Trade-Offs in a DEI Strategy*

In 2020 I conducted DEI visioning sessions with more than three hundred global leaders across industries. Even though each organization was at a different place on its DEI journey, the most senior leadership teams had almost never sat down to have an explicit conversation about what the members truly believed about DEI or their own experiences with it. The purpose of the sessions was to get leadership teams talking, including having honest conversations about what sacrifices and trade-offs would be needed to make the vision come to life.

For example, one of the most common frustrations leaders share when they set off to hire candidates from diverse backgrounds at senior leadership levels is the lack of a pipeline. In 2020 Well's Fargo CEO Charles Scharf received national backlash for his memo blaming the bank's lack of employee diversity on a "very limited pool of Black talent."[18] In a later apology message to employees, he clarified his position, explaining that there was not a lack of Black talent in finance, but instead, the industry had failed to do its part to improve diversity. "I've worked in the financial services industry for many years," he said, "and it's clear to me that, across the industry, we have not done enough to improve diversity, especially at senior leadership levels."[19]

Scharf's comments were poorly worded and ill-timed—at the height of a national racial reckoning—but many leaders feel similarly about the lack of a talent pipeline. There truly are fewer people from underrepresented groups in major industries such as finance and technology, but the systemic structures that have historically limited access and opportunity for these people must be acknowledged. Weaver shared how she has seen pipeline challenges in the wine and spirits industry, even for a Black-owned and woman-owned business. "We had to pull teeth to actually find African Americans to work for us," Weaver said. "Those résumés were not coming in. We literally had to be very, very creative to seek out African Americans, and one of the things I realized was that if I wasn't getting résumés of African Americans, then nobody in the industry was likely getting résumés of African Americans. So, the question became, 'How do we get more African Americans interested in the spirit business? How can we be creative about building this longer-term pipeline?'"

To change the status quo, leaders must acknowledge these disparities and realize that any solutions will take time and sacrifice. If an organization is committed to increasing its diversity of leadership, it may have to keep a position open longer than expected to identify a diverse slate of candidates. It may have to recruit outside of the schools it typically draws from. It may have to reevaluate the requirements it always had for the job (such as a bachelor's degree): Are the requirements actually indicators of success? An organization may even have to consider nontraditional candidates who have had career success in other industries or business functions. Leadership teams must explicitly create opportunities for the DEI strategy to be implemented. This approach will always require trade-offs. Weaver is vocal about her willingness to embrace the trade-offs to build the most diverse team:

I was very clear that we were building a family here, and we were building something to outlive all of us. I would keep a position open for two years before I put the wrong person in it. I can tell you, if we were, for instance, to fall to 40 percent women in team members, I would hold those positions open for women, because I want their percentages in my company to match that of America. That has been my goal from day one. And I'm okay with that. I'm okay that if I look at a position and say the attrition on African Americans has put us below what our percentages [is] in this country, that position is held for an African American. Take me to court over it. I'm okay with that.

## Assuming That Diverse Cultures
## Do Not Need Explicit DEI Initiatives

Achieving demographic diversity doesn't obviate the need for DEI programs. You need to continue to build that culture through programming, or else the responsibility for DEI falls to people in underrepresented communities sharing their lived experiences and navigating difficult conversations about what it is like to be gay, or Indigenous, or disabled. It's unfair to expect anyone to be the representative for their entire group. This practice also creates an unfair, monolithic sense of diversity, for example, encouraging the idea that all Indigenous people have experiences like the one person who spoke up.

The reality is that while people can share their individual experiences, most people without specific education or training are not equipped to navigate conversations about difficult DEI topics. Thus, even organizations with demographic diversity and diversity of thought benefit from professional DEI education and other initiatives to create inclusivity.

For example, as Weaver explained, even as a Black-owned company, the Uncle Nearest organization had to learn about the challenges of race in America: "We regularly have diversity training to educate our team on topics such as the Tulsa massacre and Juneteenth. We've done skills building on implicit bias to have everyone walk through their journey together and identify their own implicit biases. Every time we do training, team members share that one of their favorite parts of our culture is that we create space for everyone to learn about these topics together."

## Using History to Build Better Together

Despite its startup status, Uncle Nearest has avoided the common pitfalls that would keep it at the awareness stage. This success is due to Weaver's intentional efforts to integrate DEI from day one.

The fact that the distiller has extended its journey to the broader industry shows exceptional maturity for a young company. Uncle Nearest is at the integrated stage of its DEI journey. In 2020 Weaver had an epiphany. "The piece I think our industry was missing until now was that we were all trying to figure out how to foster diversity within the American spirits industry separately," she said.[20] The urgent demand for action against racism from the US public created the opportunity for cooperation, and Uncle Nearest Distillery and Brown-Forman, the parent company of Jack Daniel's, jointly pledged $5 million to the Nearest & Jack Advancement Initiative. The collaboration is a three-pronged initiative aimed at increasing diversity in the US whiskey industry.

One of the prongs was the creation of the Nearest Green School of Distilling at Motlow State Community College in Tullahoma, Tennessee. "When I began looking a few years ago," Weaver said, "I realized how few people of color and women were in the pipeline for master distiller roles within our industry. And I came to the conclusion that we'd need to create the pipeline if we were ever going to have more women and people of color in those roles."[21] The Jack Daniel's parent company "immediately said yes, and we began working on it together the following day."[22]

The second prong of the joint pledge funded the Leadership Acceleration Program, which offers apprenticeships to African Americans who are currently in the whiskey industry and who want to become head distillers, heads of maturation, or production managers. "We realized that what we were doing with the Nearest Green School of Distilling was not going to create an impact as large as was needed and as fast as we wanted. . . ," Weaver said. "We decided to expand our initiative to address three issues: developing a pipeline of women and people of color in the distilling business, creating a program that helps African American startups in the spirits business . . . , and helping put more African Americans and people of color into leadership roles."[23]

The last prong was the formation of the Business Incubation Program, which will provide expertise and resources to African American entrepreneurs entering the spirits business. These resources include access to marketing firms, branding executives, and expanded distribution networks. Through this program, various advisers from Brown-Forman and Uncle Nearest meet with other African American–owned whiskey makers to share their expertise with these firms.

The two companies are offering financing, resources, and their time but will not own any part of the companies they're investing this time in—they're essentially creating competitors.

But competition is okay. The goal is to create a platform where discussion is open and encouraged so that the whiskey industry can welcome a greater diversity of businesses into its fold. Weaver said, "If an African American–owned brand such as mine was willing to come alongside to help build up another African American brand so they could have the same success as Uncle Nearest, but I will own no piece of it, then it's something we can all rally around."[24]

Uncle Nearest and Brown-Forman have used the perils of a traumatic racial history between their founders to propel change a century and a half later. In a 2020 interview Weaver mused about the relationship between the two whiskey makers, one a free White man, and the other an enslaved Black man: "You had this interesting friendship and bond that was created during the most racially divided time in our nation's history. Now, to bring the names of those two people together to help solve [problems] now is the most rewarding thing I have ever done in my life, hands down."[25]

Uncle Nearest is a model of a company intentionally using its entire sphere of influence to create change in the spirits industry. This wide-ranging model is one that every company should consider as it moves through its DEI journey.

When I asked about the future of DEI for startups like Uncle Nearest and others across industries, Weaver shared her excitement that the landscape for DEI in the workplace has the opportunity to be forever changed.

> When you set this as your intention from the start, then you are able to build a culture where DEI is so innate that people will question when something is not aligned with that value. In many companies, it is not until someone comes in from the outside and points out, "Did you know your whole leadership team is White?" or "Did you realize everyone here is wearing blue button-up shirts?" But in my company, that would never happen, because everyone, from the manager to the VP level, would speak up and call out when something is not aligned with our culture. For us, it was a part of our foundation. So, I think the beauty of companies that began in the last few years [is that they] have the opportunity to let today's standard for DEI be the foundation they're being built upon. Ten years from now, this conversation [will look] very different because we have solid foundations being built right now, and that has never been the case before now.

Fawn Weaver's vision of a workplace utopia seems clear; she's busy creating it. But she added one element to the vision I didn't expect: friendship. It's not just culturally accepted to be diverse and create diversity of thought; it also creates lasting, familial bonds. She put it this way:

I saw a quote recently that said something like, "Company culture isn't buying a beer keg; it's actually creating a culture in which people want to have a beer together." Our team members go out of their way to travel to each other's markets, just to hang out. We have an annual summit, and it will be like a big, giant family reunion. And it's not because we're doing all sorts of these things to make it feel that way. Literally, just people walking through the doors are going to feel that way. This company culture is unique, and I'm not confused about what we've built. It's special. Utopia for me is exactly what I walk into every time our entire team is together.

FIGURE 4-1

**Uncle Nearest Premium Whiskey is inspired by the best whiskey maker the world never knew. Nearest Green was the first African American master distiller on record in the United States. The company has an all-women leadership team and is the fastest-growing independent American whiskey brand in US history.**

In 2020 Uncle Nearest and Brown-Forman, Jack Daniels' parent company, created the **Nearest & Jack Advancement Initiative**, pledging a combined $5 million to increase diversity in the American whiskey industry. The initiative has three prongs:

- Creating the Nearest Green School of Distilling at Motlow State Community College in Tullahoma, TN, to create a pipeline of women and people of color for master distiller roles
- Developing the Leadership Acceleration Program, offering apprenticeships to African Americans currently in the whiskey industry who want to become head distillers heads of maturation, or production managers
- Forming the Business Incubation Program, which will provide expertise and resources to African American entrepreneurs entering the spirits sector

Uncle Nearest has a clear internal culture that celebrates DEI. Its clear guiding principles serve as an operating manual for how it works.

1. We do it with excellence or we don't do it at all.
2. Every day, we pound the rock.
3. We accept each other's differences.
4. All team member opinions are welcome.
5. We are creating a culture of radical candor.
6. We are building a brand to outlive us.
7. The more we know, the more we have yet to learn.
8. We do all things best when we do them with honor.
9. We speak life, we speak light.
10. Even in business, family comes first ... and rest is extolled.

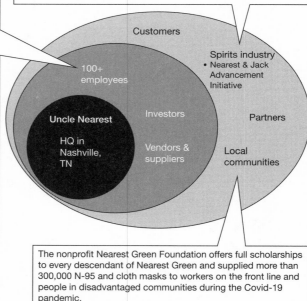

The nonprofit Nearest Green Foundation offers full scholarships to every descendant of Nearest Green and supplied more than 300,000 N-95 and cloth masks to workers on the front line and people in disadvantaged communities during the Covid-19 pandemic.

# 5

# Using Gender Diversity as a Template for All Diversity at Moss Adams

---

**COMPANY:** Moss Adams

**STAGE:** Tactical to integrated

**BEST PRACTICES:** Gender diversity programs, diversity pipeline initiatives, metrics, leadership accountability

**KEY QUOTE:** "We had data. We shared it. We're willing to put that out and hold ourselves accountable, but [the events of 2020] made me and all of us a lot more aware that the way we recruit, the way we develop team members, the way we grow leaders probably had elements of racism, buried in policies, procedures, processes. We want to be an inclusive organization. And if we're going to go there, we have to tackle this." —Chris Schmidt, retired CEO, Moss Adams

---

When Chris Schmidt made partner at the accounting firm Moss Adams in 1991, he could not help but notice how few women occupied leadership positions. He also noticed that women were leaving at significantly higher rates than men both in his organization and across the accounting and consulting industries.

"I graduated in 1981, and all my classes were full of women," he recalled. "The people that I was working with on teams [early in my career] were all women. But it was pretty clear that they weren't making it to partner and that the whole developmental process needed to be accelerated. There were times when north of 55 percent of our new hires were women. If we're hiring all of these bright, successful college students into the firm, why are our female partner ranks in the low teens? That's not logical."

At the time, many companies were focused on compliance when it came to leadership and gender. This emphasis was in part due to groundbreaking gender discrimination lawsuits such as *United Automobile Workers v. Johnson Controls, Inc.* in 1991, in which the US Supreme Court unanimously ruled that the Johnson Controls policy discriminated against women by not requiring their male counterparts to also provide proof of infertility.[1] The ruling set the statute that companies cannot discriminate against women by limiting their job opportunities because of potential reproductive hazards. More attention was also shifting to women's experiences in the workplace. For example, the widespread media coverage of Anita Hill's testimony in the Supreme Court nomination hearings of her former boss Clarence Thomas was a breakthrough in shining a light on harassment in the workplace— shocking to many except maybe the legions of women who recognized their own experiences in Hill's story.[2]

So, companies pivoted to protecting themselves from discrimination and harassment lawsuits. Moss Adams and Schmidt, though, decided to forge a different path. The company would be focusing its efforts on both the business case and the moral case for gender diversity.

"We had progressive leaders that were focused on our value system and translating that into early DEI initiatives," said Schmidt, who retired in April 2022 as the firm's CEO. "It really was about looking at the gender gap. We were hiring a lot of women, and we really needed to do much better at creating a place where they felt like they would have a long career and that they can do well, and they would be treated with respect within our value system. So, I attribute [our efforts] to both the market conditions and to leadership."

By the late 1990s, Moss Adams had created a leadership development executive series that was later branded Forum W and still exists today. The early iteration of Forum W "focused on implementing programming, developing activities, and helping women build their networks."[3]

This program was groundbreaking at the time, in part because it included men from the very beginning, and Schmidt was a proud early adopter and participant. Schmidt recalled, "We felt like we had to be specific in finding high-caliber women leaders and then cascading it into the firm so that the young female team members could see a clear career path where they could accelerate their career and feel like they belonged and that they were valued. They had sponsors, advocates, and mentors that were really going to help them grow and develop."

And the program worked well. Since Forum W's launch more than twenty-five years ago, Moss Adams has seen significant improvement in gender diversity. As of 2020, women represented 53 percent of all employees, 40 percent of national office leadership, and 25 percent of partners—above the national industry averages in each category.[4] Moss Adams is viewed as an industry leader for gender equity, enough so that even competitors often reach out to Schmidt for advice on how to improve gender equity in their own organizations.

"People call us up saying, 'Could you walk us through the framework that you used and developed on women's programs?'" he said. "I'm flabbergasted because this is just how we do things and what the expectation is. And even five years ago, when firms were calling, I'm like, 'Where have you been? It's 2016. And you're finally getting around to coming up with the systems and processes to really help this?' But I know there are still firms out there that are not really thinking about it [gender inequality] or that really don't want to deal with it right now. I have some colleagues and friends that are in firms like that, and it's a head-scratcher to me."

A head-scratcher because success at Moss Adams isn't just built on improving numbers. It's also based on the real evidence it has collected, and this evidence says that gender diversity is good for business. From the early days of its DEI journey, Moss Adams has always leaned on the business case for diversity and tactically shared with leadership the why behind its efforts.

The focus on the need for the business case for DEI often comes up in my client relationships and has been the topic of many academic debates. Some assert that highlighting the business case for DEI can pull the humanity from the effort and turns something that is right into just another business case. Why do we need to be convinced through a business case that everyone should be treated equally and have an opportunity to succeed at work? There are strong merits for this argument, yet history has shown us time and again the limits of moral conviction around DEI in the workplace. These issues of inequity were not newly emerging in 2020, even if the amount of media coverage made it seem that way. So I work with businesses on the business case, but it is framed differently. Connecting DEI to an organization's mission, values, and outcomes is a way to give the work prevalence and urgency; it's not just a business case to convince leaders that DEI is important. Further, many managers and leaders who do not understand the business imperative see DEI as just another thing on their to-do list—something that can be thought about after they have met all their other "real" obligations.

Moss Adams head of HR, Jennifer Wyne, described the business imperative of diversity:

> I talk to colleagues inside and outside the industry that feel that they don't have support and I say, "What you can do is talk facts. Understand your business. What is the business case?" To this day, we talk about the business case: Why are we doing this? Why is this important? For us, when you're hiring 55 percent women, and then you look twelve to fourteen years down the track and we only have 25 percent women in our partnership ranks, your return on investment is not great. So why is that? We try to speak to our leaders in a way in the business language that they understand and then get them hooked and work on the education piece of it. Hope is never lost, but you have to first speak the language of the leaders that may or may not see [the issue], may not understand it, may, frankly, shy away from it, because they feel like they don't know what to do with it.

Like many organizations in the tactical stage of the DEI journey, Moss Adams had an almost-laser focus on gender in terms of its DEI initiatives for twenty-five years. In 1997 women's participation in the US labor force reached an all-time high of 70 percent.[5] In 2000 women's percentage of the global labor force also peaked for the first time, at 39.5 percent, and still has not surpassed this number today.[6] Between 1980 and 2010, there was a gender revolution in management: of the 4.5 million manager jobs created, women occupied 1.9 million.[7] The changing composition of gender in the workforce required organizations to seriously consider how to achieve gender parity and inclusion.

Moss Adams was on the vanguard of gender diversity but, like many companies, failed to pay the same attention to other diversity efforts. Gender tends to be seen as the most obvious initial diversity push since women consistently represent around 50 percent of the global population.[8] That's the easy explanation most companies use for focusing there first.

Yet the often-more-honest answer is that as a society, we are often more comfortable talking about issues of gender than issues of race, sexual orientation, gender identity, and disability. Between June 2020 and April 2021, I asked more than five hundred MBA students and executives their general comfort level talking about these topics. I consistently found that people at all levels were more comfortable, by a ratio of two to one, talking about gender than they were talking about any of the other topics. When I probed to understand why people were so much more comfortable talking about gender than other topics such as race and LGBTQ+ issues, people cited more exposure to gender dynamics at work and with their parents and siblings as a baseline, whereas they might not have had close relationships with someone of a different race or sexual orientation. There was a general sense that the gender conversation had been going on for a long time, but that race and sexual orientation were relatively newer, explicit discussions in the workplace. Although the respondents' perceptions are not necessarily historically accurate—issues of race, sexuality, gender identity, disability, and others have been discussed at work for decades—the clear differences in expressed comfort on these topics should not be overlooked.

The racial reckoning in the summer of 2020 propelled the issue of race in the workplace further than it ever had been. Before then, however, when most organizations said they had a focus on DEI, they meant they were paying attention to gender diversity. Meanwhile, many other areas of diversity were left by the wayside. Moss Adams fell into this category and had to have an internal moment of honesty during the summer of 2020. Schmidt described what it was like to realize that although the firm had come so far on gender and had made a little progress in other areas, it had failed to be intentional with those other diversity areas in the same way that it was with gender:

It was quite an awakening for me when all the tragic events took place during the summer around George Floyd. I always felt like I was a good person. I took the unconscious bias test that Harvard provides and found I don't have a bias toward women. You know, I did those tests and so I thought, "Well, hey, I'm good. I can continue to do what I'm doing and mentor and lead the way I'm leading." And then I really started to make myself more aware of the bigger issues—racism, discrimination, all the things that were out there. The books that I read really helped me better understand what it's like to deal with some of the things that our team members felt. But we had never had those discussions previously, we never had listening groups, and we did not truly understand what the issues were.[9]

One key breakthrough for Schmidt, he said, was to let go of one impulse he has as a leader: "As leaders, we try to solve problems, and sometimes it's not about solving problems. It's just saying nothing and listening so that you really understand what the issues are."

Listening helped Schmidt realize that metrics are a starting point, not a goal in themselves.

And when I'm watching the events unfold across the country and here in Seattle, it really made me feel that all the issues around privilege and racism, all those DEI terms, those things are real. I spent time really setting myself around where we needed to go beyond checking the box; I really started looking at those metrics differently. We had been reporting around those metrics to the firm through the Forum W report for many years, and now we have our I&D report [a broader diversity-tracking report]. We had data. We shared it. We're willing to put that out and hold ourselves accountable, but [the events of 2020] made me and all of us a lot more aware that the way we recruit, the way we develop team members, the way we grow leaders probably had elements of racism buried in policies, procedures, processes. It caused us to just stop and say, you know, we want to be this inclusive organization. And if we're going to go there, we have to tackle this.

The reality that there was more work to do didn't make him despondent, only more focused. "I'm an optimistic person," he said. "I can be pragmatic and realistic, but I remain optimistic. If we're able to take the tragedy and use it to help improve what we're responsible for, then we are going be in a much better position as a firm in our communities and in our profession."

# Managing Backlash

Though its efforts on race may not have matched its success with gender equity, Moss Adams was not new to the racial equality conversation. In 2017, after the White supremacist rally in Charlottesville, Virginia, Moss Adams was one of few companies to publicly denounce the riot. While many CEOs had major issues with the events that took place, fear of political backlash kept many from speaking out. A *New York Times* piece by Andrew Sorkin captured the sentiment of the business community at the time: "Outraged in Private, Many C.E.O.s Fear the Wrath of the President."[10] Schmidt described speaking out during that time as a natural response for him and the rest of the Moss Adams leadership team to address White supremacy.

Though Moss Adams had a track record of supporting equality for all as a part of the company values, like many companies, it received backlash after its public statement in support of Black Lives Matter in 2020. Many companies did speak up about racial injustice for the first time and were accused of being performative allies, namely, companies that were only being opportunistic by jumping on the racial equity bandwagon.

Schmidt was frustrated by the backlash. The company had turned some attention to racial diversity as far back as 2015, when it brought in a consultant to speak to the partners and the company committed to expanding its success with Forum W to other areas in need of addressing. He described his frustration:

> I felt a little bit defensive, my initial reaction, not to the tragic events that were horrific, but to the criticism that we started to take, saying, "You need to do more." I'm like, "Have you looked and seen what we're doing? Have you read our reports? Have you seen our strategic plan around our DEI efforts?" A lot of people were criticizing, but they hadn't taken the time to even really look at the data. We were holding ourselves accountable and measuring. We had two years of reports. We'll have a third year that's coming out on what we look like, as a firm, from a diversity perspective. Now, when we sit with the board, and we're doing partner income analysis, we are looking at diversity statistics beyond just gender. We're starting to bring that information in. And that's a win.
>
> So, you get defensive, I think, when you're in a leadership role, because you want to be the best that you can be. You want the firm to be the best that it can be. The issue is not

whether it's Latinx, Asian Americans, or Black team members; it's really expanding the pipeline. We are lucky to be recruiting and operating in the West, where we have a lot of diversity. That allows us to hire, grow, and develop diverse team members beyond gender. But we need to do better, and this is just making us that much more focused in our efforts. I know we will. We just need to do our part with building the pipeline and really making sure that we have that representation. That's what we're looking for in our communities and the businesses that we're working with.

But the question can still be asked: Why didn't the organization have a more intentional focus on broader DEI earlier in its twenty-five-year DEI journey? Schmidt acknowledged that the company could have started sooner but that success with gender diversity has set it up to move fast on other DEI programs. He described the events of 2020 as shining a floodlight on the fact that the firm needed to do just that—move faster—on its broader diversity efforts:

When I came up to Seattle [from Southern California], it was mind-blowing to me that it was all White people. And at the time, back in 2003, it was surprising because we were operating in pretty diverse cities like Los Angeles, San Diego, and San Francisco. We made the decision to really focus on women, never taking our eye off diversity, knowing that we were going to bring [other diversity efforts] in a lot more aggressively when we started winning the gender battle. And some could be critical of us, and say, "Hey, why don't you run parallel?" We said, "Let's be successful, and then we can replicate that over on the broader diversity side."

Jennifer Wyne, head of HR, sympathizes with this point of view: "I think any organization can set itself up for failure if it tries to boil the ocean." But when she joined the company in 2013, she also knew that it was time to start running parallel. Her goal was to build broader diversity efforts deliberately into the company's strategic plan. Forum W was well established, and the business case for gender diversity was well understood. The same had to happen for other aspects of diversity.

"It's an interesting part of our journey," Wyne said. "We still have this conversation today about not wanting to take the foot off the pedal on the gender front, because it does cross quite a few sectors of our population, including people of color. So how do you assure our team members that we will not lose traction by expanding the program?"

Wyne was careful to note that this is no excuse for not moving forward. "[As leaders] we are not concerned about that. We know working on these efforts in tandem will only accelerate the successes. We are confident in that. I think that's where others have come along and seen that now, too."

Having the Forum W framework as a template helps, she said. "We have been able to leverage the Forum W framework very nicely and draw parallels in a way that our firm was already used to talking about business cases. Why are we talking about this, and how are we talking about that? The conversation now has shifted a bit, too, because intersectionality, it's much more complex, but it helped us to start with women, with the intent that we knew we would go broader."

## Dealing with Resisters

Though it has been twenty-five years of DEI momentum for Moss Adams, the road has not been traveled without its fair share of challenges and resisters. Chris Schmidt can be described as unyielding when it comes to dealing with people who resist the journey, especially peers in his industry:

> I will have a candid conversation with a leader and say, "You are going to become obsolete, very quickly. How could you be a good old boys' club in the world that we live in?" They may be experiencing success, but their business will not be sustainable. Some of the leaders that I talk to are mindful of that, and they know that they need to change their thinking and listen to different ways to approach this critical business issue.
>
> Yet, some are just happy, [thinking], "We're making money and I'm not going to disturb it," and I'm like, "That's your choice; the world is going to pass you by."

Again, Schmidt frames this as a business case. This whistling-past-the-graveyard approach will only mean that over time, a company will lose the war for talent. "If I am a team member and I'm making a choice to go to firm X, Y, or Z, I'm going to look at the public demographics around ethnicity and women's programs," Schmidt said. "I want to see action on behalf of that. . . . That's going to influence my decision on which firm I want to work for, and firms that don't want to wrap their mind around [DEI] are going to lose the better talent. People vote with their feet. If your values and your leadership aren't walking the talk, they won't stay."

Though these conversations must be had, not everyone resists change efforts, and most leaders do support DEI, at least in theory. Yet leaders often struggle when it comes to identifying what it really means to support change and being okay with the potential trade-offs necessary for systemic change.

Diversity does not have to be a zero-sum game, but many people in traditional seats of privilege struggle with this concept even when they support DEI from the moral and business case perspective. Doing the work can still be difficult.

"I have had so many difficult decisions and uncomfortable conversations [about DEI]," Schmidt said. He added that after promoting a woman, he was approached by critics: "I've had male partners come back and tell me, 'Hey, you've put yourself in a position where you have to put a woman there.' And I smile and say, 'And?' They just kind of look at me, and what do they say? I am clear that we need to do this."

But Schmidt continues to champion DEI work, and at some point, it becomes a natural part of doing business. He explained his position:

> For example, say you have two men and a woman, and they
> are equal, and I will basically advocate for the woman, be-

cause we need the woman in the role to continue to develop the leadership ranks. Some people will say, "That's not fair to this group." But we know that you need to put this individual in this role and support her with tools and coaching and sponsorship and all the mentoring so that she can continue to grow and develop so that other young women leaders can see that the firm isn't always going to default to men.

I've had so many of those conversations inside the boardroom, one-on-one with partners mapping what women's trajectories look like. Jen and I will be on calls, and I will text her and say, "This person seems really sharp. We need to make sure that we continue to work with her and find roles for her." At some point, it just becomes natural and second nature if you're thinking that way and that helps.

Many leaders struggle with being able to take such a strong stance on DEI when confronted by their peers. I pushed Schmidt further, trying to understand what allowed him to get to a point where he could stand up to his peers in such a direct way.

He started with a single word. "Confidence," he said. "Confidence that the woman who was being considered was ready because of the time, effort, and energy that had been put into her. Being able to tell the men who might be complaining that there's a lot of other leadership roles in the firm, there's never a shortage of leadership needs, we never have an oversupply of leaders. So, I guess, just believing in our strategies and our values, and advocating and sponsoring people who you know are going to pay dividends downstream."

# Developing the Pipeline

The confidence that Schmidt described is certainly not all blind faith. One of his leadership strengths, as described by his team, is his ability to assess the skills of individuals. "Not all business leaders necessarily are as adept at assessing skills as Chris," Wyne said. "Assessing the qualities and capabilities of somebody without necessarily working with them side by side is a talent that not all leaders possess. But it's super important in the diversity conversation because individuals who have that skill set can identify skills in somebody who is different from them. He can understand how they would succeed with the skills and experience that they bring to the table. Some people might call this ability to assess talent a soft skill, but I think it's one of the hardest skills to develop."

Research shows that most people fall prey to similar-to-me (or affinity) cognitive bias, which causes people to disproportionately favor individuals who are like themselves.[11] This bias is well documented to have an impact on how hiring and promotion decisions are often made.[12] But talent selection is only the first step in creating a diverse team. As a leader, Schmidt goes beyond the identification stage and intentionally empowers his direct reports to coach and develop diverse talent. He encourages them to speak up when they "see a spark" and to then ask, "How do we cultivate them? How do we engineer this person into this role so that she can develop, or they can develop?"

"We're getting a lot better at that," Schmidt said. "We were never bad, but we continue to improve and really put people in and support them. It does take a village for anybody who steps into a complex leader role, and we're trying to give the right training and coaching and informal mentoring so that people feel like they are supported. It's not like you're sending them off on a boat adrift. 'We want to support you, and I want to watch you grow and develop.'"

## Metrics and Accountability

Even when it's as deeply enmeshed in a culture as it is in Moss Adams, a DEI strategy is just a vision without metrics and accountability to support actual behavioral and performance changes. Moss Adams has been very clear on the power of both in its DEI journey.

Metrics come easy to Moss Adams in some ways, because it's an accounting firm. "We love to set metrics on everything and get down to the numbers," Schmidt said. "So, the simple math, when we started Forum W, was, 'If we're hiring fifty-plus percent women, is it not logical that we would have 15 percent women partners?'"

That led to many conversations about how a woman's career evolves differently, with child responsibilities, for example. The digging into the why behind the numbers helps the company improve its DEI strategy. Why are non-White and non-male hires stalling here? What's going on at year nine or ten, when there's a stall in advancement? Schmidt described the process at Moss Adams:

So we went into all of those different avenues and came back and started setting metrics and said the right number to target is 35 percent [women in leadership roles]. We had midterm and long-term goals. It's a moving target, but we set benchmarks, and we try to measure the pipeline. We look at development reports. We feel anybody who aspires to become a stakeholder or become a partner needs to see that path forward that ties into the metrics that the firm has agreed to.

Analytically, in my mind, the business world at some point should reach some type of equilibrium with all the women in the workforce. And all of these firms and professions need to continue to increase the number of women who are involved in those positions.

Wyne said that making the business case for diversity has become easier in recent years and the company digs in and leans on the external research that supports it:

If you go back ten years, there was a lot of information coming out, whether it was McKinsey [& Company], or the Conference Board, or HBR [Harvard Business Review Press], around the business performance of companies improving when there was more diversity amongst teams. Then there was also specific research around gender and when women were at the table and the results of business decisions. There was data on the bottom-line results of the companies [improving in diverse organizations]. Strategically incorporating external research adds credibility. It's not just us talking to ourselves. Being grounded in [external and internal] research data has continued to be a big part of our journey.

Schmidt sees in diversity a virtuous cycle as well. The number of women-owned businesses, for example, is increasing rapidly. What firm will those businesses pick when they need accounting and consulting? "Wouldn't it be logical to have women served by a woman partner?" he asked. "That's another business driver that we continue to see, and it's awesome to be able to have women partners and team members who can step in and serve that role."

The crucial backstop in the Moss Adams DEI program is accountability, of course. Measuring helps. Creating public-facing reports helps. But so does challenging your own results, just as you would with any other core part of the business. As Schmidt sees it, if a unit is underperforming on revenue, no one would shy away from asking that group why. The same goes for DEI, Schmidt said:

[I ask leaders,] "Are you developing these people? Are you adequately providing for succession?" When we have leaders who are only making male partners, they get called out. We start deconstructing and asking questions like, "What's going on in the pipeline? Where are the pressure points? Why is this?" We lean in on it. We start asking the tough questions.

Sometimes you must have the uncomfortable conversation, and you're looking for bias. You're looking for that decision-making framework where there might be an issue. We don't shy away from putting the pressure on leaders if they're not delivering around our business imperatives.

## Becoming Anti-Racist

As a leader who had long championed diversity in the workplace, Schmidt still found the moment of racial reckoning in 2020 difficult, no matter how much progress the company had made on gender equity and whatever initial steps it had taken with racial diversity. "It was very uncomfortable for me, as a sixty-two-year-old White male who needed help and coaching from our team members on how to deal with those uncomfortable conversations, and it was very educational for many of our leaders, and it's a journey," he said.

Like many organizations, Moss Adams started responding by listening to employees, learning about their experiences at the firm, then determining the best course of action. "We got to a point where we had many uncomfortable conversations," Schmidt recalled. "Then we asked our I&D advisory board that's made up of multiple business resource group leaders to help us with bold action steps that we could weave through the firm. So, we were listening to the team from the bottom and helping to drive the message from the top."

In this sort of sandwiched top-down and bottom-up approach, Moss Adams took the bold step of going beyond being an inclusive organization and determining it needed to become an anti-racist organization. There is a distinction between inclusivity and anti-racism. An anti-racist organization actively identifies and opposes racism by changing its policies, structures, and behaviors that perpetuate racist ideas and actions. Race and discrimination scholar Ibram X. Kendi notes, "Racial inequity is a problem of bad policy, not bad people."[13] Anti-racism begins in knowledge but must be rooted in active steps to eliminate racism.

"We made being an anti-racist firm a goal for our board for the next eighteen months," Schmidt said. "We are not going to be done in eighteen months, but [in] every board meeting that we have, there will be discussion, dialogue, and feedback around action items that our I&D board has recommended back to us."

Schmidt was not taking a hands-off approach or leaning on his HR or inclusivity and diversity leadership group to do the heavy lifting, as many CEOs have. "I committed to our executive committee and our board that anti-racism would be one of my three primary goals for the calendar year. I am responsible for driving that goal forward," he explained.

Part of the goal, Schmidt said, was to get everyone in the same place regarding where the company was on the journey and where it was headed and to make everyone comfortable with having the difficult conversations. "That's where we feel like we'll make progress faster at the firm at all levels, with that board accountability, the communication in the action items, and the responsibility that's coming up from our other team members."

Companies do not become ant-racist overnight, but Moss Adams has the advantage of a successful track record with Forum W and is applying that template. Schmidt described the value of feedback:

> The feedback that we were getting is, once we bring someone
> in—for example, if we bring a Black team member in—how

are we ensuring that that team member is sponsored, has allies, is getting coached, mentored, and developed? We are watching and looking at our metrics and stepping back and really thinking more holistically about sponsorships. Our Black team members would love for us tomorrow to quadruple the number of Black hires we have in the firm. My conversation back to them is, "Please help us work with the various projects that we have to grow the pipeline of qualified individuals, and also help us with learning and listening, so that we do a better job of retaining those team members." I love being in a room with team members who are providing us feedback. I use that as an opportunity to lay out the leadership issues that we've faced, not as an excuse, but to pull them along that conversation so that they understand what we're dealing with from a firm perspective.

Schmidt again pointed to the importance of listening but, more than that, listening with an open mind: "A lot of it is just listening, not being offended by what people are saying but asking them, imploring them, to please help us come up with better things we can do to retain, develop, grow, and build these leaders that are going to take us into the future."

It's easy to sense Schmidt's excitement about the dialogue. "The conversations have been great," he said. "A lot of them are with young people. If you're dealing with [someone early in their career], and they are confident enough to provide you feedback and an email, it's great. I've been so impressed. I've responded to every single email that's come to me from our team members around this. Sometimes I'm up late at night. But I want them to know that they're being listened to."

## The Future of Moss Adams

I asked both HR vice president Jennifer Wyne and CEO Chris Schmidt the question I ask everyone: What does a workplace utopia look like to them? Understanding how deeply enmeshed diversity can become in a culture through their experience with Forum W and gender diversity efforts, both Wyne and Schmidt focused on that stage of the journey: the stage where DEI is no longer special, where it's just something you do. At this stage, DEI becomes effortless, part of your organizational DNA.

"Utopia would be that we don't need to really have to shine the light on [DEI] intentionally at some point, because it just comes naturally, as it has on the gender front," Wyne said. "That is what I would say our nirvana would be: [DEI] is just part of our DNA where, theoretically, we wouldn't have to champion these things, we are not even thinking about it, it's just who we are and what we do."

Schmidt retired in April 2022, after I had interviewed him, but his hard work on DEI continues. And his idea of a workplace utopia informs the company to this day:

Workplace utopia, to me, is where people truly feel like, "I belong here. I am comfortable," and we don't have to go out of our way to be deliberate. There's an acceptance and a tolerance and an understanding, where it's just work. And your differences and my differences don't even matter. . . . When we are not talking about gender, or the White male who feels like he's being discriminated against or marginalized, or the team member that doesn't feel like they're understood or belong. . . . It's just, "You're my team member, and we're gonna go do some amazing things."

We have a ways to go, but that's nirvana. Maybe that's societal nirvana too. But we can only control what's happening inside the Moss Adams boundaries, and that's what we are focused on.

FIGURE 5-1

## Moss Adams provides the world's most innovative companies with specialized accounting, consulting, and wealth management services to help them embrace emerging opportunity.

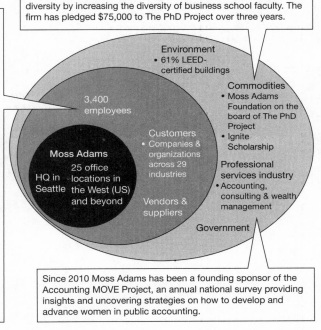

The Moss Adams Foundation sits on the board of **The PhD Project**, a nonprofit whose mission is to increase workforce diversity by increasing the diversity of business school faculty. The firm has pledged $75,000 to The PhD Project over three years.

In 2008 Moss Adams launched Forum W to strategically address the lack of gender diversity and inclusion at the firm and in its industry. Forum W is a regionally based business resource group with four priorities: dialogue, networking, mentoring, and advancement. The initiative has evolved over time and today is part of Moss Adams's DNA and culture. In 2016 Moss Adams and Forum W launched the GroWth series, a yearlong leadership development program for high-potential one-to two-year senior managers. The series is designed to strengthen the firm's pipeline of women partners.

Environment
• 61% LEED-certified buildings

Commodities
• Moss Adams Foundation on the board of The PhD Project
• Ignite Scholarship

Professional services industry
• Accounting, consulting & wealth management

Customers
• Companies & organizations across 29 industries

Vendors & suppliers

Government

3,400 employees

**Moss Adams**
HQ in Seattle
25 office locations in the West (US) and beyond

Since 2010 Moss Adams has been a founding sponsor of the Accounting MOVE Project, an annual national survey providing insights and uncovering strategies on how to develop and advance women in public accounting.

# 6

# Moving from Introspection to Global Diversity at Sodexo

---

**COMPANY:** Sodexo

**STAGE:** Compliance to sustainable

**BEST PRACTICES:** Global strategy, local implementation, training, diversity scorecard metrics

**KEY QUOTE:** "What may have initially been sort of resistance, seeing it as a legal mandate, very soon became an enabler of business growth and business success. We went from that class action legal mandate to more of a business enabler." —Rohini Anand, PhD, former global CDO, Sodexo

---

Imagine you land your dream leadership job, CDO, at one of the world's twenty largest employers, with over 420,000 employees in sixty-four countries. You are prepared to make a difference on a grand scale, empowered to integrate diversity into the professional lives of nearly half a million workers. Then, six months in, there comes an $80 million class action lawsuit that directly falls under your leadership purview.

This was the exact experience of Rohini Anand, CDO for Sodexo, a French company specializing in food services and facilities management. The forty-five-year-old company is headquartered in the Paris suburb of Issy-les-Moulineaux. Despite its size, Sodexo is a family business, founded by Pierre Bellon in Marseilles, France, and is still majority family owned today.[1]

Anand found herself at the company's forefront during one of the darkest periods for the company. In March 2001 approximately 3,400 of Sodexo's Black employees filed a class action discrimination lawsuit against their employer, charging that they were routinely barred from promotions and segregated in the company. Of the company's 100,000-plus North American employees in the year 2000, Black employees held 18 out of 700 upper management jobs and none of the 188 top corporate jobs.[2]

The company would settle the $80 million suit in 2005; it was the largest race-related job bias settlement of the era. In addition to the monetary settlement, Sodexo denied any wrongdoing through a consent decree, that is, a voluntary agreement between two parties to cease legal activities in exchange for a settlement. The company also agreed to a five-year plan to improve diversity practices. Sodexo agreed to make enhancements to its systems, policies, and practices, including the establishment of an independent panel of monitors for five years to oversee the implementation of the nonmonetary provisions of the decree.

The initial excitement Anand had about her new role was quickly overshadowed by an enormous legal mandate to turn things around quickly, under a watchful eye. As the first CDO ever at the company, she had no playbook for how to build a DEI strategy from the ground up while meeting strict compliance parameters being set by others.

"There really was no roadmap," she recalled. "I don't think people knew what to do, or how to make it happen, or where to start, or where to go from step one. There was a lot of resistance because this was seen as a legal thing. It's one more thing we have to do on top of our day jobs."

## Surprising to Executives, Not to Workers

CEO Michel Landel remembered the shock felt when the lawsuit was disclosed. "It was very painful," he recalled. "Our culture has been built around strong values and a spirit of service and progress, and the majority of promotions in our company are internal. So, when we were told employees felt that we'd discriminated against them, we were surprised."[3]

Leadership's lack of awareness about employees' DEI struggles isn't unusual; I've seen it before. In most organizations, a leadership perception gap exists between how executives and managers view the organization's inclusivity and how employees experience working there. For example, a Gartner survey had these findings:[4]

- Only 41 percent of employees agree that senior leadership acts in their best interest, compared with 69 percent of executives.

- Only 56 percent of employees agree they feel welcome to express their true feelings at work, compared with 74 percent of executives.

- Only 47 percent of employees believe leadership takes their perspective into consideration when making decisions, whereas 75 percent of senior leaders feel they do.

That is, roughly three-quarters of leaders see their organizations as inclusive, while less than half of workers do. That's a massive gap that contributes to leaders having no clear sense of what it is like to be in the lower or middle ranks of the organization, especially for employees from different backgrounds. The mere fact that they are leaders contributes to this difference: research on perspective-taking has demonstrated that possessing power itself impedes a person's ability to understand the perspectives of others.[5] Thus, it is not surprising that Sodexo's mostly White male leadership at the time lacked insight into the experience of Black employees and was shocked by the class action lawsuit.

A typical reaction when leaders are made aware of this gap—not always so dramatically through a class action lawsuit, more typically through an individual incident—is to entrench themselves and defend both themselves and their organizations, especially in public. Anand was pleased that this was not how Sodexo approached it. Instead, the company acknowledged the pain of the moment and used it as a catalyst for change.

"It was quite a rude shock for the company," she told me. "We had a French CEO at the time. And he was an extremely inclusive, open executive. And this lawsuit was a difficult time for the company." In an NPR interview, she described one result of the lawsuit: "I think it made us introspective. You never want to feel that there's even one person in the company who feels they don't have an opportunity to succeed."[6] Anand again described this sense of introspection when I interviewed her: "It made the company look within and reflect on how we got here and what we needed to do to change."

# The Introspective Process:
## Acknowledge, Be Open, Be Humble

Any company facing employee backlash and trying to introspectively understand the current DEI landscape must first acknowledge both the structural systems at play and the individual actors who bring the company culture to life. For Sodexo, part of its structural challenges stemmed from the rapid expansion through acquisition.[7]

"We went from a French company with 25,000 employees to acquiring Marriott Management Services and growing overnight to 125,000 employees," said Anand. "So, the processes and systems were not as consistent as they should have been. The company was more focused on the basics such as just getting payroll done. The result was a very decentralized organization."

Although Sodexo was a large company experiencing the challenges of getting the day-to-day tasks done, I also see these challenges with smaller, newer companies not focused on DEI from the beginning because they are just trying to get off the ground. In the early days of building a new company or navigating the transition through an acquisition, organizations must have DEI at the forefront of their vision and build it into their architecture. Otherwise, an organization will more easily end up where Sodexo did, having endured a damaging lawsuit and still having to build its culture of diversity from the ground up.

The second part of introspection involves gaining an understanding of the lived experiences for all levels and backgrounds of employees.

Listening and understanding is the only way to reestablish trust in the organization. Anand described some of the challenges she faced as she led the effort to build a culture of trust after the lawsuit. "I'm Asian American," she said. "I've known African Americans, so I was very, very conscious of my identity, and the need to build relationships and trust with the African American community. Obviously, I was aware of discrimination, but I had not experienced what they had experienced with the toxic history of slavery. So, I had to be open to learning, be humble. Instead of coming in with my own agenda, I listened. I had to make a very intentional effort to build those relationships and to build trust."

Trust in leadership is a major challenge in most organizations, never mind a company facing a suit from its own employees. According to Gallup's global database, only one in three employees strongly agrees that they trust the leadership of their organization.[8] Yet trust is a critical factor in the success of DEI efforts. Without it, diversity practices alone are likely to fail.[9]

Rebuilding trust after employees have publicly expressed frustration with the DEI climate of an organization is extremely challenging and often takes many years of intentional efforts to repair. Anand discussed how she began this journey in the early years after the lawsuit settlement: "Building trust began with candid conversations. I acknowledged that I did not know but was willing to learn and to listen. It began with admitting that this was an extremely difficult time for the company and that, while we were not perfect, we were committed to trying."[10]

## Compliance as a Foundation

After the period of introspection, Sodexo had a clear way to focus its efforts: by earning compliance with the terms of the lawsuit settlement. Compliance would yield meaningful changes in the organization and was clearly laid out. As Anand saw it, the compliance program was a good place to start because the terms were so concrete. They'd provide a foundation. "The consent decree articulated ten different things that we needed to do and was in place until 2010," she explained. "Those items in the consent decree became very much our baseline."

Being at the compliance stage does not feel good for any company. The word itself has negative connotations outside the legal field, suggesting it's the bare minimum to pass—just barely doing enough. However, compliance is where many organizations like Sodexo have started their DEI journey, either through specific legal mandates or more generally to comply with EEOC statutes. At Sodexo, for example, those initial years focused on meeting certain parts of the ten-point plan given to the company by regulators. Specifically, the company focused on designing and implementing companywide processes for talent selection and performance review.

Yet compliance is not necessarily a bad thing. It can be a good starting place for a company without a plan, because it provides so much built-in structure. It gives you goals to hit (the line between being compliant and noncompliant) and provides a kind of focus.

But leaders need to go into this exercise recognizing—indeed, trumpeting—the fact that compliance is not the endgame. It's the foundation. It's near the start of the necessary journey, not the destination.

Anand recognized the incomplete nature of compliance and, with CEO Landon, made sure that while they worked on meeting the terms of settlement, they also went further. With the structure of compliance giving a path forward, she focused on quickly growing beyond that.

To that end, the company committed to diversity training, work-life effectiveness programs, mentoring programs, employee network groups, leadership education, awards and recognition, and diversity councils. It also invested in internal and external communication through the company's website and the annual diversity report.[11]

A diversity scorecard was implemented to measure progress in increasing diversity in the management ranks and to set targets for women and minorities in leadership positions. Later, it added inclusive behaviors as part of the scoring. This scorecard was innovative for the time in the way it used incentives: 25 percent of the executive team's bonus and 10 to 15 percent of manager bonuses were tied to performance on the diversity scorecard.

Anand remembered how compliance quickly spurred actions the regulators weren't mandating. "The first year, we trained five thousand people within the organization on compliance training, what we later called the Spirit of Inclusion," she said, referring to the mandate. "But after that, action came from accountability [with the diversity scorecard]. The important piece here was that it was a protected bonus. Even if the company didn't do well financially, that bonus was still paid out. That sent a message that we're in for the long haul. Accountability is really important. How are we holding the managers and individuals accountable for really showing progress and being clear about what their progress looks like?"

In the first seven years of the implementation of the diversity score-card, the percentage of minority employees increased by 23 percent, and the number of women employees rose by 11 percent.[12] For companies finding themselves in the compliance stage, they should embrace it and then be prepared to grow beyond it by taking the time to understand what the organization desires and needs from DEI to thrive.

"I think the baseline is compliance," Anand said. "Absolutely critical. But clearly, there needs to be a compelling reason for people to change. So that's the business case, and it has to be embedded within your core business strategy. Yes, it is about social justice. And it is about [its] being the right thing to do. And we all want to do that. But unless it really is embedded within the mission, the value proposition, and your core business, it's not going to move beyond that legal and compliance space."

## Chipping Away at Resistance

A first step in moving beyond compliance is to understand how DEI impacts your business. Anand explained it this way:

> Engaging a predominantly White male executive team and getting their buy-in was one of my first priorities. They had to overcome their view that DEI was simply a legal requirement and irrelevant to the business. They also had to be convinced that it was a way to attract and engage the best talent. And they had to see DEI as a market differentiator and an enabler

of business success if we wanted a truly diverse, equitable, and inclusive organization as an outcome.

To get there, the executives had to take ownership of their own learning journeys. I had to influence these leaders, chipping away at their resistance, so that ultimately, they demonstrated their inclusive leadership.

While engaging the executive team alone is a necessary step, it was only the first step. The next was to look at all systems involved in the talent process and figure out how they were blocking progress or reinforcing bias, or doing both. That required a deep dive and partnering with many groups across a vast organization—a task made more complicated by Sodexo's recent annexation of a large company in Marriott Management Services.

Consequently, as a new leader, Anand had to build credibility with management and establish a reputation as someone who knew what she was doing and could deliver. She found herself needing to find practical ways to encourage the commitment needed to make the culture more diverse and inclusive while aligning it with the realities of a low-margin business to get the buy-in of senior leaders.

In her book on leading global DEI, Anand describes this journey from compliance to tactical efforts:

> With these advances, Sodexo gained stature as a thought
> leader in DEI. Sodexo's leadership, who had previously
> considered DEI merely a legal requirement, now saw it as
> an asset to the company. The legal requirements became an

irrelevant threshold that the company far exceeded as they realized the benefits. When the consent decree monitoring committee expired in 2010, the leadership decided to appoint an external DEI advisory board for several years after to ensure Sodexo continued to remain intentional in addressing DEI and had an external perspective to inform that commitment.[13]

Leadership's early efforts started to differentiate Sodexo meaningfully for clients as well. In this way, Sodexo's DEI strategy matured from compliance to tactical efforts.

## Thinking Globally, Acting Locally

Tactically, Sodexo faced even more challenges. It was one thing to absorb 125,000 new employees from the Marriott acquisition (and the attendant systems, processes, and culture that came with them). Sodexo also had to deal with the fact that in the United States alone, the organization was now spread out over twelve thousand locations.

"My concern was, this is such a decentralized organization," Anand explained. "Our managers work out of client sites, so how are we going to kind of build this inclusive culture?" Fortunately, the decentralization proved to be more of an amplifier than a dampener. "As we started to roll out our initiatives," she said, "our managers started sharing some of it with their clients. The clients started seeing what we were doing. So then the clients started asking for our expertise and our knowledge."

In a way, Sodexo's effort went a bit viral within its complex network of sites. Suddenly, executives saw how the DEI compliance effort was good for business. "That really expedited the engagement across the organization," Anand said. "What may have initially been sort of resistance on the part of the organization, seeing it as a legal mandate, very soon became an enabler of business growth and business success. We went from that class action legal mandate to more of a business enabler."

One unique attribute of Sodexo's DEI journey is its global nature. While the company managed negative perceptions and a significant backlash in the United States because of the class action lawsuit, it also had to build a global DEI strategy for its eighty countries under the strained circumstances.

The challenges of a global DEI strategy are significant. Diversity management requires understanding how each country defines and conceptualizes diversity from a social, legal, and political perspective.[14] For example, while gender equality is generally a global issue, other issues vary by country. In India, the caste system has historically been the focus of diversity efforts, while in the United Kingdom, race, ethnocentrism, and class issues are prevalent. South Africa has historically focused on race but also more broadly on sexual orientation, HIV status, political opinion, and culture.[15] It can be overwhelming for organizational leaders to understand the sociopolitical norms in every country their organization operates in and then to master local DEI-related legal statutes. For example, employers must evaluate what employee data is legally permissible to collect; this ruling varies by country.

All these considerations still do not guarantee cross-cultural competence—the knowledge and skills needed to effectively communicate, understand, and interact with people across cultures. Sodexo experienced this challenge when it realized it could not implement certain scorecard metrics that accounted for the ethnic composition of the workforce in France or Germany, because it was illegal to collect this data in those countries.[16] Thus, the company had to figure out how to implement the bonus system in a place where it couldn't use the data the system was based on.

Anand was promoted to global CDO in 2007 and quickly started to understand these intricacies in global DEI strategy. In general, she implemented a rigorous global approach in terms of overall goals and governance and then created flexibility lower down so that programs could be resourced and implemented at the local level in a way that comported with the local needs.

"So we have a global framework around our strategy. And that strategy then gets localized," she said. "For some, it might be to focus first on people with disabilities, like in Brazil or in France, where they have quotas around people with disabilities. For others, it might be generational considerations, for instance, engaging or retaining youth. In China, for instance, where there's a lot of mobility in the workforce, that becomes important. Figuring out what those pain points are in different parts of the world is managed locally, but it's all under a global framework."

Ultimately, there is no one-size-fits-all approach to a global DEI strategy, and many companies that have made progress in their headquarters region have lost momentum and interest when taking their efforts global. In other situations, employees outside of the organization's home country will resist DEI efforts that feel generic and indifferent to their local experiences. Amelia Ransom, leader of engagement and diversity at software company Avalara, once shared with me a peanut butter analogy for global DEI strategies. Her analogy has always stuck with me (no pun intended):

> You really have to learn what the motivations are in the places where you're doing business. It doesn't look the same. Being Black in Brazil is not the same thing as being Black in the Americas, and so we can't just spread our strategies like peanut butter around the globe. The challenges are different, the structures are different, the expectations and culture are different. So you have to actually be solving for other things. Being a woman is very different in India. The expectations on the family and all look very different from the expectations on a woman in the Americas. . . . But if you can't center it in the country and not put US expectations on what good looks like . . . You have to have something that suits your organization but also the allowance for regional expectations and regional progress and regional success."[17]

Even a seemingly simple task like localizing a workshop on courageous conversations for a multinational company can present cultural minefields that can derail the whole training. In 2021 my consulting organization set out to train people from a US technology customer service organization in ten global locations on how to have courageous conversations about racial discrimination.

In some countries, our work was dismissed as not relevant to their culture (though we know that historically, racism can be found in every region of the world), yet other countries told us our training would be impossible to implement because of cultural norms.[18] In some places, it was socially unacceptable to be confrontational, even in the face of discriminatory treatment. My team ended up having to work directly with representatives from each country to make sure the training content would land well in each location while fighting to maintain the core messages of the training so that all employees in the division would be on the same page about company expectations to speak up against discriminatory behavior.

Sodexo dealt with a common localization challenge: DEI was being stereotyped as an American issue. Some country-level CEOs derided the diversity initiative as unnecessary because, they said, "We don't have those kinds of problems here."[19] As a result, Anand and her team decided to implement a country-by-country strategy that focused on getting buy-in from country-level CEOs and their executive teams, building the business case for each country and training.

For example, the US compliance training was adapted to what the company called Spirit of Inclusion, a more global version that trained executives to identify two important dimensions of diversity in their country and how those were connected to their abilities to drive business in the future.[20] This is a strong example of how a global approach to something like DEI training must be altered for local relevance to be successful.

Another global DEI challenge Sodexo faced was uneven progress. Efforts were taking off at faster paces in some places while making no headway in other places, despite similar resources. In Europe, women resisted training on gender equality in 2007, until the company facilitated a discussion about gender that included both men and women.[21] At the same time, in India, grassroots gender-equality initiatives such as women's networking groups, a task force to tackle women's issues in the workplace, and development of male "diversity champions" were all well received and successful straightaway. One unique challenge in India, however, was that the Sodexo North American mentoring program could not be replicated, because the Indian personnel considered it socially unacceptable for the woman to reach out directly to a male mentor for support. The program had to shift its structure so that the mentor had more responsibility for the mentoring relationship. In China, the experience for women's gender initiatives was predicated on leadership commitment and partnering with external organizations to develop cross-industry women's networking events.[22]

This tailoring of approaches to fit the local norms isn't easy, of course, but it's necessary. And to prevent the loss of momentum, seeing and recognizing where there is progress is a key element of every company's DEI journey. Sodexo's slow but steady improvements demonstrate the importance of acknowledging progress. In the company's 2010 diversity and inclusion report, Anand wrote: "Our number one priority globally is to ensure representation of women at all levels of the organization, particularly at the most senior levels. Currently, 20 percent of Sodexo's senior leaders are women and we have an ambition to increase this to 25 percent by 2015. It is an ambitious target, but we know that it can be done because we have clear processes in place to help us to accomplish it."[23]

Indeed, the company exceeded its goal of having women make up at least 25 percent of its top two hundred leadership positions globally by 2015. The proportion was actually 31 percent.[24] By 2020, Sodexo had reached gender-balanced teams at most levels of the organization, including 60 percent of the board, 30 percent of the executive committee, 40 percent of all senior executives, 44 percent of managers, and 55 percent of the total workforce.

But the company is not done. Sodexo is racing toward a global goal of having women represent at least 40 percent of its leadership by 2025 and 100 percent of employees working in entities with gender-balanced management teams.[25] Sodexo's global journey toward gender equality has demonstrated the importance of setting DEI goals, having the appropriate tracking metrics, integrating systems of accountability, and having the patience to see the fruits of the collective labor. Sustainable DEI change does not happen overnight even for the most advanced companies on the journey.

## Seeing Clients Take Notice and Influence Grow

When clients started to notice Sodexo's commitment to DEI, the organization was able to catapult its efforts by partnering with clients to have an impact on the organization's broader sphere of influence beyond its own walls. For example, in 2006 Sodexo and National Basketball Association Hall of Famer Earvin "Magic" Johnson founded SodexoMagic, a community advocacy group with the following mission: "We serve to uplift communities, to advocate equity, to ensure inclusion, to be a force for change. We sustain and empower communities everywhere through healthy food and exceptional services. We stand with our employees and partners to ensure quality-of-life services that safeguard wellness for all communities to create a just and more equitable future for all people."[26]

The organization has been successful combating food insecurity in communities and helping to provide clean and safe learning environments with a highly diverse group of more than sixty-five hundred employees serving consumers at more than seventeen hundred sites in the corporate arena, health care, universities, K–12 schools, and aviation.[27,28] SodexoMagic is a key example of an organization that uses its sphere of influence to have an impact on the world of DEI beyond its employee workforce while adhering to its core mission and values. It's not about being everything to everyone or mimicking what other organizations have done. It's about being connected to how your core business can create positive impact in the world around you.

"If it's a health-care organization," Anand said, "it's about addressing health-care disparities. If it's an education organization, it's about student achievement. If it's B2B, it's about your client base. If it's B2C, it's about the customer base. Whatever it is, it really has to be core to what the organization is about. I think that helps to expedite moving further along the continuum, going from compliance to getting buy-in and breaking down resistance. The key is embedding DEI within the business and really getting the value from it holistically."

Sodexo has continued to use its internal lessons learned about DEI to partner with others to increase the external impact of the work. The company realized the value in sharing its work with the broader business community by externally sharing its case studies. In 2014 Sodexo launched an internal study of the correlation between gender-balanced management and performance. This effort became known as the Gender Balance Study, a multiyear, longitudinal analysis of gender parity at all levels of leadership globally at Sodexo, with the goal of expanding research on the business case for women in leadership more generally.[29]

As the company has matured in its DEI perspective and under the leadership of Anand, it has become a thought leader on a wide array of DEI topics. For example, in 2019 alone Sodexo USA conducted research and published three white papers on varied topics:

- "Why 'LGBTQ-Welcoming' Will Soon Be a Hallmark of the Most Successful Senior Living Communities: A Primer for Operators, Marketers & Leadership"[30]

- "Addressing Culture and Origins across the Globe: Lessons from Australia, Brazil, Canada, the United Kingdom and the United States"[31]

- "Healthcare Administrators: The 2043 Business Imperative— Advocating for Hispanic Leadership in Healthcare and Cultural Competence"[32]

In addition, Sodexo offers menu guidelines to help mangers be more culturally aware when celebrating global cultures through food choices.[33]

## Still, Resistance

You might think that Sodexo has it all figured out and is cruising on its necessary journey, virtually frictionless. While the company is a model, there's still resistance. "I've worked at Sodexo for eighteen years," Anand said. "And for eighteen years, there's always been resistance in different forms. It doesn't go away."

Change management scholars will tell you that resistance is an organic part of any major organizational change.[34] Resistance to DEI initiatives can be even more complex than resistance to other change management initiatives because of the implicit and explicit social pressures of the cultural climate. In my experience with executives, though, I encourage them to approach DEI strategy with the same rigor and candor that they bring to other business imperatives, because many leaders are still afraid to speak up. A 2020 study by the Society for Human Resource Management found that 32 percent of HR professionals, those who are supposed to be the most well versed on issues of DEI, did not feel safe voicing their opinions about racial injustice in the workplace.[35] This lack of comfort with being honest about DEI manifests itself in leaders all signing off on a new, shiny DEI strategy with no understanding of how they are expected to commit to it and no real intention to support it beyond the head nod to HR. You have to meet the leaders where they are.

"The initial resistance was really about meeting people where they were and using individual strategies to bring them along," Anand said of her two-decade effort at Sodexo. "For some, it was about getting them to mentor individuals who were different from them so that they could then learn from the experiences of the person they were mentoring. For others, it was exposing them to a learning opportunity within the organization. For others, it was engagement in the community and being able to see what those communities go through. In other instances, it was having White males carrying the messages for me. There were a bunch of different strategies in terms of breaking down the resistance."

Behind it all, of course, was the data and the business case, and those help. But Anand believes that they only get you so far. One of the most dynamic and powerful ways to get resisters on board is to expose them to the opportunity to walk in someone else's shoes, as Anand explained:

> Eventually, people have to feel it in the heart and the gut, to really change their hearts and minds. So it was exposing them to this sort of variety of experiences. For example, we had fishbowl activities with the African American Leadership Forum, where we had the executive sit on the outside of the African American ERG circle and listen while [Black employees] shared stories about their experiences. Then we had the executive [on the outside] speak to their own privilege and how they were going to be committed to DEI. It was a lot of listening to stories and putting other people's experiences through either structured activities, mentoring, or informal engagements.
>
> In addition to seeing the data through the business case of showing how it's benefiting the business and benefiting our clients, it was those kinds of things that helped leaders move beyond resistance.

## The Journey Continues

It has been more than twenty years since Sodexo faced the shattering class action lawsuit about racial discrimination. The company's DEI journey started as a compliance exercise with a brand-new CDO. Since then, Sodexo has earned numerous DEI awards, most notably being honored by DiversityInc for thirteen consecutive years since 2008, and in 2021 was named second of the top fifty companies in DiversityInc's Hall of Fame.[36]

When asked to reflect on the journey of Sodexo over the past twenty years and how she knew her work made an impact, Anand shared three areas of impact she is most proud of: metrics, culture, and the sustainability of Sodexo's DEI program:

> We struggled to get senior leaders that were people of color, and women in operational profit and loss roles. So just looking at the numbers of senior executives in those roles [who] are women and people of color today gives me a huge sense of accomplishment. When a person says to me, "Look, I had all these choices as a female engineer, but I came here because of the culture, and because of your commitment to diversity . . ." I mean, in 2002, I never thought that I would go beyond that level. But today, I'm a global executive, thanks to the culture [of Sodexo]. I knew that we had an impact when we saw [that] engagement scores of our people of color and African Americans in particular had gone up incredibly high. They had a sense of belonging to the organization. That was a sense of accomplishment. And I think that fact—that when I was not in the room, and there were other people who were advocating for DEI—I knew I had an impact.

Anand cautions leaders that the journey is not over for Sodexo and that organizations must continue to be diligent in their efforts, even once they have reached this level of success: "Although organizations can go from class action lawsuits to best in class, without intentionality and focus, it is easy to slide back. Addressing DEI is continual and relentless."[37]

Although Anand has retired as CDO of Sodexo, she still shares her lessons learned with leaders all over the world. When I asked her what a workplace utopia looks like to her, she preached vigilance:

> DEI is an iterative process; it's always evolving. The external landscape is always changing. Utopia looks like an organization not taking their foot off the pedal, constantly addressing it, not slipping back or getting complacent. We must be prepared to constantly be addressing issues and not sit back on our laurels. For example, when the pandemic arrived, a lot of organizations cut back their support for DEI and cut back their head count. And then George Floyd's murder happened, and all the other events of 2020, and now all of a sudden, companies had to retool again.
>
> But this is life, and it is going to happen. Utopia is to be constantly vigilant and to keep DEI front and center, regardless of what's happening.

FIGURE 6-1

## Sodexo provides on-site services encompassing food, facilities management, and workplace and technical management services. It also provides benefits and rewards and personal and home services, with the mission of improving the quality of life of all those it serves.

**SodexoMagic** was founded in 2006 in partnership with NBA Hall of Famer Magic Johnson to "sustain and empower communities everywhere through healthy food and exceptional services." The organization has provided either standalone or integrated solutions for major corporations and institutions, including K–12 schools and HBCUs.

Sodexo's nonprofit Stop Hunger Foundation was started in 1996 with the mission of ensuring that every child in the US would grow up with dependable access to enough nutritious food for a healthy, productive life.

In 2018 Sodexo's CEO committed to reach a global representation of 40% women in senior leadership by 2025 and made teams accountable by linking 10% of annual incentives for the executive population to this target. Additionally, Sodexo has a target that all employees work for gender-balanced management teams by 2025.

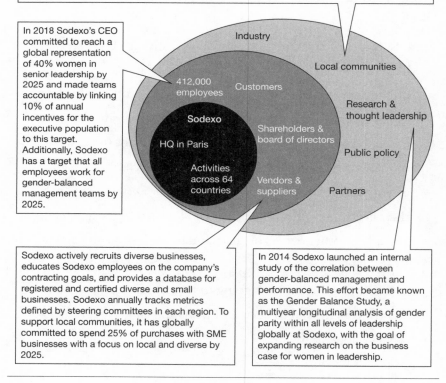

Industry

Local communities

412,000 employees

Customers

Research & thought leadership

Sodexo

Shareholders & board of directors

HQ in Paris

Public policy

Activities across 64 countries

Vendors & suppliers

Partners

Sodexo actively recruits diverse businesses, educates Sodexo employees on the company's contracting goals, and provides a database for registered and certified diverse and small businesses. Sodexo annually tracks metrics defined by steering committees in each region. To support local communities, it has globally committed to spend 25% of purchases with SME businesses with a focus on local and diverse by 2025.

In 2014 Sodexo launched an internal study of the correlation between gender-balanced management and performance. This effort became known as the Gender Balance Study, a multiyear longitudinal analysis of gender parity within all levels of leadership globally at Sodexo, with the goal of expanding research on the business case for women in leadership.

# 7

# Bringing Humanity to DEI through Leadership at Best Buy

---

**COMPANY:** Best Buy

**STAGE:** Tactical to integrated

**BEST PRACTICES:** Manager accountability, narratives, public metrics

**KEY QUOTE:** "You make a difference by touching the hearts of the employees and the leaders in the company, by bonding as a management team and saying we're going to make a difference."
—Hubert Joly, former chairman and CEO, Best Buy

---

For so many companies, deep introspection on DEI came in the wake of George Floyd's murder. The pain of the moment was felt around the world, and electronics retailer Best Buy was no exception. But there was a difference at Best Buy, too. Its headquarters is located just seven miles from the spot where Floyd was killed.

On that day, the Best Buy executive team gathered. CDO Mark Irvin remembered it clearly. "It was a catalyst moment. When people saw

George Floyd being murdered on their television screens in a way that reflected no mercy, no embrace for humanity . . . Many people didn't understand the Black experience. The rationalization that is usually used is, 'Well, this person did this or had that background.' But all of us understand mercy. All of us understand justice."

But this wasn't justice.

Irvin recalled, "I remember going back to the executive team the day Floyd's murder occurred, and I was talking to the executive team and our CEO, Corie Barry, leaned in and she said, 'We have to do better.'"

Best Buy put out both internal and external statements reinforcing Barry's words that the company had to do better. Barry wrote:

> We are, I believe, in one of the toughest times in our country's history, as we continue to battle a deadly pandemic and the resulting economic havoc while, once again, coming face-to-face with the long-term effects of racial injustice. Watching tens of thousands take to the streets to speak out against fear and inhumanity is, on one hand, inspiring for the commitment it represents and, on the other, heartbreaking for its profound need.
>
> But what's next? What do we do to change the cycle in which black men or women, with tragic frequency, are harmed by those who are supposed to protect them? Or the gut-wrenching truth that to be a person of color in America is often to not feel fully safe, seen or heard?
>
> For me, it starts with seeing the situation for what it is, acknowledging these experiences for what they are and, quite

simply, apologizing for not doing enough. As important, it includes committing the company I lead down a path of systemic, permanent change in as many ways as we can find.

I don't have the answers, but I am no longer OK with not asking the question: If everything were on the table, what could Best Buy do?[1]

Irvin fielded several communications from DEI colleagues from other companies. They said they had never seen a CEO take a stand like that. "They also told me later that we provoked their CEO to make a similar stand," he said. It was a moment of progress on the necessary journey brought on through pure leadership. A CEO's simple sentence, "We have to do better," prompted a cascade of leaders to join the chorus. "People could tell the journey this company was on was to value humanity first," Irvin said. And his and the company's response to the murder, which had happened just down the road, was definitive and forceful: "We just couldn't tolerate it."

## Making It Real

In 2012 Best Buy was a forty-six-year-old company at its nadir. The year before, the company's stock had lost 40 percent of its value. It was struggling to compete in e-commerce against behemoths like Amazon to meet new consumer expectations and demands. Internally the company was also on life support; employee turnover was at an all-time high, and morale was nonexistent.

Many people thought decorated business leader Hubert Joly was incredibly foolish for taking the job as Best Buy CEO at such a moment. It seemed as if the company were destined to go out of business. Yet Joly did take the job. He was determined to transform the company through a focus on humanity, and that's exactly what he did. Within a few years, Best Buy's stock was soaring, employee turnover was down, and the company was consistently rated one of the best to work for. Even Amazon was putting mini-stores inside Best Buy's stores. It's one of the most remarkable turnarounds in American business.

DEI was central to the cause. "The most pivotal DEI moment for Best Buy was just as Hubert was joining," Irvin said. "The company was at a place where many people would say, 'You're going out of business. You're not going to make it.' Hubert came in and was very intentional about creating the human approach, which is the reason why I joined."

Irvin had been with Target (also based in Minneapolis) and was sold on joining Best Buy after meeting Joly. "It was really my first human conversation with a CEO," Irvin said. "I was shocked at how accessible and approachable he was. Many companies in the North are very formal, but his approach began to unlock a more informal culture where you can have open and honest conversations. This human-centered approach led to our current guiding principles: Be human. Make it real. And our rallying cry: *Let's talk about what's possible.*"

Though Best Buy had some gender diversity efforts before Joly joined, many would say the company's intentional efforts around DEI began when he took the reins. Part of what made the intentional efforts seem natural is that Joly's overall philosophy for the business had elements of inclusivity built into it. Joly described this approach in his own words: "Our philosophy is that the company is a human organization, made of individuals working together in pursuit of a goal. And that goal is not profits. Instead, it is the pursuit of a noble purpose that starts with creating an environment where every individual can feel that they belong, can be themselves, and know the company will take an individual interest in them. Because I think that irrespective of size, it's still one individual at a time. That was an essential element of our transformation of unleashing what I call human magic."

This philosophy sounds noble, just as Joly uses that word. But without tactical implementation, his noble intentions would have just been words. Joly said that tactical implementation was part of Best Buy's necessary DEI journey and also part of the company's larger turnaround as a business.

"Part of the journey at Best Buy was figuring out how we create an environment in which everyone feels that their personal purpose, what drives them, connects with the purpose of the company," Joly said. "We want employees to feel they can be human, imperfect, vulnerable, and they can be the full version of themselves. That was the central idea in the resurgence and success of Best Buy."

## Public Commitments as Leadership

Although the philosophy was in place, Joly recognized that it was not enough. "Of course, you cannot stop there, because you have to look at the systemic issues around diversity and inclusion."

Like many other organizations, Best Buy started its DEI efforts with a focus on gender. Joly was an ambassador for gender diversity from the start. "For many years," he told me, "I've been passionate about gender diversity. Half of my direct reports at Best Buy were women. My successor is a woman, and when I stepped down from the Best Buy board, the majority of the board members were women." Irvin describes Joly's gender equity commitment as a pivot point in the overall DEI journey: "He championed gender diversity, and the company began to transform. From a leadership perspective, he did what no DEI team could do: he made a public commitment."

All along, one way that Joly used leadership to further his company on its necessary journey was through public commitments to DEI. In 2017 the company signed on to the Parity Pledge, promising to interview at least one qualified woman candidate for every open position at the level of vice president and above, including seats in the C-suite and on the board.[2] As of March 2019, Best Buy was one of only two *Fortune* 100 companies to have gender parity on its board of directors.[3] In April 2019 Best Buy appointed its first woman CEO, Corie Barry, to succeed Joly, bringing the number of women on the board to seven and making its board of thirteen majority female.[4] Today, Best Buy's board of directors has ten members, including six women and four men.[5]

In his book, *The Heart of Business*, Joly admits that for all the marvelous progress on gender diversity, racial diversity proved a bigger challenge for the company and for him. A series of focus groups exposed how serious the disconnect was. In his book, Joly describes how focus groups made it clear that Black employees felt stuck at entry-level positions and saw no prospects for advancement. Those who had moved from other parts of the country were also suffering culture shock in Minneapolis, where they felt displaced and sensed that their local colleagues lacked an understanding of how their life experiences were far different.

What is often undervalued in having these types of listening sessions is how difficult and painful it can be for employees to share their experiences with discrimination or exclusion at work. People of non-dominant identities in work spaces that are majority White and male can experience vastly different daily realities than members of the majority. During conversations about these experiences, there is often a dismal potential for victim blaming by people who may not have experienced the work environment in the same way. Engaging in respectful dialogue with people who hold opposing views is a major problem in society today. A global study of discourse and polarization in business by the Dialogue Project found that across the globe people struggle with respectful dialogue across differences and see it as a major problem (US 57%, Brazil 64%, India 49%, UK 28%, Germany 26%).[6] Thus, Joly's intimate conversations on race in the focus groups were challenging and at times uncomfortable but needed to happen for change to take place.[7]

Being grounded in humility helped Joly navigate these tough conversations. "I was blown away, and hurt, by what I heard in these focus groups," Joly writes. "As a white Frenchman living in Minnesota, I had had very limited exposure to the challenges that people of color face. I was also aware that my experience in driving real change when it came to diversity of all kinds was limited. I wanted to better understand the depth of systemic obstacles facing minorities, especially our African American colleagues."[8]

Irvin said he saw the exact moment that Joly connected on this issue and began to understand the difference in people's experiences. It was during a roundtable discussion with the Black Employee Resource Group (ERG). Irvin didn't remember what was being talked about, but he remembered how it just all seemed to click for Joly. "You could just tell that was a moment for him, no question about it," Irvin said. Joly appointed the then leader of the Black ERG as the head of diversity and inclusion for the organization. "And from then on," Irvin noted, "we really started to make inroads."

Then came additional public commitment. In July 2017 Joly signed the CEO Action for Diversity & Inclusion pledge and named Howard Rankin the company's first D&I officer.[9]

# Humanity Creates Momentum, Metrics Create Progress

The work of building up Best Buy's DEI program was made easier by leadership's complete buy-in. The company never considered DEI just an HR task—it still needed to actually implement programs and measure progress. It used a multitude of approaches to do this. Here are some.

## Narratives Connect DEI to the Business

DEI is not an esoteric concept that only academics and HR professionals understand. The best way to think of it is as an effort that creates the human experience of being seen, heard, and feeling valued in the workplace. By sharing stories, leaders can help people connect to those common and varied human experiences. One of Irvin's first priorities was to get leaders to see themselves as a part of the DEI journey using narratives that connected it to the business imperatives of the organization.

"So often people talk about, 'Is DEI the right thing to do?'" Irvin said. "Well, it is the right thing to do, but everyone doesn't agree with that. But everyone that leads a business does understand the economic rationale of being locked out of a vast majority of society, and the economic ramifications of that." In other words, the story Irvin wanted to tell was about how a failure to focus on DEI, whether you think it should be a priority or not, was just bad for business. And things that are bad for business are things that should be addressed. He explained his approach:

> For our leaders, I paint the story using Amazon as an example, that when things start to change, such as the rise of e-commerce, companies that don't adapt ultimately go out of business. And so it's the same story here. If there is a dramatic shift in social change and understanding, if companies maintain their posture of barriers and resistance in a workforce that doesn't mirror the society, a lot of businesses will not survive.
>
> So we started to tell stories about the demographics and the representation of the workforce. For example, as you think about the evolution from the baby boomers to the millennials, into the postmillennials, and the demographic changes that

are beginning to happen in the workforce, there are real economic implications playing out.

The economic implications of DEI that Irvin refers to are the basis
of the business case for DEI efforts for any organization. Without
recognizing the business implications of DEI, these efforts can lose
momentum when other business imperatives take precedence. For a
sustainable DEI strategy, it must have a clear connection to the organization's business strategy and performance. Narratives helped Best Buy
leaders make that connection, Irvin said: "If people can't write themselves into the story, in most cases they won't embrace the story."

## Using Business Cases to Drive
## Functional-Unit Level Change

Beyond the big-picture business case for any organization, there needs
to be a business connection for every major function in the business. I
often tell clients that managers are the most critical link to successful
DEI implementation. However, many managers do not truly understand how the efforts of organizational DEI have a direct impact on their
own responsibilities. They may even believe DEI doesn't contribute to
success, given the way success is measured for them. Thus, they are less
motivated to focus on DEI than they are their other priorities. That is,
managers have a hard time connecting the dots between DEI and their
bottom lines, annual goals, and opportunities for internal advancement.

Furthermore, most managers feel overworked already. DEI feels like
extra work. It's easy to see how managers may care about the under-

lying issues but may not act on them, because they fail to see how DEI can actually help them achieve their individual and team goals. Managers often tell me, "I care deeply about these issues, but when I am evaluated on my team's output or bottom line, it is hard to find the time for DEI." This too is a human reaction. Vroom's classic motivation theory tells us that people are motivated to increase effort based on the belief that their effort will increase performance and that high performance will lead to an outcome they value (i.e., money, recognition, status).[10, 11] Thus, if managers do not believe increased attention to DEI will lead to better performance evaluations and thus desired outcomes, it is easy to see why DEI can fall further down their to-do list even if they are well intentioned. This is why it is vital for managers to see the connection between DEI, the success of their teams, and how this work is tangibly valued and rewarded by their organization.

Unraveling these issues can be challenging. I have worked with many client teams to help illuminate how DEI has an impact on their part of the business, and while the leaders understand the needs in theory, they find it extremely difficult to put into words or data the benefits of DEI to their specific business unit. If managers cannot clearly grasp how diverse teams with inclusive cultures can help them—for example, by solving problems faster or making them more likely to catch mistakes earlier or to attract new customers—then they are unlikely to embrace activities that create an inclusive culture.

For example, one way managers can foster an inclusive environment that welcomes divergent perspectives is to appoint a different *dissenter* or *critic* in every team meeting. Such a practice creates a space where opinions that deviate from the norm are not only welcomed but also expected to be a part of the critical thinking process. Yet the downside of this change in the decision-making process is that in the short term, it can prolong meetings and increase the time it takes to make a final decision. Moreover, people in this assigned devil's advocate role may need time to create rules for authentic dissent on teams.[12] Yet countless social science studies and companies like Google and IDEO have implemented similar team roles and found them to be effective in limiting groupthink and spurring innovation.[13] If managers can connect their desired outcomes with practices of inclusion, such as assigning a dissenter in a meeting, then they will be much more likely to make it an everyday management practice and will be less likely to think of it as something extra on their list of to-dos.

Best Buy used the narrative approach to bring to life the business case for each part of the organization, especially for frontline managers. "We began to tell stories of the demographic dollars shifting," Irvin said. "And Best Buy was strategic about this as well. We have been cascading this message in a way to make sure that in every area that we've done it, we've got our marketing team fully engaged. We've got our customer office fully understanding the ramifications. For example, we tell stories about customers of different backgrounds that walked into a Best Buy and had an experience that none of us would appreciate because of unconscious bias." The stories—for example, that a bad store experience affects sales—create the connection between DEI and sales, one critical part of the business. "So we began to really spread that [message] across the organization: that one of our strategic priorities has to be to create an inclusive culture where everyone is engaged and valued and appreciated for the difference that they bring."

## *Accountability Unapologetically Drives DEI*

After getting the organization on board with DEI as a leadership challenge, it was time to see change that could be measured. Accountability is usually evaluated as the extent to which leaders do what they say they will do about DEI. But true accountability for DEI requires having some skin in the game and a willingness to take risks to get it right. "What gets measured gets done" holds true in the world of DEI.

I've seen many companies that had seemingly impressive DEI progress ongoing for years but never wanted to put metrics in place for fear that doing so would expose failures. Joly's approach eventually was to embrace metrics, no matter how unapologetically they might reflect shortcomings, because then the company could see what it needed to do. His leadership had already impelled the organization forward, but once it was on its journey, metrics would mark and drive the progress. Joly explained:

> You make a difference by touching the hearts of the employees and the leaders in the company, by bonding as a management team and saying we're going to make a difference. I believe now—something I didn't believe then—that you absolutely have to set quantitative goals. I was reluctant to do it initially, because I wanted first to touch the hearts of people. But then ultimately, once you've given them a chance to be touched, you say, 'Now let's create a goal.' Now, for many companies, that has started to change. Many companies now are setting goals, and their boards are holding them

accountable. When that happens, you can manage it as any other business priority.

Today, Best Buy has inclusive leadership behavioral metrics on vulnerability, empathy, courage, and grace. Each leader is annually evaluated on their performance of these behaviors as "off track," "on track," or "leading." Notice these metrics don't have to be statistically complicated—it's a three-point scale. But assigning any measure fosters the change both in the behavior of those being measured and in the culture of the company, which now understands that these attributes are valued in performance assessments.

"If someone is off track, we give them feedback," Irvin said. "For example, someone off track on exhibiting vulnerability means they're not open, not willing to hear different points of view, not interested, not curious. In our performance process, we look at where each leader shows up on this metric. And that has an influence on whether they might be considered for promotion and other opportunities across the organization."

Still, without the willingness to take risks and stand behind your values, even the best-written metrics can fall flat. For example, many organizations say they are committed to diversifying their leadership pipelines but have no systems of accountability in place to make sure that this happens. Or they don't hold people accountable if the goals aren't reached. Once Best Buy had metrics, its leaders realized they had to be bolder in their actions to make the metrics a reality.

"I needed to change my board because at the time, we didn't have any Black directors," Joly said. "We told the headhunters that we have made great progress on gender but not race, so for this next wave of re-cruits, don't bother giving us non-Black résumés. In this way, we went way past the Rooney Rule." Joly was referring to a National Football League initiative (promoted by former Pittsburgh Steelers owner Dan Rooney) that told teams to interview at least one minority candidate for every coaching or front-office vacancy. "I felt it was important to send a clear signal," he said. "I told the headhunters, 'If you believe you're not going to be able to give us good résumés of potential Black directors, we will just work with another firm.'"

## *Acknowledging Mistakes and Embracing Challenges*

There is a level of humility that must accompany any organization on its DEI journey. Everyone will make mistakes; it's part of how we adapt and get better. These mistakes can be terrifying when we are dealing with sensitive topics like race, especially in light of the cancel culture we live in today. Studies find that fear of saying the wrong thing often inhibits leaders, especially White men, from saying anything at all when it comes to DEI.[14] Joly, who is White, led by example, even when he made mistakes.

"When I began on this journey with my team, we said, 'We don't even know what's okay to talk about,'" Joly said. "So, I promised every-body I was going to make mistakes and I would learn. For example, in one meeting, I said, 'We have too many pale and male executives,' and a White man heard this and filed a complaint with legal. Once it came to my attention, I realized I was totally wrong to say that, and I reached out to my team to say I'm sorry if I offended anybody, and we talked.

We are all human beings, and we have to forgive ourselves and each other as we grow."

At an individual level, humility is the key ingredient in owning mistakes. But at the group and organizational level, it can be harder to recognize mistakes and course-correct. A reluctance to admit that what we have been doing is not working and to start from scratch and rebuild a more equitable system is what holds many organizations back from putting into practice the things they claim are their values. For example, during the hiring process for a senior leadership position at Best Buy, Irvin noticed that bias was creeping into the candidate evaluations. Two of the candidates were John and Ricardo. Most of the team seemed to be resonating with the experiences of John.

"I was the only person on the interview team with a diverse racial background," Irvin said, and he thought, of course the team was connecting with John over Ricardo because the team members' experiences and backgrounds were similar to John's. Not only did Irvin think this was unconscious bias at play, but he also thought their decision was maybe not the best for the organization. Diversity includes diversity of experiences and of thought. Wouldn't the team be better served by bringing in someone different instead of someone more like the people already there? Irvin explained what happened next:

> So, we're fully committed to DEI, but I saw us being led down
> an unconscious-bias journey. As we're recapping the inter-
> view, I said, "Wait a minute, help me understand. Are we hir-
> ing to double down on capabilities that we already have? Are
> we trying to round out the experiences of our team in a way
> that makes us better?"

Other leaders later said to me, "We don't know how to interview for diverse perspectives. We've always hired for who we thought was best." What they came to realize during that situation, though, is that "best" is usually based on our own experiences. That's a biased hiring strategy.

It's this type of willingness to acknowledge errors and shortcomings and, crucially, to talk about them that organizations need to do more of. One thing that prevents this level of openness is the fear that by calling out biases or other problems, you might be judging your colleagues. Irvin wanted to surface something, but he wasn't suggesting his colleagues were bad people for their behavior. And the discussion afterward ensured that they knew that his motives were sincere. Acknowledging, talking, correcting, and pivoting help organizations overcome these challenges.

## Sharpening the Saw

When Joly first joined Best Buy, the company was at the tactical stage of its journey. It had active internal DEI initiatives, many of which focused on gender diversity, but DEI was not yet a part of its core business model and could not yet be seen throughout all aspects of its work. Under Joly's and Irvin's leadership over the next decade, Best Buy homed in on DEI and matured to the integrated stage as evidenced by its employee-focused programs and initiatives that span Best Buy's large sphere of influence in local communities and the larger business community as a whole.

Though Joly stepped down as CEO in 2019, the spirit of his work lives on as a core company value and has had rippling impacts on the company's DEI journey. He established a clear value that still holds today: DEI is not an HR challenge. It's a leadership responsibility.

Today, Best Buy structures its culture around four strategic pillars of diversity and inclusion: workforce, workplace, marketplace, and community.[15] The company has received wide recognition for its efforts. In 2019 it ranked number eleven on the Historically Black Colleges and Universities (HBCU) Connect's list of top employers for HBCU students and graduates. That same year, it sponsored forty Black employees to attend the Executive Leadership Conference in Washington, DC an event held with the goal of increasing the number of Black leaders on the top five hundred corporate boards and CEO offices.[16] In 2020 Best Buy was named a Noteworthy Company for Diversity by DiversityInc (one of just two retailers on the index) and a World's Most Ethical Company by Ethisphere (they won the honor in 2021 and 2022 as well).[17, 18] It was also recognized on the Bloomberg Gender-Equality Index.[19]

Best Buy's most recent progress includes the creation of a Task Force for Racial Equality in June 2020, a group appointed by Barry to challenge the senior leadership team and board of directors to identify substantive ways the company can address inequities.[20] In December 2020 the company announced a five-year plan focused on hiring BIPOC and women employees and creating additional educational and career development opportunities and support for youth and emerging leaders.

Its commitments—again, made publicly—include a goal to fill one out of three nonhourly corporate positions with BIPOC employees, and one out of three new nonhourly field roles with women by 2025.[21]

The company also announced a $44 million commitment to expand college prep and career opportunities for BIPOC students, including the launch of a scholarship fund for HBCU students in partnership with the United Negro College Fund.[22] To enhance its inclusive culture for employees, Best Buy expanded its network of ERGs to include diversity and inclusion steering committees.[23] These cross-functional groups of leaders focus on attracting and investing in top talent and fostering inclusion.[24] In June 2021 they upped their commitment by pledging to give at least $1.2 billion with BIPOC and diverse businesses by 2025.[25]

Best Buy has also expanded its sphere of influence beyond its own walls—another natural offshoot of Joly's vision for a stakeholder-driven company that serves the community as well as employees and shareholders. For example, broadband access—especially in a pandemic—is a significant need. "It's a big issue in New York City, and in rural Minnesota, for example," Joly told me. "And of course, it affects different groups differently, right? There is enormous inequality and injustice in the country, around broadband access." His successor, Corie Barry, partnered with a few other CEOs and governors to mobilize together for a solution. The contribution of people, time, and effort to cross over and talk with competitors and other leaders is as crucial as anything else in a company's sphere of influence. "Writing a check is easy, right?" Joly said. "But doing things is even more important."

Irvin described how the company has worked to extend its influence:

> The number one thing that I'm most proud of is how we're using our voice. The entire senior leadership team, sixteen people strong, coming together after some event occurs,

saying, "What do we want to say about it? What do we want to say to our government affairs office? How do we want to influence policy? What do we want to say to our internal employees? And then how do we want to use our platform to make a difference in the communities in which we operate?" We're thinking about that constantly. We recently put out a statement about the impact to the Asian community around hate crimes. And we've also invested in organizations as well. We make a stand against hate. I think that makes a difference.

Given Best Buy's increased attention to DEI over the past few years, it would be easy to think the company has arrived. But it hasn't. The DEI journey is always evolving. DEI is about humans, and humanity is always evolving and changing; thus your organization's DEI journey will too. Best Buy is now looking at the future of its DEI efforts and how it can become increasingly intentional. Just as Iora Health focused on what unique DEI steps it could take rather than just implement generic DEI goals (see chapter 1), Best Buy wants to move forward similarly.

"You can't set out to do one hundred things," Irvin said. "It does not work to say we are just going to throw all these things down the road and just see how that all lands. In the inclusion and diversity space, and in the social-impact space at times, organizations can be involved in many things. What I'm asking us to do is sharpen that saw, be more intentional about who we are, and figure out where we can make the most decisive difference."

For example, by 2021, Best Buy had opened thirty-five teen tech centers in underserved and undervalued communities where kids can use the latest technology. The goal is to create career aspirations in technology for kids who may otherwise never get access to a place that would inspire them to go in that direction. "I think that is unique to us," Irvin observed. "So we've made a commitment to scale those teen tech centers from thirty-five to a hundred. I think it's important to not do too many things and instead be intentional enough to just do a few that represent authenticity and the DNA of the company." At the time of writing Best Buy had already increased to forty-six centers, with a continued commitment to expand to one hundred centers and reach thirty thousand teens annually by 2025.[26]

# Human Magic

I asked both Mark Irvin and Hubert Joly what a workplace utopia would look like to them. Both focused on a workplace where people could be themselves. And both effortlessly connected that to the results it brings to business.

Irvin said, "You know, if you think about the moments you've had in life, where you thought, 'I have a different voice, but my voice is valued. And I'm allowed to help us all to make a difference.' That's what I'm looking for. I'm looking for a workplace where the barriers are removed, where we actually listen to people. I don't want them to feel like they have to use similar terminology and have similar perspectives to everyone else. I want people to be their authentic selves in a way that makes us all better. That's the world that I'm fighting for."

For Joly, DEI is a big part of what will create what he calls "human magic"—what happens naturally when people, not profits, are the goal. He believes utopia is a workplace where "I am seen as a human being, which honors all parts of who I am, including the color of my skin. Because if many of us are not seen, we don't have a voice. We don't have a seat. That's why diversity and inclusion is not a sideshow; it's essential to unleashing human magic."

FIGURE 7-1

**Best Buy is the world's largest multichannel electronics retailer. Best Buy's goal is to enrich lives through technology and to ensure that every customer feels appreciated and excited about their experience.**

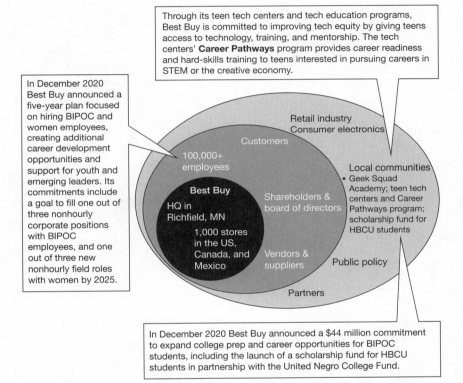

Through its teen tech centers and tech education programs, Best Buy is committed to improving tech equity by giving teens access to technology, training, and mentorship. The tech centers' **Career Pathways** program provides career readiness and hard-skills training to teens interested in pursuing careers in STEM or the creative economy.

In December 2020 Best Buy announced a five-year plan focused on hiring BIPOC and women employees, creating additional career development opportunities and support for youth and emerging leaders. Its commitments include a goal to fill one out of three nonhourly corporate positions with BIPOC employees, and one out of three new nonhourly field roles with women by 2025.

Retail industry
Consumer electronics

Customers

100,000+ employees

Best Buy

HQ in Richfield, MN

Shareholders & board of directors

Local communities
• Geek Squad Academy; teen tech centers and Career Pathways program; scholarship fund for HBCU students

1,000 stores in the US, Canada, and Mexico

Vendors & suppliers

Public policy

Partners

In December 2020 Best Buy announced a $44 million commitment to expand college prep and career opportunities for BIPOC students, including the launch of a scholarship fund for HBCU students in partnership with the United Negro College Fund.

# 8

# Breaking Traditions to Increase Inclusion at Infosys

---

**COMPANY:** Infosys

**STAGE:** Tactical to integrated

**BEST PRACTICES:** Nontraditional recruitment strategies, broader definitions of diversity

**KEY QUOTE:** "You build the services of the future; you will build the right ones as long as you build them with a diverse workforce. That, to me, is the real thing. It so happens that it's also the right thing to do. But we're not doing it for the sake of the narrative. We're doing it because it is a viable business model. And it happens to be the right thing for an equitable future." —Ravi Kumar, president, Infosys

---

In 2017 Infosys, a technology company based in India, had earned $10.2 billion in revenue, largely by helping companies around the world create and execute digital transformation strategies. President

Ravi Kumar was excited about a new strategy to expand its US presence. He made a huge pledge to hire ten thousand employees from the United States that year. As an India-based technology company, Infosys had traditionally hired very little in the United States. "When we made an announcement that we're going to create ten thousand in the US," he said, "it was actually a surprising announcement, because people said, 'We don't find good technology talent in the US.' That's how it has been."

Still, the company was excited about the pivot to expand its US workforce, but Kumar knew the strategy would have to pivot from how Infosys recruited talent in India, where the company runs the largest corporate training university in the world. "Our ten-thousand pledge was built on hiring from schools and colleges, which by itself was very new to us because we don't traditionally hire a lot from schools," Kumar explained. "We hire experienced talent from the market. So that by itself was a big leap. Before 2017 we hired zero from schools. And in 2017, we hired a thousand people from schools."

By 2021, Infosys was one of the largest direct recruiters from US schools, hiring four thousand employees. To do this, the company took a unique approach. Not only did it hire at the top colleges and universities, as did many of its competitors, but it went heavily after an untapped source of talent: community colleges.

Kumar explained how the strategy was born out of necessity: "Skills of the future are going to be depleted very rapidly. We realized that the jobs of the future are not just going to be core digital jobs. As digitization goes up, you will need a lot of backbone jobs, like data operations and end-user security operations. Given the need for back bone jobs, we started looking for alternative ways to bring talent into the workforce, and we found community colleges could be a great source for talent."

This was a unique strategy—to go after a largely untapped market in the technology space. Traditionally, graduates with two-year associate's degrees experience higher unemployment rates than do those from four-year bachelor's degree programs, yet they make up one-third of the available undergraduate talent pool in the United States.[1] Further, community colleges offer a more diverse and experienced talent pool, as many students already have workforce experience. Community colleges enjoy a more diverse population in general. Half of students enrolled in community colleges are racial and ethnic minorities, and more than two-thirds of these students come from families earning below $50,000.[2]

Employers say finding people with adequate technical and digital skills is a challenge.[3] But research shows that associate's degree graduates are well positioned to be adaptable to the future needs of organizations and that those with relevant experience perform equally as well as, or better than, college graduates do on the job.[4]

For Infosys, it was like discovering an untapped vein of rich ore to mine. It seemed like a simple formula to gain US talent: recruit from community colleges, pay them higher than market value, and easily reach the goal of hiring ten thousand people in the United States.

But Kumar and his recruitment team experienced the opposite of a simple task. What threw up the roadblock?

## When Pay Isn't the Only Motivator

Kumar and his team discovered only a lack of interest in their company from community colleges. "The first time our recruiters went to community colleges," he recalled, "they came back saying people are not willing to join. I was actually shocked that with a compensation structure, which was 25 to 30 percent more than anybody else was offering, people didn't apply. I thought it was a slam-dunk thing."

Kumar said the team learned that people didn't even know what the promoted jobs were. Infosys would advertise a cybersecurity job, and people would say, "We don't even know what that is. What are you talking about?" The team pressed, focused mostly on pay as a lever, but the effort was futile. Even when Infosys promised higher pay, people were still not interested.

In retrospect, Kumar and the recruiters seemed to be pulling on the wrong lever all along. No matter what, they kept focusing on how competitive their wages were. And the more resistance they met, the more the recruiters tried to point out how much more money they were offering, thinking that this enticement, above all, would motivate people to join the company.

Kumar and the recruiters worked closely together to figure out what was causing the issue. They eventually realized that many of these community college graduates simply didn't know anyone who had done a remotely similar job. They had no role models in technology. They had no people to ask about their experiences in the field. Working for Infosys was remarkably unfamiliar territory to the recruits, and unfamiliarity creates uncertainty. Better to focus on something you understand or at least know you can learn about through trusted friends and family. The lack of role models is a huge psychological impediment for people trying to see themselves succeeding in a role. Research has shown that women and minorities are more likely to feel capable of success in a job or leadership role when they have models with similar backgrounds to look up to.[5]

The associate's degree holders' reluctance was brought into high relief when compared with what Infosys recruiters were experiencing at four-year colleges. For these colleges, Kumar said, "we didn't have the same problem, because while they have not seen technology jobs before, they know somebody who is doing a technology job. They were able to participate in the process."

All the focus on competitive pay would never move the needle. Pay wasn't the issue, Kumar learned. "The issue is, do they have the confidence to do this?"

Infosys tacked to a new strategy, finding the organizations that were trusted in the communities where these students came from. "We realized we needed the nonprofits who work in these communities, who have trusted relationships, to be that bridge," Kumar said. "We also started to work with companies that were more interconnected with the communities and use them as the bridge to funnel talent into our organization." For example, Infosys has partnered with the California nonprofit MV Gate to host family code nights, evening events hosted by K–5 elementary schools where children and their parents pair up to carry out their first hour of coding together.[6] Other community partners along a long list include Girl

Scouts of America, Girls Who Code, and the Boys & Girls Clubs of America.[7]

## DEI in a Time of Expansion

Infosys was founded in Pune, India, in 1981 by seven engineers with $250 of investment capital. It is now a $72 billion company, recognized as a global leader in tech services and consulting, with almost a quarter million employees worldwide in more than fifty countries.

For years, Infosys has known only growth and expansion. Expanding beyond India, the company opened its first international office in 1987 in Boston. In 1993 Infosys became the first IT company from India to be listed on the NASDAQ. That was followed by more expansion, first a European headquarters in the United Kingdom and then a global development center in Toronto in 1995. By 2000, Infosys had offices or development centers in Germany, Sweden, Belgium, Australia, France, Hong Kong, Canada, the United Kingdom, and the United States. Its growth in revenues and locations continued at a steady pace from 2000 to around 2003, reaching $2 billion in revenue less than two years after reaching $1 billion. It reached 50,000 employees by 2006 and doubled that within three years.[8]

Infosys's DEI journey has had to scale at the same rate as the company's own breakneck rate of growth. By most measures, the journey has been successful, through that simplest of strategies that most companies espouse but do not always live up to: focus on your people, your talent. Infosys seems to have pulled it off, though. Its successes were first acknowledged in 2001, when Infosys was rated as "Best Employer" by *Business World/Hewitt*.[9]

In 2012 *Forbes* ranked Infosys among the world's most innovative companies. Infosys was also recognized among the twenty-five performers in the Caring for Climate initiative, the world's largest corporate sustainability endeavor.[10]

While technology is generally a male-dominated field, Infosys has increased gender diversity through its sponsorship programs that aim to strengthen the talent pipeline of female leaders in business. These efforts include the Infosys Women's Inclusivity Network for women and their allies and the company's innovative Restart with Infosys program.[11] The Restart program focuses on bringing back women after career breaks by helping them develop relevant skills, providing real-life project experiences, and mentoring. In fact, Infosys also provides support for mothers through its return-to-work post-maternity programs. Through these efforts, Infosys has managed to see 89 percent of its women employees return to work after maternity leave.

The work Infosys has done to increase gender diversity has not gone unnoticed. In 2019 the company won the AccelHERate 2020 and DivHERsity Awards in three categories: top five in Most Innovative Practices, Women Leadership and Development Programs (large enterprises); top twenty in DivHERsity (large enterprises); and top twenty in Most Innovative Practices, Women Leadership Development.[12] And after all the growth and expansion, Infosys has not suffered declines in its reputation. It ranked third on the 2019 *Forbes* World's Best Regarded Companies list and was recognized as a 2020 Top Employer in Australia, Singapore, and Japan.[13][14] Infosys was also declared one of the best companies for women in India and ranked number one for anti-sexual-harassment practices among 357 companies in India at a conference sponsored by the publishers of *Working Mother* and Avtar. As a champion of inclusion, Infosys was listed—on the Working Mother & Avtar Most Inclusive Companies in India Index in 2021. Infosys was also honored by Great Places to Work and *Fortune* as one of the 2021 Best Big Companies to Work.[15, 16]

What's most impressive about these gender diversity efforts is that Infosys has managed to have such an impact on gender diversity all while the company has been in hypergrowth mode. Since 2010 the company has reached many firsts, such as crossing $10 billion in revenue in 2016 and increasing to $15 billion in 2021 while also serving 185 clients on the *Fortune* 500 list.[17] The company has managed to keep an eye on its diversity efforts by being willing to experiment with novel approaches and celebrating every milestone as a big deal.

Gender parity is a clear global issue that makes sense for a company like Infosys to focus on. Today the company has an ambition of creating a gender diversity workforce with 45 percent women by 2030 (in 2022 around 38 percent of employees were women).[18]

Yet, creating racial equity and inclusion has been more of a challenge for the organization, which has more than 156 nationalities represented. Some employees have raised concerns that despite its multinational presence, the company's workforce is disproportionally South Asian and Indian, more than 90 percent, to be exact.[19] In the United States, the company has not been immune from EEOC claims of racial and gender discrimination.[20]

When I interviewed a Black woman who was a former Infosys employee in the United States, she described the challenges of having few Black role models in the firm and, often painfully, being the only Black person on her teams. "I was the only Black American woman in my cohort of twenty-five people when I joined the firm," she recalled. "Yet, I talked to other Black employees who have since also left, and we each had similar experiences. Even though I had an MBA and significant consulting experience before Infosys, I was put on teams to take notes. . . . I did not feel valued. Whenever I did have ideas, they were not really taken seriously."

Like many companies, particularly large global entities, Infosys has done a stellar job in some areas but still has work to do to make sure all employees have inclusive experiences. Part of embracing the complicated nature of DEI is embracing the fact that no organization, and no person for that matter, is perfect. But seeking perfection should not prevent a company from trying.

## Breaking Old Models

Infosys lives in the world of technology and is therefore constantly looking ahead at what's next. Kumar sees a world in which technological realities make diverse workforces necessary. In a future diverse world in which technology has transformed the need for talent, you simply won't be able to compete if you have a homogeneous workforce pulled from four-year colleges.

"One of the reasons why people are not able to find jobs is that there is often a prerequisite for a degree, which is not needed," Kumar said. "Everybody wants a degree, but if you really look at the roles and responsibilities of the job, you don't need a degree."

What's more, Kumar said, tech moves so fast that a four-year degree is virtually obsolete in two years. "So, by the time you come out of college, you are automatically going to look for newer skills."

At the heart of this disconnect, education has become divisive rather than bridging, Kumar believes. "The whole debate of diversity and inclusivity and equitable access to jobs has happened because of education. The cost of education has gone up almost 150 percent since around 2000. Education has not been the bridge that it historically was to a good career. "It has actually created the divide," Kumar said.

Kumar thinks technology and its rapid reinvention is, in a way, fostering diversity by breaking down old models of education and career entry and presenting new opportunities, such as those at community colleges. "We are lucky that digital technologies have a shorter life," he said. "They're challenging the traditional four-year degree. It led us to hiring without a degree and hiring based on learnability."

Infosys has expanded its recruiting beyond community college graduates to offer specialized training to some students who are working low-wage jobs and going to school to make a midcareer shift. Basically, the company can say to students, "Come take our courses rather than general courses at community college." Kumar explained, "We said, 'Why couldn't we go and run programs for the specific jobs rather than only going to community colleges?' So, we recently started a program where we look for people in a midcareer shift. If you have high potential but you're working on a low-skilled job, we are willing to take you to a high-skilled job."

Hiring from the diverse pool of talent at community colleges has proved beneficial to the business, Kumar said. "Our internal numbers show that if I hire an undergrad from school, the attrition rate is higher than the rate from community colleges. The talent we get from community colleges has a bigger emotional connection with us because we've invested in them. It's a really viable business model because they don't attrition out."

## The Future Is Diverse by Default

For Infosys, the DEI journey is really about business continuity. Without DEI, there is no continuity. Kumar said:

> When you build the products of the future, which cater to every constituent in the society, you see that diversity and inclusivity will create better products and will create more efficient ways of building better products. You build the services of the future; you will build the right ones as long as you build them with a diverse workforce [because they'll be serving a diverse client base]. That, to me, is the real thing. It so happens that it's also the right thing to do. But we're not doing it for the sake of the narrative. We're doing it because it is a viable business model. And it happens to be the right thing for an equitable future.

To that end, Kumar is as focused on looking to the future as he is on meeting certain demographic profiles in the present. Many companies are focused on demographics to improve their diversity, and while this is foundationally important, they should also be thinking about cognitive diversity, socioeconomic diversity, and other facets of the breadth of diversity that will help prepare their workforce for the future.

"I don't think we will have to force the diversity and inclusivity metrics on people," Kumar said. "It will just happen by natural force" because there's a viable business model here that is just waiting for people to take advantage of it. In the future, they will have to. The demand for talent will be too intense to leave any stone unturned, never mind a massive opportunity like the one Infosys has found in community colleges.

## Influencing the Future of Education

Infosys is a company at the tactical to integrated stage in its DEI journey. It has clearly been thoughtful about DEI across its multiple spheres of influence. Specifically, its out-of-the-box thinking with non-traditional recruitment strategies and its broader definitions of diversity (e.g., community college graduates versus traditional four-year college graduates) has helped to increase their workforce diversity and they have also reached outside of their internal company to impact the larger global community. Yet, as noted, the company must be intentional to create inclusive experiences for all its employees, not just those from community college backgrounds. With so many new initiatives, it will take time to see the long-term impact of these efforts and whether the company can continue to mature to the sustainable stage of its journey.

Infosys's noteworthy sphere of influence has matured; it extends beyond its own employees. Infosys has tactically used its sphere of influence to expand its learning and training ecosystem beyond four-year college programs and even beyond the diverse and valuable community college programs it has successfully fostered.

In addition to being an early champion of the talent hidden in plain sight at community colleges, Infosys has partnered with organizations such as Merit America, Per Scholas, and Woz U and a network of academic institutions that have fostered the connection between tech companies and communities with little experience in the tech industry. The Infosys Foundation, a not-for-profit initiative established in 1996, continues its reach into underprivileged communities by supporting "programs in the areas of education, rural development, health care, arts and culture, and destitute care."[21]

The company still also works with colleges directly, but in ways that continue to challenge the traditional four-year model. Infosys partnered with Arizona State University on "stackable credits," a program that allows people to earn credits toward a degree while working at the company. Efforts like these represent a different approach to skills and career development. "The experiential learning, it's like an apprenticeship," Kumar said. "And if you do well, we will promote you to the next job and make sure you progress on an ongoing basis."

Kumar also extends the sphere of influence to state governments, running a career pathways forum for the governor of Connecticut. As Kumar sees it, without participating in, or even creating and driving, your sphere of influence, you won't get far in DEI. "If you want to make a huge impact, it can't be done just by enterprises," he said. "It has to be done by enterprises, academic institutions, and state governments."

Infosys's DEI efforts are deliberately connected to and informed by what's going on in the world. Kumar makes sure that as the world changes, inclusivity is not forgotten, especially in crises. The Covid-19 pandemic led to more workers in technology who could rapidly upskill in a remote environment. Infosys recognized this as an opportunity for talent but also intentionally focused on communities hit hardest by Covid-19 job losses such as minorities, women, and nondegree holders.

Infosys and its partners created Reskill and Restart, a free online platform that matches potential employees to roles in tech, non-tech and support functions. The platform is unique because it also offers training programs in technology, which helps skill people for future jobs while also connecting them with current job opportunities to provide experience.[22] This approach helps solve the pervasive cycle job seekers encounter: trying to get a job to gain experience but finding that all jobs require previous experience to be selected.

This includes people without bachelor's degrees. The macro trend that Kumar believes is most important in the future is the shrinking life cycle of technical skills and how it doesn't mesh with an education system based on a four-year undergraduate program. It has him convinced that you can use training and learning aptitude to get people into good career-building roles without requiring a bachelor's degree or any other degree. Infosys has piloted a program with Google to this end. "We have already hired a hundred people without degrees, and we found very good results," Kumar said. "So, we're going to scale. Now, that is a big part of DEI."

For Infosys, talent is much more about aptitude to learn versus a degree. In an interview with *Forbes*, Kumar shared his perspective on the value of intentionally hiring nontechnology, nondegree talent as a strategy:

We know there are millions of Americans who lack a traditional college degree: they may be stuck in low-potential jobs, but they have very high potential. For instance, we can hire someone with no technology experience for a data operations role, which is an entry-level role in our company. In just a couple of years, with the right training, education, and support that we're able to provide, that individual can move into a skilled data scientist role. And we are doing that at scale.[23]

Kumar is looking more and more outward, beyond his own company. For any company that has a culture of scaling at high speed, it's no surprise they would take the same approach to DEI. "We've been experimenting with these things. And every time we've had initial success, we celebrated it so much. We also spoke about it for others to learn from. Now, my endeavor is no longer about Infosys doing it. My endeavor is, 'Can every enterprise do it? Can my customers do it?' Because there is a vantage point: if everybody does it, that becomes mainstream. Then all the hard work I'm doing to evangelize diversity will be done by a bunch of organizations together."

# Challenges

Infosys's necessary journey continues. The United States was one of the first non-Indian markets where the company really ramped up its DEI efforts and the community college, nondegree hiring programs that have contributed to both the company's overall diversity and its competitive advantage. Infosys is starting similar programs in Australia, the United Kingdom, and Germany.

But repeating these programs is not a simple one-to-one experience. You can't just transplant these programs. "The US is very uniquely different," Kumar noted. "It's fascinating how on one side the US has the American dream, where anybody can become anything. On the other side equally, you have a situation where the access to the future jobs is not there for many parts of the community." That, Kumar said, makes the United States a great experimental ground for reimagining hiring, training, and career building in a more diverse and equitable way. And fortunately, right now, he said, "There's a lot of openness to experiment with that."

Another challenge Kumar sees is getting the hiring managers themselves to think beyond the traditional way of doing business, in which you check certain boxes such as a bachelor's degree before even allowing candidates into the pool. Many of these managers are products of a system that rewarded four-year degrees, so a different approach seems counterintuitive to them. Kumar has seen some resistance to some of the new ideas that are driving diversity in the workforce. He believes this resistance may require mandates before it is overcome, but he hopes that it's accompanied by organic acceptance and recognition of the success of this new way of bringing talent to the company. "The hiring managers are not convinced yet," he said. "They want to see more data points. And that's because we're all so wired to think in a [certain] way. So I do think there will be a top-down push on this, but there has to be a natural force that has to come from behind, too. Can we solve this at one shot? Maybe not. Do we have the natural forces coming together now? Yes. And there has to be somebody who has to stand up and say, 'Okay, for these jobs, we will not ask for a degree.'"

Unsurprisingly, Kumar focuses on questioning the status quo when he's asked what a workplace utopia would look like to him: "My workplace utopia would be one where we naturally ask these questions that break the traditions. We are asking, 'Why do you need a degree? Because we always said you need a degree?' We are asking, 'Why does it need to be that you have to go to a physical workplace? Because it always happened that way?' And the perfect workplace for me would be one where we don't even have to ask those questions. We hire based on skills. We hire based on talent."

FIGURE 8-1

## Established in 1981, Infosys is a NYSE-listed global consulting and IT services company with more than 259,000 employees.

Launched in association with India's National Association of Software and Service Companies, Infosys funded the **National Digital Literacy Mission's** center in Chikkballapur, Karnataka. The center is South India's first such facility for people with disabilities. Infosys aims to make the mission's programs inclusive and accessible to all.

The Restart with Infosys program focuses on bringing women on career breaks back into the corporate workforce by providing skill-building, mentoring, and real-life project experience opportunities. In addition, Infosys's post-maternity programs have enabled 89% of women employees to return to work after maternity leave.

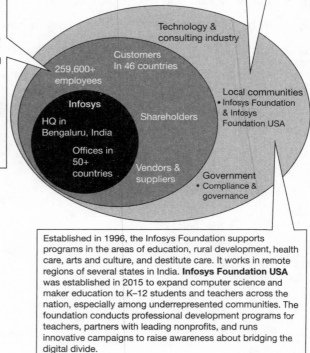

Established in 1996, the Infosys Foundation supports programs in the areas of education, rural development, health care, arts and culture, and destitute care. It works in remote regions of several states in India. **Infosys Foundation USA** was established in 2015 to expand computer science and maker education to K–12 students and teachers across the nation, especially among underrepresented communities. The foundation conducts professional development programs for teachers, partners with leading nonprofits, and runs innovative campaigns to raise awareness about bridging the digital divide.

# 9

# Going from DEI Mandates to Company Mission at Denny's

---

**COMPANY:** Denny's

**STAGE:** Compliance to integrated

**BEST PRACTICES:** Focus on de-biasing hiring, becoming embedded in the community, firm-wide trainings, zero-tolerance policies, creation of the first CDO role, supplier diversity, partnering with peers to foster continuous improvement

**KEY QUOTE:** "We don't believe in hiding from this shameful part of our history." —John C. Miller, CEO of Denny's[1]

---

"Denny's is offering a new sandwich called the Discriminator. It's a hamburger. You order it, then they don't serve it to you."[2] When late-night talk show host Jay Leno made this joke on *The Tonight Show* in May 1993, it was an easy way to get a laugh. Denny's, one of the largest US food chains with thousands of locations, was mired in numerous racial scandals, and its reputation was sinking fast. At the time, 50 percent of Black Americans associated Denny's with racial discrimination.[3]

Now, imagine you are a Black woman from Spartanburg, South Carolina—home of Denny's headquarters—and you are asked to come work for Denny's to help bring about change. Do you take the job? Do you shun the chain? Can you change a company that had so clearly failed in its culture and practices? It seems like a big ask to put this on one woman, but it was exactly the situation April Kelly-Drummond found herself in when the mayor of Spartanburg encouraged her to take a job at the company in 1994.

To set the context, the climate of race relations in the United States was in turmoil at the time, much like the situation in 2020. In 1991 the brutal beating of Rodney King by four Los Angeles Police Department officers was caught on camera and widely broadcast across the nation. A year later, when all four officers were acquitted, the decision sparked riots in L.A. and triggered a national discourse on racial discrimination.

At the time, Denny's was a forty-year-old business started in Lakewood, California, and known for 24-7 service. It found itself at the center of multiple claims of discrimination against Black customers. The first reported act of discrimination came on December 31, 1991, when eighteen college students visited a Denny's restaurant in San Jose, California.[4] The Black students were asked to pay a "sitting fee" of $2 and to pay for their meals in advance before they would be seated and served, yet their nine White classmates were already in the restaurant and were not made to pay a sitting fee or asked to pay for their meals in advance.[5] Two years later, on the morning of April 1, 1993, six Black Secret Service agents stopped for breakfast at a Denny's in Annapolis, Maryland, and were denied service for almost an hour while their White colleagues at a nearby table were promptly served "within minutes and went on to their second and third cups of coffee."[6] These and other reported incidents led to a class action case by members in forty-nine states. The suit was the largest case at the time under the public accommodations section of the 1964 Civil Rights Act.[7]

At first, explains journalist Anne Faircloth in a piece for *CNN Money*, Denny's top management characterized these incidents "as isolated misunderstandings, inevitable for a chain that serves one million meals a day."[8] The company contested the lawsuits. Denny's made performative moves, signing a pledge with the National Association for the Advancement of Colored People to hire minorities and to increase purchases from minority-owned businesses.[9] But at the same time, the company did not acknowledge the presence of any underlying racial issues in the organization. Court testimony during the lawsuit made it hard to square this assertion. Customers and employees indicated pervasive issues of racism in the company culture. Faircloth describes what one server observed while she worked for the chain: "Sandy Patterson, a White waitress who worked at several Denny's in California, stated in her court declaration that use of the N word was 'not uncommon,' nor were the terms 'them,' 'those people,' or 'that kind' in referring to blacks. [Patterson said,] 'I was told by management that we did not want to encourage black customers to stay in the restaurant.'"[10]

By 1995, Denny's settled the class action lawsuits, paying more than $54 million to 295,000 customers. Denny's also signed a consent decree, which required the company to create written antidiscrimination policies, inform the public of these policies, provide antidiscrimination training to all employees, and monitor and report any future discrimination incidents.[11]

The year before the settlement, in 1994, when Kelly-Drummond was asked to join Denny's, she was rightfully skeptical. She had no idea that the company would go on to make history as the first company to employ a CDO and become one of the best companies to work for minorities.

In the thirty years since Denny's was the butt of late-night jokes, the company has learned many lessons in its struggle to recapture sales from minority customers, repair its reputation in local communities, and create an environment where people from local communities felt comfortable working and dining in their restaurants. Denny's has 1,650 franchised restaurants in 146 international locations.[12] Today, Denny's describes its aspiration to be "America's Diner for Today's America."[13]

It hasn't been a simple, straightforward journey for the company to make its transformation. But it got to a new place, largely through the efforts of Kelly-Drummond, who did take the job the mayor asked her to take and who would eventually become CDO of Denny's.

## "How Dare You?"

After the lawsuits and settlements in the 1990s, Denny's found itself squarely in the compliance stage of its DEI journey. In this case, compliance was legally mandated through the consent decree the court had put in place. The public nature of Denny's case led many other companies to voluntarily set themselves into a compliance mindset. They saw the negative impact on publicity and public perception that the lawsuits against Denny's and other companies in the 1990s and the first years of the twenty-first century created. The compliance stage of a DEI journey aims to mitigate that risk. It exists primarily to keep the company out of legal trouble.

Denny's could have just settled there; many other companies did. But instead, it turned the legal mandates into a foundational stepping-stone to more advanced stages on its journey, in large part because of Kelly-Drummond's efforts.

She arrived at the company at its nadir, she said: "We found ourselves asleep at the wheel without a roadmap when it comes to effective diversity management. In short, Denny's was at a historic low point."

When Kelly-Drummond first joined the company, there was no DEI department. She joined the Public Affairs Department, first as a part-time assistant to determine whether this was where she wanted to be. Part of her job was to be a spokesperson for the company at conferences and events and help recruit new team members. It was an uphill climb.

"It was not easy for me as an African American female having to go out and talk about a brand that had such an awful stigma at the time," she recalled. In one sense, she was excited because the court decree meant she had opportunities to effect change right away. She could prioritize diversity in employee hiring and franchisee opportunities. But the public wasn't having it. At one hiring conference, this response was made abundantly clear. She remembered, "People would not even stop by my table. Even if I was offering a lot of money, I remember people saying, 'I am not patronizing Denny's,' and 'How dare you work at a company that discriminates?'"

The hostility could have caused her to give up; less determined people might have seen it as hopeless. But Kelly-Drummond didn't quit. For one thing, she remained with the company in those early years because she saw the genuine changes happening inside the organization. She believed that her voice was being heard and respected there, even if the public wasn't on board yet.

"I was in the room," she said, "and my voice was important and that was the change. I was able to say that I worked at Denny's with pride, not because of what I was getting paid and not because of a particular title, but because I felt like I could be the voice of the people. I was able to go to bed at night saying, 'I know this company has changed. I'm seeing the change and the difference.' I saw that Denny's was making strides, and that was important to me—to be able to be a part of it."

## Representation in the Room

For Kelly-Drummond, the demographic shift to a more diverse pool of workers and leaders was not an end in itself. Large-scale progress would be driven by the diverse thinking and perspectives that can only be created if you have a variety of people in the room.

"When I first started the company, we had all White male leadership, and there was groupthink in the room," she said. "You had no entrepreneurs, no franchise owners, no people of color, or other diverse groups in the room where leadership made decisions. When we started having diversity in the room, you had different ideas, beliefs, and perspectives, and it changed the company. It changed the way that we thought about how we reach out to our consumers, which in turn changed the products we pushed out, all because of the diversity in the room."

Denny's also had to come to terms with the fact that their problems of race and discrimination were not isolated one-off instances, as the company had originally tried to claim. Rather, they reflected a culture of discrimination and other unacceptable behaviors that had to be rooted out. For example, stereotypes that non-White patrons tip less than White patrons have been shown to lead to differential treatment by servers.[14] In the same *CNN Money* article, Faircloth recounts another Denny's employee's testimony. Robert Norton, a former Denny's manager in San Jose, testified that when he began managing there, he "observed staffers 'routinely' closing the restaurant when 'they were concerned about the number of Black customers' entering . . . 'Blackout' was used by Denny's management to refer to a situation where too many Black customers were in the restaurant." Norton also testified that "when he discontinued the policy, his district manager threatened to fire him."[15]

Making the problem worse, one bad apple can ruin the bunch, as the old saying goes. Research has shown that when racist comments are made in restaurants, servers are more likely to be racist in their actions toward customers even if they themselves do not participate in the racist banter or if they do not agree with it personally.[16] Thus, in the case of Denny's, the culture of racism and discrimination was pervasive and often contagious. Part of the reckoning that Denny's had to have during this time was to acknowledge that unconscious (and sometimes conscious) bias was a real problem the organization was facing in its restaurants.

Kelly-Drummond said bold policies were needed to move beyond this culture. "We had to be very sensitive to where you sat African Americans or any [other] people of color. We had to make sure that the timing of their food coming out did not make people feel like they were being discriminated against. So guiding principles and zero-tolerance policies had to be put into training, and we had to hold our team members accountable."

The consent decree mandated that all employees attend diversity training within 90 days of joining Denny's and a second session within 270 days, but Denny's tightened those requirements to 75 days and 225 days.[17] The training taught about unconscious biases and the importance of empathizing with customers.

The training became so effective that in 1999 Denny's was released from the oversight of the civil rights monitor a year earlier than the consent decree had mandated. Even after the release of the oversight, Denny's itself enforced the mandate. The company continued to investigate every incident of discrimination, even placing a toll-free number in every restaurant to encourage others to help identify problems. Denny's still has a no-tolerance policy for discrimination; there are strict disciplinary standards for any employees demonstrating these behaviors, and any customer who discriminates against others or who uses discriminatory language is asked to immediately leave the restaurant.[18]

Denny's demonstrated that the compliance stage of the DEI journey can lead to impactful DEI practices. What's more, moving beyond compliance to the tactical stage of the journey, where DEI efforts go beyond the bare minimum and merely legal, is where real change starts to take place.

# How Leadership Shapes Change

Denny's transformation may not have been as dramatic had its leadership not changed and then brought about structural shifts to foster continued progress. In 1995 James B. Adamson became CEO. As one of his first actions, he separated diversity efforts from the previous Public Affairs Department, giving the diversity objective its own leadership structure and initiatives.

Adamson created the nation's first CDO position, that is, a senior executive officer who reported to a CEO, and hired Rachelle Hood-Phillips, his former colleague from Burger King, to fill the position. The creation of this role was a major step forward in diversity management. Back then, most diversity officers were not considered a part of the most senior executive team of a company. Kelly-Drummond recalled the rigorous process the leadership team went through to create the new department and to figure out the next steps for the journey: "I remember we consulted and benchmarked with professors, other corporations, and civil rights leaders to guide us during this time. I can recall being in the room when we were talking about things like, what we should call this department? It was public affairs at first. And then we thought, 'Let's make it diversity affairs.' Then we had to determine the title of the leader of the department, and we named it chief diversity officer, which was the first in the country."

As historic an act as it was, Denny's did not fall into the trap of pushing its diversity efforts onto the CDO and considering it a done deal. Many companies think that hiring a CDO will automatically solve their DEI challenges. This simplified assumption could not be further from the truth. Successful DEI requires both top-down and bottom-up efforts. Though the DEI strategy may be the focus of the CDO, this executive can be successful only if leaders at every level and across departments see themselves as part of the DEI journey. Continued support of the CDO in terms of resources, implementation partners, and support across the organization is a critical part of the process.

Hood-Phillips and Adamson worked together to go beyond what was required by the consent decree. For example, 25 percent of senior management's incentive bonus was tied to the advancement of women and minorities.[19] Furthermore, Adamson was publicly vocal about his commitment to the DEI efforts and set a clear tone by telling employees at his first meeting that he was "going to do everything possible to provide better jobs for women and minorities. And I will fire you if you discriminate. Anyone who doesn't like the direction this train is moving had better jump off now."

Within a few months of Adamson's appointment as CEO, eight of the company's top twelve officers left. Among their replacements were a Hispanic man and a Black woman.[20]

In this moment, Denny's represented an organization evolving from the compliance stage to the tactical stage of its DEI journey. They moved past compliance concerns and started to think about DEI in a strategic way as connected to the values and goals of the organization.

Kelly-Drummond shared how the top-down and bottom-up approach has continued to be pivotal for Denny's (see figure 9-1). Adamson explained that leadership at the top and people all throughout the organization have to be committed. "It isn't just at the board level or

FIGURE 9-1

## DEI beyond human resources: top-down and bottom-up approaches

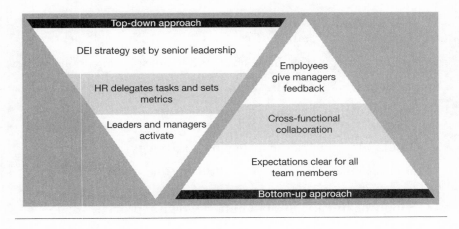

the CEO suite," he said. "It also has to be the people who are making the day-to-day decisions. You have the directors down to even the people in the restaurants, so it's at the top all the way down that have the same mindset and ideas of treating people with respect, and to make sure that you have opportunities for all."

The culture Adamson and Kelly-Drummond set remains strong to this day. John C. Miller, who has been CEO since 2011, remains an active part of Denny's DEI strategy implementation, working with the current CDO, Kelly-Drummond, who's still with the company nearly three decades after uneasily taking a job in public affairs at Denny's low point. Kelly-Drummond told me, "Miller reminds us nearly every day about our commitment to our communities around the country and challenges us to ask what more we can do to grow business and be good corporate citizens and partners to those local, regional, and national organizations."

## Rising to Best in Class

Over the past thirty years, Denny's has successfully implemented numerous DEI strategies that have led to its current standing as one of the best places to work.[21] Looking back, we can see three focus areas that have been pivotal to the company's improvement:

- **Talent:** tackling bias in hiring, broadening its recruitment efforts, and building the promotion pipeline

- **Supply chain:** seeking out minority-owned providers of goods and services

- **Continuous improvement:** learning from outside partners' expertise[22]

Today, Denny's DEI progress has been widely acknowledged as a model of growth, maturity, and success by civil rights leaders, community groups, and many publications, including *Fortune*, *Hispanic Business*, *Black Enterprise*, *Asian Enterprise*, *Family Digest*, and *Latino Magazine*. The company has won numerous awards, and as mentioned earlier, it has been named one of the best places to work for minorities.[23] Its demographic diversity is a source of pride: 75 percent of team members are minorities, 58 percent of restaurants are minority owned, and 56 percent of board members are minorities—44 percent are women.[24]

Denny's has spent nearly $2 billion with underrepresented suppliers since it developed the Supplier Diversity Program in 1993. In 2020 diverse and disadvantaged businesses represented 13.2 percent of Denny's purchases, and Hispanic businesses represented Denny's largest spending segment by $3.4 million, with African American business spending ranked second largest.[25]

Since 2006 Denny's has published annual diversity reports as well as quarterly internal DEI newsletters that have contributed to rebuilding employee morale. Denny's has pursued a level of transparency in its DEI approach by ensuring public accountability in its efforts.

Under the leadership of Miller, the organization's diversity efforts were expanded to include equity and inclusion. Denny's became one of the first companies to sign the CEO Action for Diversity & Inclusion coalition in 2017, the largest CEO-driven business commitment to advance DEI in the workplace (see chapter 2). Miller also created a roadmap for the organization, naming five guiding principles to promote diversity and align DEI goals with all functional areas of the company. Notice how these principles seem to reflect a core strategy for the company, and that core strategy happens to be deeply infused with the language and practices of good DEI. More companies could benefit from aligning company principles with DEI in a similar way:[26]

- **Guests First:** They're more than just customers or consumers. They are our guests, and we invite them into our homes with open arms. They are the very reason we are in business and the center of everything we do.

- **Embrace Openness:** Open means so much more than just being open for business 24-7. It means being open to all people, appetites, and budgets. It says we are open-minded and open to new ideas. Honest, warm, and inviting. Open is the way we think and act every hour of every day.

- **Proud of Our Heritage:** We are the classic American diner and proud of everything that means. Since 1953 we have served quality food and healthy portions at a fair price. No matter where we are, our light is always on, inviting guests around the world to a place where everyone is welcome.

- **Hungry to Win:** At Denny's, we are constantly looking ahead. We are always moving forward, striving for more, hungry for greatness. We are open to fresh, innovative thinking. We believe we will succeed through teamwork, accountability, and pushing the boundaries of ourselves and our brand.

- **The Power of We:** Our Denny's family is our most important asset. We trust, support, and respect each other and work together for the greater good. We recognize the contributions of all and empower each and every one of us to achieve great things. Together, we will celebrate our successes and have fun doing it.

These efforts have been laudable, but in light of my experience, they're not what truly sets Denny's apart. In analyzing its journey, I uncovered four key indicators that have propelled Denny's to the integrated stage of its DEI journey.

## *Telling Its Story, Truthfully*

One of my clients joked that what DEI really needs is a panel of leaders talking about "how we failed at DEI" to really spark change. As Brené Brown shares in her research, shame is one of the most universal feelings we all have as humans; what allows us to overcome that shame is vulnerability.[27] It is difficult for individuals to be vulnerable about their imperfections and even harder for organizations to openly share how they got DEI wrong in the past.

Individuals may have to account for one flaw or mistake, but organizations must be honest about their systemic flaws and continuous mistakes. For Denny's, these cumulative mistakes led to one of the largest class action discrimination lawsuits of its kind. Many companies would be afraid to own these kinds of mistakes. They would not realize that telling the story and owning it is a necessary part of the journey to sustainable change that can ripple throughout the company, the industry, and beyond. Even as I wrote this book, many companies I approached said they were not far enough along their DEI journey, or they still had some work to do before they would feel comfortable sharing their story. Denny's took the opposite approach, telling its story on many platforms over decades, and its honesty is what sets the company apart.

"We don't believe in hiding from this shameful part of our history," wrote Miller, Kelly-Drummond, and their colleague Fasika Melaku-Peterson, vice president of learning and development. "It is most productive to discuss it openly and honestly. By sharing the steps we've taken to rectify past mistakes and become what we hope is a model organization for DEI, we can hopefully help others do the same."[28]

If leaders do not see themselves in the journey of other companies, they cannot really imagine what can be possible. Denny's has been committed to not only owning the mistakes of its past but also sharing its journey for the benefit of other organizations. While most companies are afraid of taking responsibility for their own mistakes, Kelly-Drummond advises the best thing a company can do, especially when it has made a mistake, is to be open and seek the help of its industry peers. "My suggestion to anybody who gets a call tomorrow from someone who says, 'Hey, we have a DEI situation,' is to be transparent, have an open dialogue, network with other companies and other organizational leaders. Listen, understand, communicate, and don't be afraid to reach out to others and say, 'Hey, I need assistance with this.'"

## *Sacrificing More Than Money*

As discussed earlier in the book, since 2020 giving money to social justice causes has become the major play for companies that want to publicly demonstrate commitment to DEI. One year after the murder of George Floyd, racial-equity monetary commitments from companies reached $200 billion.[29] Critics argue that for many companies, these donations did not represent a real sacrifice as they were often given to nonprofit organizations that allowed their donations to become tax deductions. What's more, simply donating will offload to others any work needed to improve the situation.

Beyond charitable giving, many companies have struggled to take meaningful action to improve racial disparities in their organizations and their communities. By October 2021, sixteen months after these pledges, 40 percent of employees of color reported their companies had not improved DEI practices.[30]

Denny's is a role model for putting in the work beyond financial support for DEI by contributing vital human capital resources to the real work of change. In 2020 it joined the CEO Action for Racial Equity Fellowship, and CEO John Miller has committed internal resources such as the company's legal team to serve on committees that sometimes meet weekly to work on strategies for advancing racial equity and social justice. Both Kelly-Drummond and Miller themselves also dedicate their time to serving on various committees in the fellowship. This is a remarkable and largely unheard-of move for senior-level executives to be so hands-on with external DEI efforts. Kelly-Drummond described the level of deep executive involvement:

> We care about really getting down to the root causes of social injustice and not being afraid to talk about it. It's important for CEOs to not just sign up for these causes but to invest people from their companies to come together to put together ideas and draw up a blueprint plan to implement policies and join forces with human rights leaders to where we can implement change and make a huge impact.
>
> That is the next step that all companies should look at: going beyond your four walls and just giving dollars to support but actually investing in the efforts. At Denny's, our CEO has committed two years for us to be involved with the fellowship for racial equity, and my chief legal counsel is on the policy committee that meets two or three times out

of the week. I serve on the Education Committee, so every day, Monday through Friday, I am on a call with the Education Committee. We also have a vice president of operations on a committee. In general, we make sure we have those expert teams in the room to help further the overall cause. Other corporations bring in other resources such as IT, but the beauty is, we all get together and talk about ideas to help change the systemic racism in the country. Bringing all those perspectives in the room is a brilliant idea, and I am really proud to be a part of it. It's true dedication.

## Becoming Embedded in the Community

An organization trying to get to the integrated stage of its journey considers its entire sphere of influence and looks around at its impact on nearby communities. The food service industry has a unique social contract with the towns and cities where the restaurants are located. Unlike many companies, food service organizations must hire from local communities to be successful. Denny's recognizes the need not only to hire people in the community but also to provide opportunities for them to develop into business leaders.

"The difference for us from any other *Fortune* 500 company is that we provide service directly to the community and we want to make sure our company is a reflection of that community," said Kelly-Drummond. As mentioned earlier, Kelly-Drummond is from Spartanburg, South Carolina, where Denny's is headquartered, and she still lives there. "We hire people who are in your neighborhood," she explained. "Maybe it's a student who decides they don't want to go to college but wants to learn about a business and a trade to become a business owner. We have a Managers in Training program that employees can go through to learn about the entire business, including learning about how to be an owner. We create space for people in the community who want a leg up to have an opportunity to go to corporate America or develop within the business, such as owning a franchise."

Denny's recognizes this connection to community as both a part of its journey and something that is good for the business. It invests in the community and gets real talent development out of that investment while also creating meaningful DEI results.

## Innovation through Inclusion

It's this simple: inclusive cultures are six times more likely to be innovative.[31] Research shows that diversity of thinking can improve innovation on teams by 20 percent and decrease risk by 30 percent.

But innovation does not happen just because you have a group of demographically diverse individuals on the same team. Sharing new ideas can be a frightening experience. What if other people shut down your idea, or even worse, what if it's an idea that fails? Yet creative thinking is needed for companies to evolve and grow in a competitive landscape. Companies looking to innovate often miss out on novel insights from their own employees by failing to create a psychologically safe environment for employees to share their ideas.[32] Denny's has overcome this challenge by continuously creating opportunities for its employees and franchisees to contribute to the evolution of the organization. Kelly-Drummond explained:

> Like our famous Grand Slam Breakfast, some of our best innovations come from our franchisees. That has always been true, and I'd say even more so recently during the pandemic, as we've had to pivot quickly to meet shifting consumer demands and local and state regulations. Curbside pickup was one of our most successful pandemic innovations, and that idea came from a franchisee. Our franchisee Rahul Marwah was the first to provide groceries and home meal kits to his communities.
>
> We want to support collaboration and results across our franchisee family. Dawn Lafreeda started at Denny's as a server when she was a teenager. Now she is one of our largest individual franchisees. She has built an empire with incredible business results while persistently advocating for women's and LGBTQ+ rights, helping Denny's on our pathway to diversity and inclusion. Our brand and our workplace culture have benefited tremendously from her insight on social issues as well as her business savvy.

## Holding Up a Mirror

In looking at how far Denny's has come since it was riddled with discrimination claims and had to focus on compliance, a company in its position could easily decide it has done enough to prove itself in the DEI landscape. Denny's hasn't done that, though, and that's perhaps the most important aspect of its maturity into the integrated stage of its journey. The company realizes that the journey does not end.

"The goal is always improvement and forward progress, not to find a comfortable stopping point," Kelly-Drummond said. "Leaders in this space need to be comfortable consistently critiquing themselves and looking for holes in their strategy or its implementation."

In addition to realizing DEI has no finite ending point, organization leaders must be humble enough to check in on their efforts and realize when some part of their strategy needs to be adjusted or changed altogether. "We must take proactive steps to create inclusive cultures and be held accountable to build a diverse talent pipeline," Kelly-Drummond said. "We must hold a mirror up, evaluate what we are doing well, what we need to take away, and what we need to do more of. Then we must act boldly—take action as a result of this knowledge. This is the only way to drive change and accelerate progress. Over the years, advancing DEI has existed, but meaningful change is happening, led by advocates championing DEI across geographic and cultural boundaries."

When I asked Kelly-Drummond the question I ask all leaders—"What is your vision of a workplace utopia?"—she said she focuses on holding that mirror up and making Denny's not just diverse but also diverse like the communities it operates in: "Ultimately, our desire is to have a workforce that represents the makeup of the communities we serve at all levels of management and in our board. We know this nation is becoming increasingly diverse. By many accounts, more than half of America's population will be mainly diverse within the next twenty-five years. We know in many of the cities we serve, they are majority-minority communities. Here at Denny's, we want to keep pace with the changes in this country. We believe it represents our core mission, vision, and values, and it's great for business."

FIGURE 9-2

## Denny's is a table-service diner-style restaurant chain with locations in many countries.

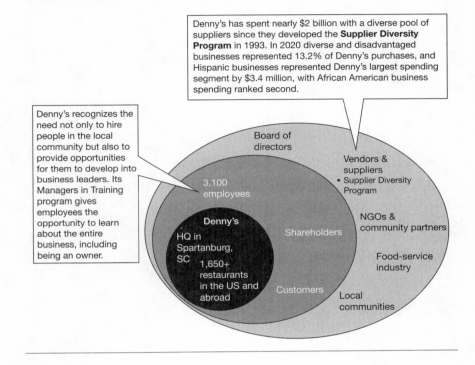

Denny's has spent nearly $2 billion with a diverse pool of suppliers since they developed the **Supplier Diversity Program** in 1993. In 2020 diverse and disadvantaged businesses represented 13.2% of Denny's purchases, and Hispanic businesses represented Denny's largest spending segment by $3.4 million, with African American business spending ranked second.

Denny's recognizes the need not only to hire people in the local community but also to provide opportunities for them to develop into business leaders. Its Managers in Training program gives employees the opportunity to learn about the entire business, including being an owner.

Board of directors

Vendors & suppliers
• Supplier Diversity Program

3,100 employees

NGOs & community partners

Denny's
HQ in Spartanburg, SC

Shareholders

Food-service industry

1,650+ restaurants in the US and abroad

Customers

Local communities

# CONCLUSION

# Forward Motion

*For me, becoming isn't about arriving somewhere or achieving a certain aim. I see it instead as forward motion, a means of evolving, a way to reach continuously toward a better self. The journey doesn't end.*

—Michelle Obama, *Becoming*

Thank you for traveling these journeys with me. I hope they were inspiring and instructive. Still, you may be wondering what's next for you. You may be an organizational leader who has a large influence on your company's DEI journey and wants to get going now that you've seen others in action. You may be simply wondering about your own individual DEI journey. With so much to still be done, what can you really do?

No matter your position or where you are starting from, I encourage you to consider the three guiding lights of your DEI journey: purpose, pitfalls, and progress.

## Purpose: What's the Vision for DEI? What Am I Trying to Achieve?

On any journey, you start by defining a destination: What do you want to achieve? In this book, we see each company grappling with how it is going to embody DEI. Iora Health, for example, a company just beginning its journey, needed to align as a leadership team on what it was truly trying to achieve. Through their envisioning exercise, the team members realized they should connect their company mission—to restore a sense of humanity to health care—to the psychological safety of their team members. That was core to Iora's purpose and DEI journey. Other companies, like PwC, were deeper into their journey but had to stop and take a hard look at whether they were actually doing enough and what their DEI legacy was going to be. Many companies do much good work for DEI but get stuck at the tactical stage because they are not sure what they are ultimately trying to achieve within and beyond their four walls. They still lack a crystal-clear DEI purpose. Still other companies get caught up comparing themselves with others to determine what they should be doing in DEI. While benchmarking is helpful, without a clear purpose and connection back to your own organization's mission and culture, your efforts will always be misaligned with what your company truly needs.

I encourage any of you reading this book, before you create your next big ERG program, or launch a firm-wide training, stop and ask yourself, "What am I really trying to achieve?" Make your vision a reality by writing it down, and then make sure the key stakeholders will endorse it. The whiskey maker Uncle Nearest showed us the power of vision. While navigating uncharted waters in the spirits industry, the company has committed to doing it with DEI at the center of its business, even if that means having to pass on lucrative opportunities not aligned with this vision. Once you are clear on where you are going, it becomes much easier to avoid getting lost on pathways leading you away from your goals.

I see people grappling with the same challenges on a personal level. They want to show up as an ally, so they read as many books as they can and listen to all the relevant DEI podcasts. Yet they never take a moment to get clear on what they want to change about their own current state or the impact they hope to make. If you want to be a better ally, you need to create a purpose—a vision for what you want to contribute and the impact you hope to make. Then continue to educate yourself and take action to make that vision come to life.

## Pitfalls: What Is Holding Us Back from Achieving Our Vision?

I have been most inspired by the humility and honesty demonstrated by the companies that were brave enough to share their journeys in this book. No company is perfect when it comes to DEI, but so many companies are afraid to admit they are less than perfect. So they tout their DEI aspirations and efforts, never stepping back to understand the areas where they may have fallen short in the past. Without this type of honest self-reflection, we cannot truly make progress. Some companies you read about, like Denny's and Sodexo, made huge mistakes that they couldn't hide from. Under such circumstances, many other companies would have simply settled their lawsuits and tried to sweep the bad publicity under the rug. And many companies have done just that. Yet, as described in earlier chapters, Denny's and Sodexo leaned into the moment and took it as an opportunity to dig deep to find the root of the discrimination and exclusion in their companies. They met the moment, did the work, and have since transformed their companies into world-class leaders in DEI.

Those moments of self-reflection about what's holding us back do not have to occur on the world stage. We should be self-reflecting on our pitfalls much more often. We should honestly note that, for example, our employee referral system may be hindering our ability to diversify our talent pipeline; that the informal conversations on the golf course may be introducing inequity in our promotion process; that our personal discomfort with tough topics like race or privilege keeps us from engaging in necessary conversations. If DEI is about elevating humanity in the workplace, we must also recognize that to be human is to be imperfect. Only when we can be honest about our pitfalls as organizations and as individuals can we make the changes needed to build inclusive workplaces and to be the DEI advocates that we proclaim to be. It's not easy, but it is a vital part of the journey.

## Progress: How Can We Make Sure We Are Progressing?

Despite our most earnest intentions, the challenges workplaces face around DEI will not get solved overnight. The double-edged sword of seeing DEI as a business imperative is that we treat it like our other business initiatives. We put a plan in place, create metrics for success, and expect to get high-performance results just as we would in our marketing and finance functions. But we forget about the human part of this work. Just because we put our best foot forward does not mean we will get it right on the first try. We are creating workplaces and communities for real people, not for the sake of marketing slogans and data points. Consequently, leaders become frustrated and give up if they have put the effort in DEI but it does not seem to be changing things quickly enough.

Let me be clear. Your organization should absolutely have a DEI strategy that considers the organization's entire sphere of influence. You need short-term and long-term metrics for success, and you need clear structures of accountability. These are how you show progress. Yet seeking perfection is the enemy of progress, especially in DEI. This is not a product launch. This is not a new line of business. DEI is a core cultural transformation. So, to make sure you are not getting stuck, recognize that you are on a journey that will sometimes go forward but will sometimes have setbacks. The goal is progress—progress toward achieving your vision. Commit to progress over perfection. This means experimenting with things you have never done before. Infosys tried experimentation when it decided to go outside industry norms and focus on recruiting community college students. And while new ways of doing something are exciting, progress also means being self-reflective and honest about when things are not working. Be brave enough to change course on your DEI journey if something is not working, just as Moss Adams did when, realizing its efforts for gender equity would not necessarily create racial equity, the company charted a new pathway.

We must each define what progress looks like on our own journeys. For companies, progress may be specific metrics such as recruitment numbers or employee engagement scores. For individuals, progress can be harder to define but is equally important to consider. Some people who have been working on their cultural competence and DEI get frustrated whenever a new DEI term or topic, such as gender-fluid identity, emerges. They will say to me, "Things are always changing. How can I ever know it all?" The reality is that it's impossible to know everything there is about DEI and get it right 100 percent of the time. But again, perfection should not be the goal; forward motion is the aim.

I encourage you to think of progress on your journey as the acts of inclusion that you can do each day. Noticing you are now more comfortable using your colleagues' desired pronouns is progress. Taking the opportunity to learn when someone points out a microaggression, and committing to not making the same mistake in the future, is progress. Raising your hand to question the status quo when it's easier to stay silent is progress. Embrace your own journey and commit to progress, however long it takes. Remember Lao Tsu's words: "The journey of a thousand miles begins with one step."

## Where the Journey Goes from Here

I started this book by sharing the history of DEI in the workplace. You may have noticed that although some things have changed over the years, too much has stayed the same. The racial reckoning events of 2020 brought DEI to the forefront and demanded change in a way that we had never seen before. Yet, two years after that moment, the constant question I get is, "Has anything really changed?"

The answer is yes. There has been progress. For example, diversity disclosure is becoming a new standard for businesses. In 2017 only 3 percent of *Fortune* 500 companies publicly disclosed full diversity data. In 2021 *Fortune* became a change agent by partnering with Refinitive to make DEI disclosure and performance a critical metric in *Fortune* 500 ranking.[1] Of the full 500 companies, 262 reported some level of race and ethnicity data in 2021.[23] Yet the percentage of full disclosure still hovered at 3.6 percent (18 companies). Steps forward, yes, but so much more work to be done.[4]

To fully address the question of what has changed since 2020, I propose that we need a total mindset shift on DEI. We fantasize about a magical end point, where we wake up one day and everything is different, racism is eradicated, sexism is abolished, and homophobia is expunged. That is not the reality of DEI. Companies and industries need transparent reviews of policies and tactical metrics to track progress, and this open, honest assessment is only one aspect of change. The intangible cultural aspects of DEI require us to not only know the right things to do but also be able to activate these behaviors over and over. We must learn and acknowledge the inherent biases we have and actively work to manage those biases each day. We must be willing to admit to the past structures of inequity and must commit the necessary time and resources to rebuild those structures from the ground up. The real work of DEI goes beyond identifying the gaps; it's about leaning into the actions of inclusion over and over again. Seeing progress at the organizational, industry, and societal levels takes time, and it's not always easy to see the impact of our efforts.

Instead of thinking of DEI as a marathon with a specific end point, I urge you to think about DEI as an integrated and permanent piece of workplace culture. Because even once your organization has achieved demographic diversity and established equity in its policies like gender pay, there will always be more work to do. We will always need to make sure team members at every level feel seen and valued.

I have often said that DEI is about elevating humanity, and the very nature of humanity is to evolve. Although I believe there will always be a need for DEI, my hope is that we will evolve from the current conversations to the next frontier of DEI. We might look at topics such as how Generation Z, the most diverse workforce population, is reshaping societal (and business) norms about identity.[5] Or we might consider how the remote global workforce can be more inclusive than ever before or how mental health initiatives are necessary for inclusion and optimal performance. DEI will and should evolve, but it's not going away. And we shouldn't want it to disappear. DEI allows every person to thrive in the workplace, so let's embrace the journey.

. . .

As I look toward the future of our workplaces, I am hopeful. I've asked all the brave and wonderful people who contributed to this book what their workplace utopia looks like, and now I'll share mine. My workplace utopia is not one in which everything is perfect. Rather, it's one where everyone is trying to get better and doing so in a place that encourages that. It's a place where I can thrive fully as myself. I laugh with colleagues and my students. I raise my hand when something doesn't feel right. I embrace emotion when a situation has touched me. But this utopia can exist only in environments with a commitment to equity and inclusion. Where someone like me, or like you, is welcomed and able to thrive. I hope we each continue to do the work on the necessary journey to elevate humanity, embrace differences, and create workplaces where we can each feel a bit of our own utopia every day.

# APPENDIX

## Spheres of Influence Model

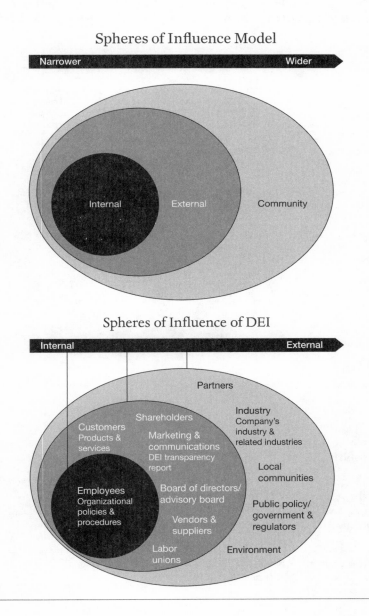

Narrower → Wider

Internal
External
Community

## Spheres of Influence of DEI

Internal → External

Partners

Customers
Products &
services

Shareholders

Marketing &
communications
DEI transparency
report

Industry
Company's
industry &
related industries

Local
communities

Employees
Organizational
policies &
procedures

Board of directors/
advisory board

Vendors &
suppliers

Public policy/
government &
regulators

Labor
unions

Environment

# Company Profiles

**FIGURE A-1**

## Iora Health works to restore humanity to health care, aiming to deliver robust, dynamic primary care that transforms patients' lives.

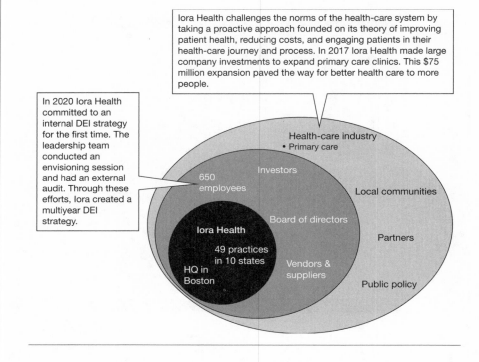

Iora Health challenges the norms of the health-care system by taking a proactive approach founded on its theory of improving patient health, reducing costs, and engaging patients in their health-care journey and process. In 2017 Iora Health made large company investments to expand primary care clinics. This $75 million expansion paved the way for better health care to more people.

In 2020 Iora Health committed to an internal DEI strategy for the first time. The leadership team conducted an envisioning session and had an external audit. Through these efforts, Iora created a multiyear DEI strategy.

Health-care industry
• Primary care

Investors

650 employees

Local communities

Board of directors

Iora Health

Partners

49 practices in 10 states

HQ in Boston

Vendors & suppliers

Public policy

**TABLE A-1**

## Iora Health

| | |
|---|---|
| **FOUNDED** | December 2010 (acquired by One Medical, September 2021) |
| **COMPANY SIZE** | 650 employees (December 2020) |
| **HQ** | Boston |
| **COMPANY SECTOR OR INDUSTRY** | Health care Facilities and services |

*(continued)*

| | |
|---|---|
| **PRODUCTS** | N/A |
| **SERVICES** | Primarily for individuals 65 and older on Medicare<br>• Primary care<br>• Chronic care<br>• Wellness classes<br>• Mental health services |
| **COMPANY STRUCTURE** | Private for 10 years, now part of One Medical (a public company)<br>7 rounds of investing[1]<br>29 executives<br>11 board members[2] |
| **COMPANY REVENUE** | 2021 revenue more than $300M |
| **ORGANIZATIONAL INFLUENCE SPHERES** | Employees<br>• Executive team: 7 men, 3 women (7 executives White, 3 of South Asian descent)<br>• Leadership team: 8 men, 12 women<br>• Compliance team is all women<br>Patients<br>• Curated care for patients over 65<br>• "Delivering robust, dynamic primary care" by changing the status quo of patient care[3]<br>• Reaching more clients through word of mouth<br>Investors<br>• Funded by 15–20 investors[4]<br>49 physician practices<br>• Expanded relationship with Humana to provide Medicare members access to care[5]<br>• Partnered with more than 12 national and regional Medicare Advantage Plans and employers<br>• Expanded reach to more geographic regions through unique employer, insurer, health systems, and union partnerships[6]<br>Technology<br>Health coaches<br>Institutional rules and regulations<br>Health laws and policies |
| **COMPETITORS** | Oak Street Health<br>ChenMed/JenCare<br>Village MD |

FIGURE A-2

## Slack's mission is to make people's working lives simpler, more pleasant, and more productive. Slack is a channel-based messaging platform where people communicate, collaborate, and get work done.

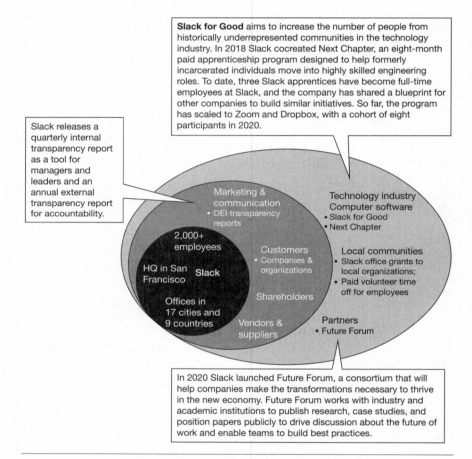

**Slack for Good** aims to increase the number of people from historically underrepresented communities in the technology industry. In 2018 Slack cocreated Next Chapter, an eight-month paid apprenticeship program designed to help formerly incarcerated individuals move into highly skilled engineering roles. To date, three Slack apprentices have become full-time employees at Slack, and the company has shared a blueprint for other companies to build similar initiatives. So far, the program has scaled to Zoom and Dropbox, with a cohort of eight participants in 2020.

Slack releases a quarterly internal transparency report as a tool for managers and leaders and an annual external transparency report for accountability.

Marketing & communication
• DEI transparency reports

Technology industry
Computer software
• Slack for Good
• Next Chapter

2,000+ employees

HQ in San Francisco **Slack**

Customers
• Companies & organizations

Local communities
• Slack office grants to local organizations;
• Paid volunteer time off for employees

Offices in 17 cities and 9 countries

Shareholders

Vendors & suppliers

Partners
• Future Forum

In 2020 Slack launched Future Forum, a consortium that will help companies make the transformations necessary to thrive in the new economy. Future Forum works with industry and academic institutions to publish research, case studies, and position papers publicly to drive discussion about the future of work and enable teams to build best practices.

TABLE A-2

## Slack

| | |
|---|---|
| **FOUNDED** | 2009 |
| **COMPANY SIZE** | 2,045 employees |
| **HQ** | San Francisco |
| **COMPANY SECTOR OR INDUSTRY** | Computer software |
| **PRODUCTS** | Channels<br>Integrations<br>Security |
| **SERVICES** | Customer service |
| **COMPANY STRUCTURE** | Public |
| **COMPANY REVENUE** | $630.4M (2020) |
| **ORGANIZATIONAL INFLUENCE SPHERES** | Employees<br>• 44.9% women globally<br>• 46.1% of managers are women<br>• 29.9% of leadership positions are women<br>• 13.9% underrepresented minorities in US<br>• 12.1% of managers are underrepresented minorities<br>• 9.2% of leadership positions are underrepresented minorities<br>• 28.3% Asian<br>• 7.9% Hispanic<br>• 4.4% Black[7]<br>Investors<br>Customers |
| **COMPETITORS** | Microsoft Teams<br>Flock<br>WhatsApp<br>Skype for Business |

## PwC is a global network of firms delivering world-class assurance, tax, and consulting services. The firm's purpose is to build trust in society and solve important problems.

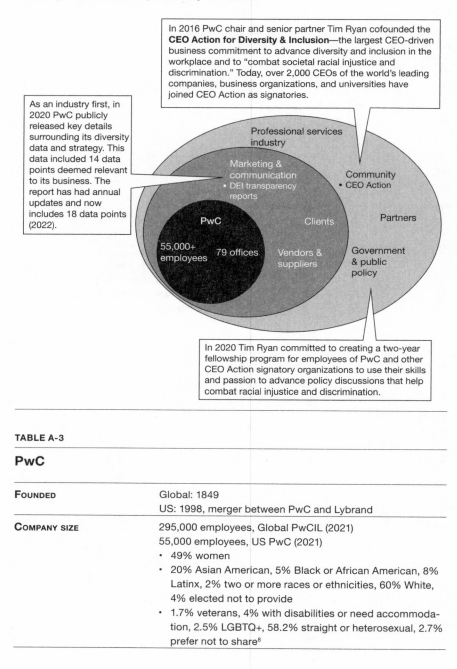

In 2016 PwC chair and senior partner Tim Ryan cofounded the **CEO Action for Diversity & Inclusion**—the largest CEO-driven business commitment to advance diversity and inclusion in the workplace and to "combat societal racial injustice and discrimination." Today, over 2,000 CEOs of the world's leading companies, business organizations, and universities have joined CEO Action as signatories.

As an industry first, in 2020 PwC publicly released key details surrounding its diversity data and strategy. This data included 14 data points deemed relevant to its business. The report has had annual updates and now includes 18 data points (2022).

Professional services industry

Marketing & communication
• DEI transparency reports

Community
• CEO Action

PwC

Clients

Partners

55,000+ employees

79 offices

Vendors & suppliers

Government & public policy

In 2020 Tim Ryan committed to creating a two-year fellowship program for employees of PwC and other CEO Action signatory organizations to use their skills and passion to advance policy discussions that help combat racial injustice and discrimination.

---

TABLE A-3

## PwC

| | |
|---|---|
| **FOUNDED** | Global: 1849<br>US: 1998, merger between PwC and Lybrand |
| **COMPANY SIZE** | 295,000 employees, Global PwCIL (2021)<br>55,000 employees, US PwC (2021)<br>• 49% women<br>• 20% Asian American, 5% Black or African American, 8% Latinx, 2% two or more races or ethnicities, 60% White, 4% elected not to provide<br>• 1.7% veterans, 4% with disabilities or need accommodation, 2.5% LGBTQ+, 58.2% straight or heterosexual, 2.7% prefer not to share[8] |

| HQ | US headquarters: New York, NY |
|---|---|
| COMPANY SECTOR OR INDUSTRY | Professional services<br>Industrial services<br>Commercial support services |
| PRODUCTS | Business integrity products<br>• Customer Link<br>• DoubleJump Interchange<br>• Future Cast<br>• Insights Platform<br>• Media Intelligence<br>• Performance Analyzer[9] |
| SERVICES | Consulting solutions<br>Trust solutions<br>Products and technology<br>Business services |
| COMPANY STRUCTURE | Private partnership<br>PwC: a US member firm of PricewaterhouseCoopers International Limited (PwCIL), a network of individually owned and independent accounting firms<br>PwCIL "does not practice accountancy or provide services to clients; rather its purpose is to act as a coordinating entity for member firms in the PwC network"[10]<br>US: chair and 22 board members who oversee different US regions<br>Leadership: privately owned (5th-largest privately owned company in US)<br>Network leadership team and board of PwCIL "develop and implement policies and initiatives to achieve a common and coordinated approach among individual firms where appropriate"[11] |
| COMPANY REVENUE | $45.142B (June 2020 to June 2021) |
| ORGANIZATIONAL INFLUENCE SPHERES | Employees<br>• Demographics: 295,000 global[12]<br>• Diverse pool of employees who accurately reflect client base and who can relate to, and meet the needs of, clients<br>• PwC's network of talent from schools around the world<br>• Strong focus on culture and purpose to deliver results[13]<br>Customers/clients[14]<br>• 200,000 clients, including 100,000 entrepreneurial and private businesses[15] |

*(continued)*

# Appendix

| | |
|---|---|
| **ORGANIZATIONAL INFLUENCE SPHERES** | • PwC's diversity of clients gives it an advantage over competitors<br>• PwC's large presence among *Fortune* 500 companies<br>• Attention to corporate sustainability for clients<br>Leadership/shareholders<br>• CEO Action for Diversity & Inclusion, with more than 2,200 CEO signatories representing 85 industries and more than 13 million US employees[16]<br>• Oversight of strategic direction; use of competitor data to drive decisions<br>Governments and regulators<br>• Member of Global Public Policy Committee[17]<br>• Does not act as a corporate multinational<br>• PwC LLP regulated by the Financial Conduct Authority<br>• Ensures compliance with existing regulations in all countries of business<br>• Help shape new policies<br>• Cocreate better regulatory landscape<br>Suppliers<br>• Suppliers keep PwC updated with latest tech products to serve clients<br>• PwC's flexibility creates supplier negotiation power<br>NGOs/NPOs: stay ahead of sustainability challenges and solutions<br>Local communities: offices in 156 countries[18]<br>• Responsible business leadership program to invest in local populations<br>• Corporate social responsibility<br>• Inclusivity and environmental sustainability[19]<br>Media[20]<br>• PwC's presence among the media to keep consumers informed<br>• Keeping up with trends in the industry and competitors |
| **COMPETITORS** | Deloitte<br>Ernst & Young<br>Grant Thornton<br>KPMG |

**FIGURE A-4**

## Uncle Nearest Premium Whiskey is inspired by the best whiskey maker the world never knew. Nearest Green was the first African American master distiller on record in the United States. The company has an all-women leadership team and is the fastest-growing independent American whiskey brand in US history.

In 2020 Uncle Nearest and Brown-Forman, Jack Daniels' parent company, created the **Nearest & Jack Advancement Initiative**, pledging a combined $5 million to increase diversity in the American whiskey industry. The initiative has three prongs:

- Creating the Nearest Green School of Distilling at Motlow State Community College in Tullahoma, TN, to create a pipeline of women and people of color for master distiller roles
- Developing the Leadership Acceleration Program, offering apprenticeships to African Americans currently in the whiskey industry who want to become head distillers heads of maturation, or production managers
- Forming the Business Incubation Program, which will provide expertise and resources to African American entrepreneurs entering the spirits sector

Uncle Nearest has a clear internal culture that celebrates DEI. Its clear guiding principles serve as an operating manual for how it works.

1. We do it with excellence or we don't do it at all.
2. Every day, we pound the rock.
3. We accept each other's differences.
4. All team member opinions are welcome.
5. We are creating a culture of radical candor.
6. We are building a brand to outlive us.
7. The more we know, the more we have yet to learn.
8. We do all things best when we do them with honor.
9. We speak life, we speak light.
10. Even in business, family comes first ... and rest is extolled.

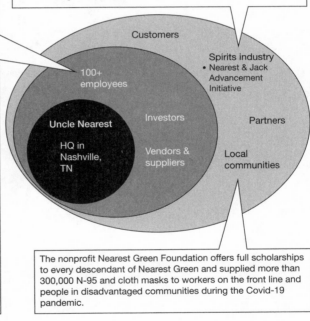

The nonprofit Nearest Green Foundation offers full scholarships to every descendant of Nearest Green and supplied more than 300,000 N-95 and cloth masks to workers on the front line and people in disadvantaged communities during the Covid-19 pandemic.

# Appendix

## Uncle Nearest

| | |
|---|---|
| **FOUNDED** | July 2017 |
| **COMPANY SIZE** | 100+ employees |
| **HQ** | Shelbyville, TN |
| **COMPANY SECTOR OR INDUSTRY** | Beverages and spirits |
| **PRODUCTS** | Uncle Nearest 1884 Small Batch Whiskey<br>Uncle Nearest 1856 Premium Aged Whiskey<br>Uncle Nearest Master Blend Whiskey |
| **COMPANY STRUCTURE** | Uncle Nearest Inc., privately owned by Grant Sidney Inc., which is wholly owned by Fawn Weaver[21] |
| **ORGANIZATIONAL INFLUENCE SPHERES** | Employees<br>Distributors in 50 US states and three UK cities[22]<br>Nearest Green Foundation<br>Uncle Nearest Venture Fund: $50M investment in minority-founded and minority-owned spirit brands[23]<br>Nearest & Jack Advancement Initiative |
| **COMPETITORS** | Jack Daniel's<br>Jim Bean<br>Johnnie Walker |

FIGURE A-5

## Moss Adams provides the world's most innovative companies with specialized accounting, consulting, and wealth management services to help them embrace emerging opportunity.

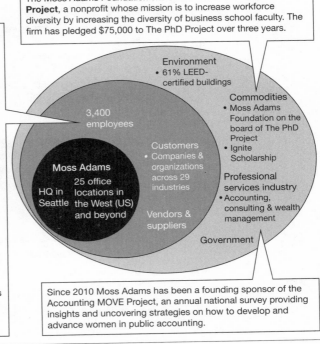

The Moss Adams Foundation sits on the board of **The PhD Project**, a nonprofit whose mission is to increase workforce diversity by increasing the diversity of business school faculty. The firm has pledged $75,000 to The PhD Project over three years.

In 2008 Moss Adams launched Forum W to strategically address the lack of gender diversity and inclusion at the firm and in its industry. Forum W is a regionally based business resource group with four priorities: dialogue, networking, mentoring, and advancement. The initiative has evolved over time and today is part of Moss Adams's DNA and culture. In 2016 Moss Adams and Forum W launched the GroWth series, a yearlong leadership development program for high-potential one- to two-year senior managers. The series is designed to strengthen the firm's pipeline of women partners.

Environment
• 61% LEED-certified buildings

Commodities
• Moss Adams Foundation on the board of The PhD Project
• Ignite Scholarship

Professional services industry
• Accounting, consulting & wealth management

3,400 employees

Customers
• Companies & organizations across 29 industries

Moss Adams
HQ in Seattle
25 office locations in the West (US) and beyond

Vendors & suppliers

Government

Since 2010 Moss Adams has been a founding sponsor of the Accounting MOVE Project, an annual national survey providing insights and uncovering strategies on how to develop and advance women in public accounting.

TABLE A-5

## Moss Adams

| | |
|---|---|
| **Founded** | 1913 |
| **Company size** | 3,400 employees (2021) |
| **HQ** | Seattle |
| **Company sector or industry** | Professional services |
| **Services** | Accounting<br>Consulting<br>Wealth management |

(continued)

# Appendix

| | |
|---|---|
| **COMPANY STRUCTURE** | Private |
| **COMPANY REVENUE** | $820M (2020) |
| **ORGANIZATIONAL INFLUENCE SPHERES** | Employees (2020)<br>• 0.4% American Indian/Alaskan Native, 1.9% Black, 6.8% Hispanic or Latinx, 14.8% Asian American, 65% White[24]<br>• 53% of all employees, 40% of national office leadership, and 25% of partners are women<br>Employees<br>• Inclusive health care, including transgender surgery benefits<br>• Ranked 13 out of 50 for best accounting firms for diversity<br>• Top company for working mothers and dads<br>Communities<br>• Ignite Sholarships provided to first- and second-year college students from diverse backgrounds pursuing accounting or related degree<br>• Guide, Pilot, Steer internships offered<br>• PhD Project pledge of $75,000<br>Government<br>Environment<br>• 61% LEED-certified buildings<br>Started tracking progress toward reducing carbon footprint |
| **COMPETITORS** | HIREtech<br>Berkeley Research Group<br>The Social Investment Consultancy<br>LMC International[25] |

**FIGURE A-6**

## Sodexo provides on-site services encompassing food, facilities management, and workplace and technical management services. It also provides benefits and rewards and personal and home services, with the mission of improving the quality of life of all those it serves.

**SodexoMagic** was founded in 2006 in partnership with NBA Hall of Famer Magic Johnson to "sustain and empower communities everywhere through healthy food and exceptional services." The organization has provided either standalone or integrated solutions for major corporations and institutions, including K–12 schools and HBCUs.

Sodexo's nonprofit Stop Hunger Foundation was started in 1996 with the mission of ensuring that every child in the US would grow up with dependable access to enough nutritious food for a healthy, productive life.

In 2018 Sodexo's CEO committed to reach a global representation of 40% women in senior leadership by 2025 and made teams accountable by linking 10% of annual incentives for the executive population to this target. Additionally, Sodexo has a target that all employees work for gender-balanced management teams by 2025.

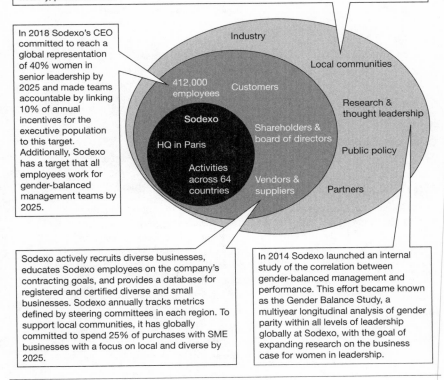

Sodexo actively recruits diverse businesses, educates Sodexo employees on the company's contracting goals, and provides a database for registered and certified diverse and small businesses. Sodexo annually tracks metrics defined by steering committees in each region. To support local communities, it has globally committed to spend 25% of purchases with SME businesses with a focus on local and diverse by 2025.

In 2014 Sodexo launched an internal study of the correlation between gender-balanced management and performance. This effort became known as the Gender Balance Study, a multiyear longitudinal analysis of gender parity within all levels of leadership globally at Sodexo, with the goal of expanding research on the business case for women in leadership.

# Appendix

## Sodexo

| | |
|---|---|
| **FOUNDED** | Global 1966 |
| **COMPANY SIZE** | 412,000 employees (2022) |
| **HQ** | Issy-les-Moulineaux, France |
| **COMPANY SECTOR OR INDUSTRY** | Food and facilities management |
| **PRODUCTS** | Cleaning; security; grounds maintenance; mailroom; document management; laundry; waste management; space design; transportation; employee benefits, rewards, and recognition; public benefits; fuel, fleet, and expense management |
| **SERVICES** | Concierge services<br>Construction and technical services<br>Food services<br>Facilities management services<br>Benefits and rewards services<br>Personal and home services<br>Vending services |
| **COMPANY STRUCTURE** | Public<br>Board of directors (10 members)<br>19 executives |
| **COMPANY REVENUE** | €17.4B ($19.3B) |
| **ORGANIZATIONAL INFLUENCE SPHERES** | Global employees across 80 countries<br>Consumers: 2025 target of having 100% consumers offered healthy lifestyle options[26]<br>More than 4,475 suppliers as part of the supplier diversity program in US and Canada<br>SodexoMagic[27]<br>Sodexo Stop Hunger Foundation[28] |
| **COMPETITORS** | Compass Group USA<br>Serco<br>Aramark<br>G&K Services |

**Best Buy is the world's largest multichannel electronics retailer. Best Buy's goal is to enrich lives through technology and to ensure that every customer feels appreciated and excited about their experience.**

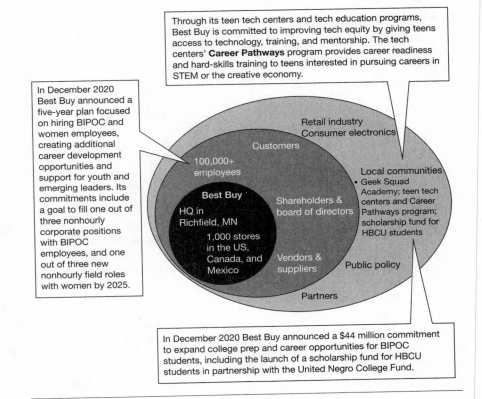

Through its teen tech centers and tech education programs, Best Buy is committed to improving tech equity by giving teens access to technology, training, and mentorship. The tech centers' **Career Pathways** program provides career readiness and hard-skills training to teens interested in pursuing careers in STEM or the creative economy.

In December 2020 Best Buy announced a five-year plan focused on hiring BIPOC and women employees, creating additional career development opportunities and support for youth and emerging leaders. Its commitments include a goal to fill one out of three nonhourly corporate positions with BIPOC employees, and one out of three new nonhourly field roles with women by 2025.

Retail industry
Consumer electronics
Customers
100,000+ employees
Best Buy
HQ in Richfield, MN
1,000 stores in the US, Canada, and Mexico
Shareholders & board of directors
Local communities
• Geek Squad Academy; teen tech centers and Career Pathways program; scholarship fund for HBCU students
Vendors & suppliers
Public policy
Partners

In December 2020 Best Buy announced a $44 million commitment to expand college prep and career opportunities for BIPOC students, including the launch of a scholarship fund for HBCU students in partnership with the United Negro College Fund.

TABLE A-7

## Best Buy

| | |
|---|---|
| **FOUNDED** | 1966 |
| **COMPANY SIZE** | 100,000 employees<br>~1,000 stores in the US, Canada, and Mexico |
| **HQ** | Richfield, MN |
| **COMPANY SECTOR OR INDUSTRY** | Retail<br>E-commerce<br>Consumer electronics |

*(continued)*

| | |
|---|---|
| **PRODUCTS** | Appliances |
| | Computers and tablets |
| | TV and home theater |
| | Audio |
| | Car electronics |
| **SERVICES** | Geek Squad Technical Support |
| **COMPANY STRUCTURE** | Public |
| | Many levels of management: retail stores, districts, regions |
| **COMPANY REVENUE** | $43.64B FY 2020 |
| **ORGANIZATIONAL INFLUENCE SPHERES** | Employees (2019) |

Employees (2019)
- 26% women
- 22% Hispanic, 14% African American, 5% Asian American
- Ranked third in the world for employee training, learning, and development
- Employees reflect population of communities they serve (percentage of Black and Hispanic employees at or above US average)

Vendors

Customers/community
- Providing customers with a one-stop shop for technology purchases with in-house tech support
- Partnering to close the technology gap across North America

Elected officials
- "Develops and advocates for public policy positions that directly impact business"[29]
- Donates to both Democratic and Republican political organizations

Investors
- Increased demand and stock during Covid-19 pandemic
- Focused on digital growth

NGOs
- Membership in more than 25 organizations to advance progress in focus areas
- Giving back through programs such as Geek Squad Academy and teen tech centers

| | |
|---|---|
| **COMPETITORS** | Amazon |
| | Alibaba |
| | Sears |
| | Walmart |
| | Target |
| | Lowe's |
| | Office Depot |
| | Home Depot |
| | BJ's Wholesale Club |

## Established in 1981, Infosys is a NYSE-listed global consulting and IT services company with more than 259,000 employees.

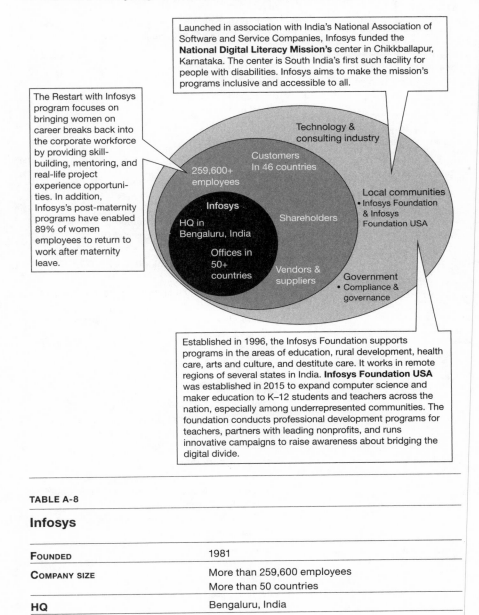

Launched in association with India's National Association of Software and Service Companies, Infosys funded the **National Digital Literacy Mission's** center in Chikkballapur, Karnataka. The center is South India's first such facility for people with disabilities. Infosys aims to make the mission's programs inclusive and accessible to all.

The Restart with Infosys program focuses on bringing women on career breaks back into the corporate workforce by providing skill-building, mentoring, and real-life project experience opportunities. In addition, Infosys's post-maternity programs have enabled 89% of women employees to return to work after maternity leave.

Technology & consulting industry

Customers In 46 countries

259,600+ employees

Infosys
HQ in Bengaluru, India

Shareholders

Offices in 50+ countries

Vendors & suppliers

Local communities
• Infosys Foundation & Infosys Foundation USA

Government
• Compliance & governance

Established in 1996, the Infosys Foundation supports programs in the areas of education, rural development, health care, arts and culture, and destitute care. It works in remote regions of several states in India. **Infosys Foundation USA** was established in 2015 to expand computer science and maker education to K–12 students and teachers across the nation, especially among underrepresented communities. The foundation conducts professional development programs for teachers, partners with leading nonprofits, and runs innovative campaigns to raise awareness about bridging the digital divide.

TABLE A-8

## Infosys

| | |
|---|---|
| **FOUNDED** | 1981 |
| **COMPANY SIZE** | More than 259,600 employees<br>More than 50 countries |
| **HQ** | Bengaluru, India |
| **COMPANY SECTOR OR INDUSTRY** | Global consulting<br>IT services |

*(continued)*

| | |
|---|---|
| **PRODUCTS** | AI platform |
| | EdgeVerve Systems Finacle: global banking platform |
| | Panaya CloudQuality Suite |
| | Skava |
| **SERVICES** | Consulting |
| | Data analytics |
| | Blockchain |
| | Digital marketing |
| | Digital commerce |
| **COMPANY STRUCTURE** | Public |
| | 13 subsidiaries[30] |
| **COMPANY REVENUE** | $13.1B |
| **ORGANIZATIONAL INFLUENCE SPHERES** | Customers/clients: 1,562 customers |
| | Employees |
| | • 36% of global workforce women |
| | • 33% of board members women[31] |
| | • 144 nationalities |
| | • Recognized as top employer in all regions of business |
| | • Willing to invest in a diverse population of hires who come from community colleges[32] |
| | • World-class training infrastructure: Global Education Centre |
| | Investors |
| | Vendor-partners |
| | Government |
| | Customers |
| | • Global reach with well-known clients |
| | • Digital expertise and leading technologies |
| | Recognized as one of the top ten fastest-growing IT services brands (2021) |
| | Sustainable performance |
| | Community |
| | • Infosys Foundation USA: expanding computer science education |
| | • Working to eradicate hunger and malnutrition |
| | Compliance and governance |
| **COMPETITORS** | Tech Mahindra |
| | IBM |
| | NTT Data |
| | Accenture |
| | Tata Consultancy |
| | Atos |
| | DXC Technology |

FIGURE A-9

## Denny's is a table service diner-style restaurant chain with locations in many countries.

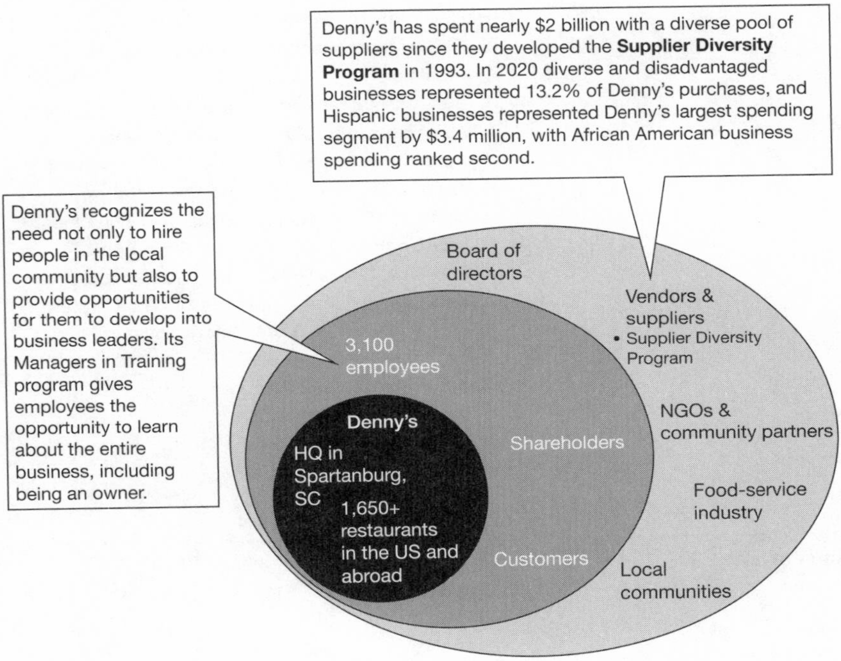

Denny's has spent nearly $2 billion with a diverse pool of suppliers since they developed the **Supplier Diversity Program** in 1993. In 2020 diverse and disadvantaged businesses represented 13.2% of Denny's purchases, and Hispanic businesses represented Denny's largest spending segment by $3.4 million, with African American business spending ranked second.

Denny's recognizes the need not only to hire people in the local community but also to provide opportunities for them to develop into business leaders. Its Managers in Training program gives employees the opportunity to learn about the entire business, including being an owner.

Board of directors

3,100 employees

**Denny's**

HQ in Spartanburg, SC

1,650+ restaurants in the US and abroad

Shareholders

Customers

Vendors & suppliers
• Supplier Diversity Program

NGOs & community partners

Food-service industry

Local communities

TABLE A-9

## Denny's

| | |
|---|---|
| **FOUNDED** | 1953 in Lakewood, CA, by Harold Butler and Richard Jezak; started as Danny's Donuts<br>Became Denny's in 1961 |
| **COMPANY SIZE** | 3,100 employees<br>1,647 total restaurants: 153 international and 1,494 domestic locations (2020) |
| **HQ** | Moved to Spartanburg, SC, in 1991 |
| **COMPANY SECTOR OR INDUSTRY** | Food services industry |
| **COMPANY STRUCTURE** | Public company<br>Franchisor and operator |

(continued)

# Appendix

| | |
|---|---|
| **COMPANY REVENUE** | $288.6 million (2020)<br>$541.4 million (2019)<br>$630.1 million (2018)[33] |
| **ORGANIZATIONAL INFLUENCE SPHERES** | Employees<br>• CEO: John C. Miller<br>• 75% of team members are minorities<br>Franchisees<br>• 96% of total restaurants are franchise owned<br>• As of December 29, 2021, Denny's had 1,640 franchised, licensed, and company restaurants around the world, including 153 restaurants in Canada, Puerto Rico, Mexico, the Philippines, New Zealand, Honduras, the United Arab Emirates, Costa Rica, Guam, Guatemala, El Salvador, Indonesia, and the United Kingdom[34]<br>• 58% of restaurants are minority owned<br>• 6% of restaurants are LGBTQ owned<br>Board of directors (9 directors)<br>• 5 directors are minorities<br>• 4 directors are women<br>Shareholders<br>Vendors and suppliers<br>Local communities |
| **COMPETITORS** | IHOP<br>Waffle House<br>Cracker Barrel<br>Friendly's |

# ACKNOWLEDGMENTS

*If you want to go fast, go alone; but if you want to go far, go together.*

—African proverb

This African proverb is a direct reflection of my life. I was brought up to value community, and I owe my deepest gratitude to the people who are part of my personal and professional communities. I am deeply grateful to all who have helped me with this project and continue to help me on my own necessary journey.

Family is my foundation.

To my father, Colonel Charles C. Washington, who was the smartest man I have ever known and who inspired me to become a college professor. Thank you for teaching me the value of working hard and playing harder. I lost you to Alzheimer's and Covid-19 while writing this book. You are forever in my heart.

To my mother, Victoria Motely Washington, my first role model, my loudest cheerleader, my rock in all storms. I am grateful you raised me to always do my best. You helped me develop my own standard of excellence by always asking me, "Did you do your best?" It's the question I still ask myself each day. Thank you for being there at every sporting event, awards ceremony, and step-show whether big or small. Your love is my constant guiding light.

Uncle Thomas, the hardest-working person I know, thank you for pouring wisdom into me all my life, making your nieces and nephews memorize "If," by Rudyard Kipling. I am grateful for your leading by example in life. I am also grateful for your now reminding me in your retirement not to work not too hard, like you did.

Aunt Francine, I am your namesake. Thank you for teaching me the importance of family community, how to share with your four sons, and most importantly how to lead with love at all times. I pray to show up in life with a portion of the grace you display.

My grandmother Ella, whom I never met but who has always lived in my heart. I hope to have made you proud to have bestowed your name on me. Thank you for the foundation of our family. To my extended family, thank you for loving me, always showing up to support me, and being a refuge from the world.

This book could not have been written without my dear friend Faith Gaines texting me one day during the summer of 2020 with the wild idea of my writing a case study book. From the moment you planted that seed, you have been a believer in this project, and I am thankful for you.

To Dr. Laura Morgan Roberts, I owe the start of my career and many of the pivotal moments in my life. I am so glad I thought to follow you out of that lecture at Morehouse College more than fifteen years ago. Thank you for being an example, a sponsor, a mentor, and a friend.

Carolyn Adkerson, for the many hats you wear in my life but most importantly for being my friend—showing up in times of need, physically or with a meme to make me laugh. Thank you for always supporting my wild ideas and often being the reason they can come to life. This book would not have been possible without your daily support, encouragement, and willingness to put out fires so I had the space to write.

*A sweet friendship refreshes the soul.*

—Proverbs 27:9

Mckenzie Patrice Gadis. When I talk about being able to be my fullest and truest self, it is because of our friendship and sisterhood since our first year at Spelman. Thank you for your selfless support of my dreams, your prayers, our laughs, and our shared life moments. From the beginning stages of this book, when it was just a proposal, you rolled up your sleeves to help me bring my ideas to life.

Drs. Erika V. Hall and Alison Hall Birch, my confidants and friends going back to our simultaneous PhD journeys. Erika convinced me that Northwestern was the best choice for graduate school and helped me navigate its complex waters. Alison, you were my very first PhD accountability partner. The safe space we give each other to vent, be vulnerable, talk about the challenges in academia, and celebrate each other is priceless. Not many people have friends who can vet hairstyles before teaching and discuss the implications of a major academic finding all in the same conversation. From sending the bottle of Moët to my dissertation defense all those years ago to your daily words of encouragement, your support is always felt and cherished.

In writing this book, I found support from those who dove in with me to help me bring my dream to full fruition.

Acknowledgments

Jasmine Sanders, my line sister, helped me find the words to describe the importance of a workplace utopia. Thank you for enthusiastically vetting ideas and lending your skills to help with the proposal that became this book.

Alyse Smith, thank you for encouraging me to keep going every time I felt that the hill was too high to climb. Your positivity is contagious and helped me get to the finish line with this book.

Lauren Sills, noble actions speak louder than any words. You continue to show me this as a cheerleader of this project from the beginning and in your willingness to put yourself on the line to advocate for me to come into your company. Your friendship is a safe space to share all the wins and losses in life, and I cherish it.

I am grateful for Abu Dumbuya's unwavering support for my ideas since our days in Chicago. Constantly believing in me and showing up to support me, from attending my dissertation defense to pushing me to boldly share my gifts with the world, you have always had faith in me and have extended your networks to support me.

To my life tribe Tiffany Gibson Meekins, Kendra N. Lee, Amina Bunkeddeko, Michaela Cooke, Jaimie Miller, Sabria Brown, Sydney English, Ashley Mayes, Kristin Johnson, Francesca Fontenot, Preston Smith, Shia Hendricks, Leron Gresham, and so many others, thank you for your unwavering support, the gift of honest feedback, and never letting me give up on myself.

Attending Spelman College remains the best decision I have made in my life. Spelman instilled in me that it is my choice, but I must choose to change the world. The college gifted me with lifelong sisters, sparked my first interest in DEI, and continues to be a pillar in my life. I hope to pay it forward through the Elevating Excellence DEI scholarship that I established and by being a role model to future generations of Spelman sisters. Thank you to the Spelman community of sisterhood that always shows up and out for me.

Following the footsteps of my mother and becoming a member of Alpha Kappa Alpha Sorority, Incorporated, forever changed me. The sorors of the Mu Pi Chapter at Spelman College and the sorors who have touched every stage of my life have been a precious gift. I am grateful for the support of our beloved sorority and how each of you continues to show me how "we help each other."

My Eminence line sisters activate with the speed, precision, and force of the world's best military operations. Thank you for rallying behind me and this work. I know nothing is impossible with the support of your sisterhood behind me.

*We make a living by what we get. We make a life by what we give.*

—Unknown

Thank you to my editor Scott Berinato, who has believed in this project from the very beginning. You helped me find my writer's voice; I am deeply proud of our work together. And thank you to the entire Harvard Business Review Press editorial, production, and marketing teams for fully supporting the vision for this book.

My gratitude goes to my colleagues at Georgetown McDonough School of Business for their championing of this project. Deans Paul Almeida, Dennis Quinn, Patricia Grant, and Prashant Malaviya; Drs. Brooks Holtom, Michael O'Leary, Cathy Tinsley, Evelyn Williams,

Acknowledgments

Jenn Logg, and George Comer; and all the others on faculty and staff at MSB have encouraged me to keep going as I brought this dream to life. The Georgetown community is a deeply special place and embodies the epitome of our *cura personalis* mission, "care for the entire person."

The consulting work of the Ellavate Solutions team is the driving force behind much of the work shared in this book. Carolyn Adkerson, Hildana Haileyesus, Jayce Esposito, and the broader Ellavate team, thank you for your commitment to our mission to elevate, inspire, and impact the landscape of DEI in our work. Thank you for trusting my leadership and allowing me to learn from you every day.

Thank you to the PhD Project family and specifically those who gave early feedback on the book idea: Drs. Quinetta Roberson-Connally, Nicholas Pearce, Atira Charles, Anthony C. Hood, and Courtney McCluney, and those who always continue to inspire and support Drs. Danielle King, Sekou Bermiss, and Stephanie Creary.

To Sue Synodis and the other readers of the early manuscript, thank you for your time to make this book relatable and relevant in your various lanes of expertise.

My students are the think tank behind so much of the work that went into this book. They challenge my theories and lend their life experiences to help better inform how DEI affects them each day. I especially thank the research assistants who contributed to this book: Leena Jube, Sarena Young, Lydia Kickham-Dawes, Betanya Mahary, Julian Ernesto Gonzalez Medina, Ninette Martin, and Vincella Myah Smith. Thank you for always pushing me to think bigger!

This is a book of stories about companies, so I am deeply indebted to all the companies you read about here. I thank each person in the companies that courageously allowed me to interview people for this book. It is not easy for an organization to open up about the necessary journey. Many companies said no to having their DEI journey on display for the world to see in these pages. I am deeply grateful for those organizations and their brave leaders who said yes and who continue to lead by example. Without their candor, vulnerability, and commitment to DEI, this book would not have been possible.

There are so many other people who have supported me as a person, a scholar, and an author through the years. I thank you all, and if I've not mentioned you here by name, you are still in my heart. Please know that each of you has contributed to my journey, and I am grateful to be in community with you. Thank you.

*My mission in life is not merely to survive, but to thrive; and to do so with some passion, some compassion, some humor, and some style.*

—Maya Angelou

# NOTES

## INTRODUCTION

1. Norton, 2020. Quotation from US Equal Employment Opportunity Commission, "EEO-1 Data Collection," accessed April 12, 2022, www.eeoc.gov/employers/eeo-1-data-collection.

2. "The United States Commission on Civil Rights Statement on Affirmative Action," clearinghouse publication 54, Commission on Civil Rights, Washington, DC, October 1977.

3. US Equal Employment Opportunity Commission, "Title VII of the Civil Rights Act of 1964," accessed April 13, 2022, www.eeoc.gov/statutes/title-vii-civil-rights-act-1964.

4. US Equal Employment Opportunity Commission, "Timeline of Important EEOC Events," accessed April 18, 2022, www.eeoc.gov/youth/timeline-important-eeoc-events.

5. For pregnancy rulings, see US Department of Justice, "Laws Enforced by the Employment Litigation Section: Title VII of the Civil Rights Act of 1964," updated March 10, 2021, www.justice.gov/crt/laws-enforced-employment-litigation-section. For sexual orientation and gender identity, see Phillip M. Schreiber, "Supreme Court Extends Title VII Protections to Sexual Orientation and Transgender Status," Holland & Knight, June 15, 2020, www.hklaw.com/en/insights/publications/2020/06/supreme-court-extends-title-vii-protections-to-sexual-orientation.

6. The Pregnancy Discrimination Act of 1978. Pub. L. 95-555. www.csus.edu/indiv/g/gaskilld/business_computer_ethics/the%20case%20against%20affirmative%20action.html.

7. Elissa Nesbitt and Becky Dziedzic, "Diversity at Xerox," press release, Xerox, accessed April 18, 2022, www.xerox.com/downloads/usa/en/n/nr_Xerox_Diversity_Timeline_2008.pdf.

8. Doug Rossinow, "It's Time We Face the Fact That Ronald Reagan Was Hostile to Civil Rights," History News Network, April 20, 2015, https://historynewsnetwork.org/article/158887.

9. Erin Kelly and Frank Dobbin, "How Affirmative Action Became Diversity Management: Employer Response to Antidiscrimination Law, 1961 to 1996," *American Behavioral Scientist* 41, no. 7 (April 1998): 960+, https://link.gale.com/apps/doc/A20563254/AONE?u=anon~e640a8e7&sid=googleScholar&xid=8189b9c5.

10. Chester E. Finn, "'Affirmative Action' Under Reagan," *Commentary*, April 1982, www.commentary.org/articles/chester-finn/affirmative-action-under-reagan/.

11. William B. Johnston and Arnold H. Packer, *Workforce 2000: Work and Workers for the 21st Century* (Washington, DC: US Department of Labor, Employment and Training Administration, 1987), https://files.eric.ed.gov/fulltext/ED290887.pdf.

12. Frank Swoboda, "The Future Has Arrived, Survey Finds," *Washington Post*, July 20, 1990, www.washingtonpost.com/archive/business/1990/07/20/the-future-has-arrived-survey-finds/f50858de-6804-4cdd-b963-f499c8804c90/.

13. William B. Johnston and Arnold H. Packer, abstract to *Workforce 2000: Work and Workers for the 21st Century*, in Americans for the Arts, "National Arts Administration and Policy Publications Database (NAAPPD)," accessed April 18, 2022, www.americansforthearts.org/by-program/reports-and-data/legislation-policy/naappd/workforce-2000-work-and-workers-for-the-21st-century.

14. Ronald Reagan, "Proclamation 5724: National Job Skills Week, 1987," October 8, 1987, American Presidency Project, compiled by John Woolley and Gerhard Peters, www.presidency.ucsb.edu/documents/proclamation-5724-national-job-skills-week-1987.

15. Rohini Anand and Mary-Frances Winters, "A Retrospective View of Corporate Diversity Training from 1964 to the Present," *Academy of Management Learning & Education* 7, no. 3 (2008): 356–372, www.wintersgroup.com/corporate-diversity-training-1964-to-present.pdf.

16. Anand and Winters, "Corporate Diversity Training."

17. R. Roosevelt Thomas Jr., "From Affirmative Action to Affirming Diversity," *Harvard Business Review*, March–April 1990, https://hbr.org/1990/03/from-affirmative-action-to-affirming-diversity.

18. Rachel Soares et al., "2010 Catalyst Census: Fortune 500 Women Executive Officers and Top Earners (Report)," *Catalyst*, December 6, 2010, www.catalyst.org/research/2010-catalyst-census-fortune-500-women-executive-officers-and-top-earners.

19. Richard L. Zweigenhaft, "Diversity among *Fortune* 500 CEOs from 2000 to 2020: White Women, Hi-Tech South Asians, and Economically Privileged Multilingual Immigrants from Around the World," WhoRulesAmerica.net, University of California at Santa Cruz, January 2021, https://whorulesamerica.ucsc.edu/power/diversity_update_2020.html.

20. Anand and Winters, "Corporate Diversity Training."

21. Charanya Krishnaswami and Guha Krishnamurthi, "Title VII and Caste Discrimination," *Harvard Law Review*, June 20, 2021, https://harvardlawreview.org/2021/06/title-vii-and-caste-discrimination/.

22. Knowledge@Wharton, "What Professional Soccer Can Tell Us about Immigration, Work and Success," World Economic Forum, December 23, 2021, www.weforum.org/agenda/2021/12/immigrant-employees-performance-business/.

23. Kristine Beckerle, "Boxed In: Women and Saudi Arabia's Male Guardianship System," Human Rights Watch, July 16, 2016, www.hrw.org/report/2016/07/16/boxed/women-and-saudi-arabias-male-guardianship-system.

24. For diversity initiatives, see Michael L. Wheeler, "Diversity Training," research report 1083-94R, Conference Board, New York, 1994. For lawsuits, see Chanelle Leslie, "10 of the Biggest EEOC Settlements Ever," *HRM America*, June 6, 2014, www.hcamag.com/us/news/general/10-of-the-biggest-eeoc-settlements-ever/156010.

25. Carole Katz, "Cost of Ignoring Diversity in Workplace Can Be Greater Than Embracing It," *Pittsburgh Business Times*, July 18, 2005, www.bizjournals.com/pittsburgh/stories/2005/07/18/focus4.html.

26. Sundiatu Dixon-Fyle, et al., "Diversity Wins: How Inclusion Matters," McKinsey & Company, May 19, 2020, www.mckinsey.com/featured-insights/diversity-and-inclusion/diversity-wins-how-inclusion-matters#.

27. "Future Forum Pulse," Future Forum, April 2022, https://futureforum.com/pulse-survey/.

28. Timothy Bella, "'Just Do It': The Surprising and Morbid Origin Story of Nike's Slogan," *Washington Post*, September 4, 2018, www.washingtonpost.com/news/morning-mix/wp/2018/09/04/from-lets-do-it-to-just-do-it-how-nike-adapted-gary-gilmores-last-words-before-execution/.

29. For Ric Muñoz ad, see Martin Kessler, "The Story of Ric Muñoz and Nike's 1995 HIV-Positive Runner Ad," *WBUR*, October 12, 2018, www.wbur.org/onlyagame/2018/10/12/nike-colin-kaepernick-ric-munoz. For the girls' sports ad, see Jessica Tyler, "Nike's Colin Kaepernick Ad Isn't the First Time the Brand's Commercials Have Made a Social Statement: See Some of the Most Memorable Campaigns in Its History," *Business Insider*, September 7, 2018, www.businessinsider.com/nike-ads-make-social-statements-2018-9.

30. Tyler, "Nike's Colin Kaepernick Ad."

31. Nike, "For Once, Don't Do It," video, YouTube, May 29, 2020, www.youtube.com/watch?v=drcO2V2m7lw.

32. Lauren Thomas, "Read Nike CEO John Donahoe's Note to Employees on Racism: We Must 'Get Our Own House in Order,'" *CNBC*, June 5, 2020, www.cnbc.com/2020/06/05/nike-ceo-note-to-workers-on-racism-must-get-our-own-house-in-order.html.

33. "Nike Sweatshops: Inside the Scandal," *New Idea*, November 15, 2019, www.newidea.com.au/nike-sweatshops-the-truth-about-the-nike-factory-scandal.

34. Lori Deschene, "Nike Settles Racism Suit," *CBS News*, August 20, 2007, www.cbsnews.com/news/nike-settles-racism-suit/.

35. Edward Helmore, "Nike Hit with Lawsuit from Four Women Who Allege Gender Discrimination," *Guardian*, August 10, 2018, www.theguardian.com/business/2018/aug/10/nike-lawsuit-women-gender-discrimination.

36. Edgar Alvarez Barajas, "The 'Black at Nike' Instagram Accused the Brand of Racism. Then It Vanished," *Input Magazine*, July 16, 2020, www.inputmag.com/style/black-at-nike-instagram-account-removed-vanished-racism-diversity-inclusion.

37. Thomas, "'Get Our Own House in Order.'"

38. Brian Krzanich, quoted in Lydia Dishman, "The 10 Best and Worst Leaders of 2015," *Fast Company*, December 28, 2015, www.fastcompany.com/3054777/the-10-best-and-worst-leaders-of-2015.

39. Dishman, "10 Best and Worst Leaders."

40. Autumn Cafiero Giusti, "Why Intel Is Working Double Time on Its Diversity Goals," *Chief Executive*, September 21, 2017, https://chiefexecutive.net/intel-working-double-time-diversity-goals/.

41. Samara Lynn, "Brian Krzanich, Intel CEO, Diversity in Tech Advocate, Resigns over Affair," *Black Enterprise*, June 21, 2018, www.blackenterprise.com/brian-krzanich-intel-ceo-diversity-resigns-over-affair/.

42. Erin Carson, "Intel's New Diversity Goals: Put Women in 40% of Technical Posts by 2030," *CNet*, May 14, 2020, www.cnet.com/news/intels-new-diversity-goals-put-women-in-40-of-technical-posts-by-2030/.

43. Amanda Stansell and Daniel Zhao, "Diversity Now: How Companies and Workers Are Bringing Nationwide Social Justice Protests to the Workplace," Glassdoor, July 15, 2020, www.glassdoor.com/research/diversity-jobs-reviews.

44. Stansell and Zhao, "Diversity Now: How Companies and Workers Are Bringing Nationwide Social Justice Protests to the Workplace," https://www.glassdoor.com/research/diversity-jobs-reviews/.

## CHAPTER 1

1. Iora Health, "Iora Health Closes $126 Million Series F Funding Round," *Cision PR Newswire*, February 10, 2020, www.prnewswire.com/news-releases/iora-health-closes-126-million-series-f-funding-round-301001846.html.

2. Vijay Govindarajan and Ravi Ramamurti, "Transforming Health Care from the Ground Up," *Harvard Business Review*, July–August 2018, https://hbr.org/2018/07/transforming-health-care-from-the-ground-up.

3. Craig R. Scott and Stephen A. Rains, "Anonymous Communication in Organizations: Assessing Use and Appropriateness," *Management Communication Quarterly* 19, no. 2 (2005): 157–197, https://doi.org/10.1177%2F0893318905279191.

4. Officevibe Content Team, "12 Mind-Blowing Employee Survey Statistics," October 2, 2021, https://officevibe.com/blog/employee-surveys-infographic.

5. Iora Health, *Iora 10 Years: Celebrating 10 Years of Impact* (Boston: Iora Health, 2020), https://online.pubhtml5.com/fqas/mguc/#p=1.

6. Heike Bruch, et al., "Strategic Change Decisions: Doing the Right Change Right," *Journal of Change Management* 5, no. 1 (2005): 97–107, https://doi.org/10.1080/14697010500067390.

7. Ben & Jerry's, "Silence Is NOT an Option," accessed February 9, 2022, www.benjerry.com/about-us/media-center/dismantle-white-supremacy.

8. Bruch, et al., "Strategic Change Decisions."

9. Andrew D. F. Price and K. Chahal, "A Strategic Framework for Change Management," *Construction Management and Economics* 24, no. 3 (2006): 237–251, https://doi.org/10.1080/01446190500227011.

10. Rune Lines, "Influence of Participation in Strategic Change: Resistance, Organizational Commitment and Change Goal Achievement," *Journal of Change Management* 4, no. 3 (2004): 193–215, https://doi.org/10.1080/1469701042000221696.

11.. "One Medical Announces Agreement to Acquire Iora Health," press release, One Medical, June 7, 2021, https://investor.onemedical.com/news-releases/news-release-details/one-medical-announces-agreement-acquire-iora-health.

12.. "One Medical Announces."

13. Rushika Fernandopulle now serves as the chief innovation officer at One Medical.

## CHAPTER 2

1. Theresa M. Welbourne, et al., "The Case for Employee Resource Groups: A Review and Social Identity Theory-Based Research Agenda," *Personnel Review* 46, no. 8 (2017): 1816–1834, https://doi.org/10.1108/PR-01-2016-0004.

2. Daniel Victor, "Pepsi Pulls Ad Accused of Trivializing Black Lives Matter," *New York Times*, April 5, 2017, https://www.nytimes.com/2017/04/05/business/kendall-jenner-pepsi-ad.html.

3. Steve Robson, "Team behind controversial Pepsi ad accused of 'lack of diversity' as it emerges 'ALL those credited are white,'" *Mirror*, April 6, 2017, https://www.mirror.co.uk/news/world-news/team-behind-controversial-pepsi-ad-10169148.

4. Josh Terrell, et al., "Gender Differences and Bias in Open Source: Pull Request Acceptance of Women versus Men," *Peer Journal of Computer Science* 3 (2017): e111; Claudia Goldin and Cecilia Rouse, "Orchestrating Impartiality: The Impact of 'Blind' Auditions on Female Musicians," *American Economic Review* 90, no. 4 (September 2000): 715–741.

5. Jessica Nordell, "How Slack Got Ahead in Diversity," *Atlantic*, April 26, 2018, www.theatlantic.com/technology/archive/2018/04/how-slack-got-ahead-in-diversity/558806/.

6. Team at Slack, "Diversity at Slack, an Update on Our Data, April 2018," Slack, April 17, 2018, https://slack.com/blog/news/diversity-at-slack-2.

7. Team at Slack, "Diversity at Slack, an Update, April 2021," Slack, April 21, 2021, https://slack.com/blog/news/diversity-at-slack-2021.

8. Team at Slack, "Diversity at Slack, an Update, April 2020," Slack, April 28, 2021, https://slack.com/blog/news/diversity-at-slack-2020.

9. Team at Slack, "Diversity at Slack, an Update, April 2020."

10. Future Forum, "Win the Battle for Talent," accessed April 18, 2022, https://futureforum.com/.

11. Sheela Subramanian, "The End of Business as Usual: The Power of Empathetic Management in an Age of Uncertainty," Future Forum, October 5, 2021, https://futureforum.com/2021/10/05/how-to-manage-through-uncertainty-playbook/.

12. Frances Brooks Taplett, et al., "It's Frontline Leaders Who Make or Break Progress on Diversity," Boston Consulting Group, March 5, 2020, www.bcg.com/en-us/publications/2020/frontline-leaders-make-break-progress-diversity.

## CHAPTER 3

1. Haley Draznin, "PwC Chairman: CEOs Have a Responsibility to Help Make America More Inclusive," *CNN*, November 26, 2018, www.cnn.com/2018/11/26/success/pwc-chairman-diversity-boss-files/index.html.

2. For the Sterling killing, see Kevin Litten, "In Alton Sterling Shooting, Baton Rouge Police Officers Won't Face Federal Charges: Reports," *New Orleans Times-Picayune*, May 7, 2017, www.nola.com/news/crime_police/article_1f5bb5ce-7d65-5958-aa2f-8123dfbfb8ba.html. For Castile killing, see Mitch Smith, "Video of Police Killing of Philando Castile Is Publicly Released," *New York Times*, June 20, 2017, www.nytimes.com/2017/06/20/us/police-shooting-castile-trial-video.html.

3. Manny Fernandez, et al., "Five Dallas Officers Were Killed as Payback, Police Chief Says," *New York Times*, July 8, 2016, www.nytimes.com/2016/07/09/us/dallas-police-shooting.html.

4. Megan Slack, "Supreme Court Strikes Down Defense Marriage Act," Whitehouse President Barack Obama, archives, June 26, 2013, https://obamawhitehouse.archives.gov/blog/2013/06/26/supreme-court-strikes-down-defense-marriage-act.

5. PwC, "LGBT Partner Advisory Board," CEO Action for Diversity & Inclusion, accessed April 18, 2022, www.ceoaction.com/actions/lgbt-partner-advisory-board/.

6. PwC, "Start: PwC's Diversity Internship Experience," accessed January 11, 2021, www.pwc.com/us/en/careers/entry-level/programs-events/start.html.

7. "Disability Equality Index," AAPD, https://www.aapd.com/disability-equality -index/.

8. PwC, "Leading with Trust, Transparency and Purpose: FY21 PwC Purpose Report," accessed March 30, 2022, www.pwc.com/us/en/about-us/purpose-and-values/ assets/fy21-pwc-purpose-report-full-report.pdf. The 2020 report acknowledged limitations with the data: "We have not had a robust self-identification campaign in the recent past, so the figures for veterans, LGBTQ+, and individuals with disabilities are likely not fully representative of our workforce" (PwC, "Building on a culture of belonging," 2020, https://www.pwc.com/us/en/about-us/diversity/assets/diversity-inclusion -transparency-report.pdf).

9. Draznin, "CEOs Have a Responsibility."

10. CEO Action for Diversity & Inclusion, "Bringing Business, Communities and Policy Together to Drive Change," CEO Action for Racial Equity Fellowship, accessed January 12, 2021, www.ceoaction.com/racial-equity/.

11. Kavya Vaghul, "A Small Fraction of Corporations Share Diversity Data but Disclosure Is Rapidly on the Rise," Just Capital, January 19, 2021, https://justcapital.com/ news/a-small-fraction-of-corporations-share-diversity-data-but-disclosure-is-rapidly-on -the-rise/.

12. PwC, *Global Annual Review 2021*, accessed January 12, 2021, www.pwc.com/gx/ en/about/global-annual-review-2021/clients.html.

13. Tim Ryan, "PwC: The New Equation," PwC, promotional film and transcript, accessed January 12, 2021, www.pwc.com/us/en/the-new-equation.

14. Ryan, "PwC: The New Equation."

15. PwC, "PwC Announces the New Equation," press release, PwC, June 15, 2021, www.pwc.com/us/en/about-us/newsroom/press-releases/pwc-announces-the-new -equation.html.

16. PwC, "Trust Leadership Institute: It's Time for a New Era of Leadership Trust," 2017, accessed April 18, 2022, www.pwc.com/us/en/about-us/tomorrow-takes-trust/trust -leadership-institute-overview.html.

17. Clara L. Wilkins, et al., "You Can Win but I Can't Lose: Bias against High-Status Groups Increases Their Zero-Sum Beliefs about Discrimination," *Journal of Experimental Social Psychology* 57 (2015): 1–14, https://doi.org/10.1016/j.jesp.2014.10.008.

18. Clara L. Wilkins and Cheryl R. Kaiser, "Racial Progress as Threat to the Status Hierarchy: Implications for Perceptions of Anti-White Bias," *Psychological Science* 25, no. 2 (2014): 439–446, www.jstor.org/stable/24539817.

19. Manny T. Martinez, et al., "Former Dallas Police Officer Is Guilty of Murder for Killing Her Neighbor," *New York Times*, October 1, 2019, www.nytimes.com/2019/10/01/ us/amber-guyger-trial-verdict-botham-jean.html.

20. Georgetown University, McDonough School of Business, "Building Towards Workplace Utopia: A Conversation with Tim Ryan, U.S. Chair and Senior Partner, PwC," video, YouTube, December 3, 2020, www.youtube.com/watch?v=WA2ul4CG0WI&t=8s.

21. https://www.cnn.com/2019/10/04/us/botham-jean-pwc-portrait-trnd/index .html. https://www.kait8.com/2020/09/04/botham-jean-business-scholarship-recipients -announced/.

## CHAPTER 4

1. Uncle Nearest, "The Best Whiskey Maker the World Never Knew," Uncle Nearest, Inc., accessed November 30, 2021, https://unclenearest.com/history/.

2. Clay Risen, "Jack Daniel's Embraces a Hidden Ingredient: Help from a Slave," *New York Times*, June 25, 2016, www.nytimes.com/2016/06/26/dining/jack-daniels-whiskey -nearis-green-slave.html.

3. Cynthia Graber and Nicola Twilley, "The Secret History of the Slave behind Jack Daniel's Whiskey," *Gastropod* (podcast), January 28, 2019, https://gastropod.com/the -secret-history-of-the-slave-behind-jack-daniels-whiskey/.

4. Fawn Weaver, quoted in Graber and Twilley, "Slave behind Jack Daniel's Whiskey."

5. Elizabeth G. Dunn, "A Black Whiskey Entrepreneur Will Help Bankroll Others Like Her," *New York Times*, June 1, 2021, www.nytimes.com/2021/06/01/dining/drinks/ uncle-nearest-whiskey-black-owned.html.

6. Uncle Nearest, "More about Uncle Nearest," Uncle Nearest Inc., accessed November 30, 2021, https://unclenearest.com/; Melita Kiely, "Breaking Boundaries: Fawn Weaver, Uncle Nearest CEO," *Spirit's Business*, October 1, 2020, www.thespiritsbusiness .com/2020/10/fawn-weaver-on-creating-uncle-nearest-whiskey/.

7. Uncle Nearest, "Most Awarded American Whiskey or Bourbon 2019, 2020, and 2021," Uncle Nearest Inc., accessed April 18, 2022, https://unclenearest.com/awards.

8. "Groundbreaking Study of Black Business Owners in the Wine Industry Reveals the Immediate Need for Inclusion & Equity," *Wine Industry Network Advisor*, July 27, 2021, https://wineindustryadvisor.com/2021/07/27/study-black-business-owners-reveals -need-inclusion-equity.

9. Jasmine Vaughn-Hall, "This Is America: Black Excellence Is an Ancestral Declaration That Exceeds Hashtags," *USA Today*, February 19, 2021, www.usatoday .com/story/news/2021/02/18/america-black-excellence-declaration-exceeds-trends/ 6788074002/.

10. Beverly D. Tatum, "'Why Are All the Black Kids Still Sitting Together in the Cafeteria?' and Other Conversations about Race in the Twenty-First Century," *Liberal Education* 103, no. 3–4 (2017).

11. Gallup and Purdue University, "Great Jobs, Great Lives: The 2014 Gallup-Purdue Index Report," 2014, www.gallup.com/services/176768/2014-gallup-purdue-index-report .aspx?_ga=2.2523127.69906958.1641933029-1307002563.1641933029.

12. Barbara S. Lawrence and Neha Parikh Shah, "Homophily: Measures and Meaning," *Academy of Management Annals*, 14, no. 2 (August 10, 2020): 513–597, https:// doi.org/10.5465/annals.2018.0147.

13. Lawrence and Shah (2020: 3); Gokhan Ertug, et al., "What Does Homophily Do? A Review of the Consequences of Homophily," *Academy of Management Annals* 16, no. 1 (May 2021): 38–69.

14. Thomas M. Rand and Kenneth N. Wexley, "Demonstration of the Effect, 'Similar to Me,' in Simulated Employment Interviews," *Psychological Reports* 36, no. 2 (1975): 535–544.

15. Michael A. Stoll, et al., "Why Are Black Employers More Likely Than White Employers to Hire Blacks?," discussion paper 1236-01, Institute for Research on Poverty, University of Wisconsin–Madison, September 2001, www.researchgate.net/publication/ 228772136.

16. For Black American spending, see Kori Hale, "The $300 Billion Black American Consumerism Bag Breeds Big Business Opportunities," *Forbes*, September 17, 2021, www .forbes.com/sites/korihale/2021/09/17/the-300-billion-black-american-consumerism-bag -breeds-big-business-opportunities/?sh=69b0cdf534fc.

17. Ranjay Gulati, "The Soul of a Start-Up," *Harvard Business Review*, July–August 2019, https://hbr.org/2019/07/the-soul-of-a-start-up.

18. Uncle Nearest, "Join Our Team," Uncle Nearest Inc., accessed April 18, 2022, https://unclenearest.com/join-our-team.

19. Stephen Gandel, "Wells Fargo CEO Apologizes for Blaming Lack of Diversity on 'Limited Pool of Black Talent,'" *CBS News*, September 23, 2020, www.cbsnews.com/ news/wells-fargo-ceo-black-talent-limited.

20. Gandel, "Wells Fargo CEO Apologizes."

21. Fawn Weaver, quoted in Ted Simmons, "Jack Daniel's and Uncle Nearest Launch New Diversity Initiative," *Whisky Advocate*, June 15, 2020, www.whiskyadvocate.com/jack -daniels-uncle-nearest-diversity-initiative/.

22. Fawn Weaver, quoted in Simmons, "Jack Daniel's and Uncle Nearest."

23. Fawn Weaver, quoted in Simmons.

24. Fawn Weaver, quoted in Simmons.

25. Gabrielle Pharms, "Inside the Uncle Nearest and Jack Daniel's Partnership to Diversify the Spirits Industry," *Alcohol Professor*, June 26, 2020, www.alcoholprofessor .com/blog-posts/inside-the-uncle-nearest-and-jack-daniels-partnership-to-diversify-the -spirits-industry.

26. Pharms, "Uncle Nearest and Jack Daniel's."

## CHAPTER 5

1.. "United Automobile Workers v. Johnson Controls, 499 U.S. 187 (1991)," Justia US Supreme Court, accessed April 18, 2022, https://supreme.justia.com/cases/federal/ us/499/187/.

2. Terry Gross, "Anita Hill Started a Conversation about Sexual Harassment: She's Not Done Yet," interview with Anita Hill, *Fresh Air* (NPR), September 28, 2021, www.npr .org/2021/09/28/1040911313/anita-hill-belonging-sexual-harassment-conversation.

3. Moss Adams, "2018 Annual Report," accessed April 18, 2022, www.mossadams .com/getmedia/1609719f-764c-4cb3-9ae0-98bfdbcfadac/2018-forum-w-annual-report.

4. Moss Adams, "Inclusion and Diversity: 2019 Annual Report," accessed April 18, 2022, www.mossadams.com/getmedia/efca1604-247f-4f1d-8158-5c8b69ee4554/ inclusion___diversity_2019_annual_report.pdf.

5. The World Bank, "Labor Force Participation Rate, Female (% of Female Population Ages 15–64) (Modeled ILO Estimate)—United States," chart, accessed April 18, 2022, https://data.worldbank.org/indicator/SL.TLF.ACTI.FE.ZS?end=2019&locations=US& start=1990. Data from International Labour Organization, ILOSTAT database, retrieved on June 15, 2021.

6. The World Bank, "Labor Force, Female (% of Total Labor Force)," chart, accessed April 18, 2022, https://data.worldbank.org/indicator/SL.TLF.TOTL.FE.ZS?end=2019& start=1990. Data from International Labour Organization, ILOSTAT database, retrieved on June 15, 2021.

7. William Scarborough, "What the Data Says about Women in Management between 1980 and 2010," hbr.org, February 23, 2018, https://hbr.org/2018/02/what-the-data-says-about-women-in-management-between-1980-and-2010.

8. The World Bank, "Population, Female (% of Total Population)," chart, accessed April 18, 2022, https://data.worldbank.org/indicator/SP.POP.TOTL.FE.ZS. Data from International Labour Organization, ILOSTAT database, retrieved on June 15, 2021.

9. The "unconscious bias test" Schmidt is referring to is the Implicit Association Test, which measures the strength of associations between concepts (e.g., Black people, gay people) and evaluations (e.g., good, bad) or stereotypes (e.g., athletic, clumsy). The main idea is that making a response is easier when closely related items share the same response key. See Project Implicit, "Preliminary Information," Harvard University, accessed April 18, 2022, https://implicit.harvard.edu/implicit/takeatest.html.

10. Andrew Ross Sorkin, "Outraged in Private, Many C.E.O.s Fear the Wrath of the President," *New York Times*, August 14, 2017, www.nytimes.com/2017/08/14/business/dealbook/merck-trump-charlottesville-ceos.html.

11. Greg J. Sears and Patricia M. Rowe, "A Personality-Based Similar-to-Me Effect in the Employment Interview: Conscientiousness, Affect-Versus Competence-Mediated Interpretations, and the Role of Job Relevance," *Canadian Journal of Behavioural Science* 35, no. 1 (January 2003): 13–24, http://dx.doi.org/10.1037/h0087182; Lynn A. McFarland, et al., "Examination of Structured Interview Ratings Across Time: The Effects of Applicant Race, Rater Race, and Panel Composition," *Journal of Management* 30, no. 4 (2004): 435–452, https://doi.org/10.1016/j.jm.2003.09.004.

12. Michele J. Gelfand, et al., "Discrimination in Organizations: An Organizational-Level Systems Perspective," in *Discrimination at Work: The Psychological and Organizational Bases*, ed. Robert L. Dipboye and Adrienne Colella (New York: Psychology Press, 2005), 89–116.

13. Ibram X. Kendi, *How to Be an Antiracist* (New York: One World, 2019), 231.

## CHAPTER 6

1. Sodexo, "Who We Are," accessed April 18, 2022, https://us.sodexo.com/about-us.html.

2. Associated Press, "Sodexho Settles Discrimination Suit for $80M," *Fox News*, January 13, 2015, www.foxnews.com/story/sodexho-settles-discrimination-suit-for-80m.

3. David A. Thomas and Stephanie J. Creary, "Shifting the Diversity Climate: The Sodexo Solution Case Study," Case 412-020 (Boston: Harvard Business School, July 2011), 4–5.

4. Mary Baker and Teresa Zuech, "Gartner HR Research Identifies Six Gaps between Leader and Employee Sentiment on the Future Employee Experience," press release, Gartner, August 5, 2021, www.gartner.com/en/newsroom/press-releases/2021-08-04-gartner-hr-research-identifies-six-gaps-between-leader-and-employee-sentiment-on-the-future-employee-experience.

5. Adam D. Galinsky, et al., "Power and Perspective-Taking: A Critical Examination," *Journal of Experimental Social Psychology* 67 (2016): 91–92.

# Notes

6. "Introspection after Allegations of Discrimination," in *Diversifying the American Workplace*, special series, *NPR*, January 12, 2010, www.npr.org/templates/story/story.php?storyId=122456071.

7. Sean Madigan, "Sodexho Marriott Services Sold to French Parent for $1.1B," *Washington Business Journal*, June 15, 2001, www.bizjournals.com/washington/stories/2001/06/11/daily34.html.

8. Jim Harter, "Why Some Leaders Have Their Employees' Trust, and Some Don't," Gallup Workplace, June 13, 2019, www.gallup.com/workplace/258197/why-leaders-employees-trust-don.aspx.

9. Stephanie N. Downey, et al., "The Role of Diversity Practices and Inclusion in Promoting Trust and Employee Engagement," *Journal of Applied Social Psychology* 45, no. 1 (2015): 35–44.

10. Rohini Anand, *Leading Global Diversity, Equity, and Inclusion: A Guide to Systemic Change in Multinational Organizations* (Oakland, CA: Berrett-Koehler, 2021), 18.

11. Thomas and Creary, "Shifting the Diversity Climate," 5.

12. Pamela Babcock, "Diversity Accountability Requires More Than Numbers," SRHM, April 13, 2009, www.shrm.org/resourcesandtools/hr-topics/behavioral-competencies/global-and-cultural-effectiveness/pages/morethannumbers.aspx.

13. Anand, *Leading Global Diversity, Equity, and Inclusion*, 11.

14. Lisa H. Nishii and Mustafa F. Özbilgin, "Global Diversity Management: Towards a Conceptual Framework," *International Journal of Human Resource Management* 18, no. 11 (2007): 1,883–1,894.

15. Alain Klarsfeld, et al., "Introduction: Equality and Diversity in 14 Countries: Analysis and Summary," in *International Handbook on Diversity Management at Work: Country and Thematic Perspectives on Diversity and Equal Treatment*, 2nd ed., ed. Alain Klarsfeld, et al. (Cheltenham, UK: Edward Elgar, 2014), doi: 10.4337/9780857939319.00005.

16. Thomas and Creary, "Shifting the Diversity Climate," 7.

17. Amelia Ransom, "What Does D&I Look Like for a Global Organization?," interview by Ella F. Washington and Camille Lloyd, podcast, *Cultural Competence*, January 26, 2021, min. 18:41, https://podcasts.apple.com/us/podcast/what-does-d-i-look-like-for-a-global-organization/id1543925509?i=1000506665230.

18. UN General Assembly, "Elimination of Racism, Racial Discrimination, Xenophobia and Related Intolerance: Comprehensive Implementation of and Follow-Up to the Durban Declaration and Programme of Action," 2011, https://digitallibrary.un.org/record/3896183?ln=en.

19. Thomas and Creary, "Shifting the Diversity Climate," 7.

20. Thomas and Creary, 8.

21. Thomas and Creary, 10.

22. Thomas and Creary, 12.

23. Rohini Anand, "Diversity and Inclusion Report: Message from Rohini Anand, Senior Vice President and Group Chief Diversity Officer," Sodexo, Fiscal 2010 annual publications, accessed April 18, 2022, https://s3-us-west-2.amazonaws.com/ungc-production/attachments/11349/original/2010_Diversity_Inclusion_report.pdf?1311372930.

24. Sodexo, "At White House Event Sodexo Announces Exceeding Leadership Gender Balance Goals," press release, Sodexo, *3BL Media*, April 12, 2016, www.3blmedia.com/news/white-house-event-sodexo-announces-exceeding-leadership-gender-balance-goals.

25. Sodexo, "Sodexo Included in the 2021 Bloomberg Gender-Equality Index, Recognizing Our Commitment to Advancing Women in the Workplace," press release, Sodexo, January 27, 2021, www.sodexo.com/media/2021-bloomberg-gender-equality-index.html.

26. SodexoMagic, "About Us," Sodexo, accessed October 12, 2021, https://us.sodexo.com/services/sodexo-magic/about-us.html.

27. Dasha Ross-Smith, "SodexoMagic and Goodr Partner to Combat Food Insecurity and Waste," press release, Sodexo, *GlobeNewswire*, November 18, 2021, www.globenewswire.com/news-release/2021/11/18/2337588/0/en/SodexoMagic-and-Goodr-Partner-to-Combat-Food-Insecurity-and-Waste.html.

28. Nicole Pierce, "SodexoMAGIC Donates 1,000 'Welcome Back to School—Safe at Home' Safety Kits to Chicago Public Schools Students upon Returning to In-Person Learning," press release, Sodexo, *GlobeNewswire*, March 23, 2021, www.globenewswire.com/news-release/2021/03/23/2197720/0/en/SodexoMAGIC-Donates-1-000-Welcome-back-to-School-Safe-at-Home-Safety-Kits-to-Chicago-Public-Schools-Students-Upon-Returning-to-In-Person-Learning.html.

29. Sodexo Operations, "Sodexo's Gender Balance Study, 2018: Expanded Outcomes over 5 Years," Sodexo USA, Gaithersburg, MD, accessed April 18, 2022, www.sodexo.com/files/live/sites/com-wwd/files/02%20PDF/Case%20Studies/2018_Gender-Balance-Study_EN.pdf.

30. Samuel Wells, "Why 'LGBTQ-Welcoming' Will Soon Be a Hallmark of the Most Successful Senior Living Communities: A Primer for Operators, Marketers & Leadership," Sodexo USA, Gaithersburg, MD, accessed April 18, 2022, https://assets2.hrc.org/thelei/documents/LGBTQSeniorsSodexoWhitePaper.pdf.

31. Laura Shipler Chico, "Addressing Culture and Origins across the Globe: Lessons from Australia, Brazil, Canada, the United Kingdom and the United States," Sodexo, accessed April 18, 2022, www.sodexo.com/files/live/sites/com-wwd/files/02%20PDF/Reports/Addressing%20Culture%20and%20Origins%20Across%20the%20Globe.pdf.

32. "Healthcare Administrators: The 2043 Business Imperative—Advocating for Hispanic Leadership in Healthcare and Cultural Competence," Sodexo USA, accessed April 18, 2022, https://us.sodexo.com/files/live/sites/com-us/files/industry/healthcare/D%26IHealthcareLeadershipWhitePaper_2019_final.pdf.

33. Sodexo, "Diversity & Inclusion Annual Report: Creating a Better Future," Sodexo Quality of Life Services, 2019, https://tracks.sodexonet.com/files/live/sites/com-us/files/inspired-thinking/research-reports/2020/D_26I_Annual_Report_Final.pdf.

34. John P. Kotter and Leonard A. Schlesinger, "Choosing Strategies for Change," *Harvard Business Review*, July–August 2008, https://hbr.org/2008/07/choosing-strategies-for-change.

35. Society for Human Resource Management, "Together Forward @Work: The Journey to Equity and Inclusion," summer 2020, https://shrmtogether.wpengine.com/wp-content/uploads/2020/08/20-1412_TFAW_Report_RND7_Pages.pdf, 11.

36. Sodexo, "Sodexo Listed in DiversityInc's Hall of Fame and Named as a Top Company for Black Executives and Top Company for Talent Acquisition for Women

of Color," press release, Sodexo, May 24, 2021, https://us.sodexo.com/media/news-releases/2021-awards-diversity-inc.html.

37.  Anand, *Leading Global Diversity, Equity, and Inclusion*, 12.


CHAPTER 7

1.  Corie Barry, "A Note From Best Buy's CEO: We Will Do Better," June 3, 2020, https://corporate.bestbuy.com/a-note-from-best-buys-ceo-we-will-do-better/.

2.  Best Buy, "Best Buy Strengthens Its Commitment to Gender Equity," October 13, 2017, https://corporate.bestbuy.com/best-buy-strengthens-commitment-gender-equity.

3.  Chris Havens, "Gender Equality Is a Priority at Best Buy," Best Buy, March 5, 2019, https://corporate.bestbuy.com/gender-equality-is-a-priority-at-best-buy.

4.  Eve Tahmincioglu, "Best Buy to Get Woman CEO; Majority Female Board," *Directors & Boards*, April 17, 2019, www.directorsandboards.com/news/best-buy-get-woman-ceo-majority-female-board.

5.  Best Buy, "Board of Directors," accessed April 18, 2022, https://investors.bestbuy.com/investor-relations/governance/board-of-directors/default.aspx.

6.  "The Dialogue Divide Research Report," The Dialogue Project, 2020, https://www.dialogueproject.study/.

7.  The Dialogue Project (n.d.), The Dialogue Divide Research Report, accessed February 6, 2022, www.dialogueproject.study/research.

8.  Hubert Joly and Caroline Lambert, *The Heart of Business: Leadership Principles for the Next Era of Capitalism* (Boston: Harvard Business Review Press, 2021).

9.  Best Buy, "Hubert Joly Signs CEO Pledge for Diversity and Inclusion," July 25, 2017, https://corporate.bestbuy.com/hubert-joly-signs-ceo-pledge-diversity-inclusion/.

10.  Robert G. Isaac, et al., "Leadership and Motivation: The Effective Application of Expectancy Theory, *Journal of Managerial Issues*, 2001, 212–226.

11.  Victor Vroom, *Work and Motivation*, Wiley and Sons, 1964.

12.  Charlan Jeanne Nemeth, et al., "Improving Decision Making by Means of Dissent," *Journal of Applied Social Psychology* 31, no. 1 (2001): 48–58.

13.  Muqtafi Akhmad, et al., "Closed-Mindedness and Insulation in Groupthink: Their Effects and the Devil's Advocacy as a Preventive Measure," *Journal of Computational Social Science* 4 (2021): 455–478, https://doi.org/10.1007/s42001-020-00083-8; Colin MacDougall and Frances Baum, "The Devil's Advocate: A Strategy to Avoid Groupthink and Stimulate Discussion in Focus Groups," *Qualitative Health Research*, 7, no. 4 (1997): 532–541, https://doi.org/10.1177/104973239700700407; Tom Kelley, *The Ten Faces of Innovation: IDEO's Strategies for Beating the Devil's Advocate and Driving Creativity throughout Your Organization* (New York: Crown Business, 1997).

14.  Greatheart Leader Labs, "The Study on White Men Leading through Diversity and Inclusion," executive summary, January 2013, www.whitemensleadershipstudy.com/pdf/WMLS%20Executive%20Summary.pdf.

15.  Best Buy, "Tomorrow Works Here," job search web page, accessed April 18, 2022, www.bestbuy-jobs.com/diversity.

16.  Becca Johnson, "Best Buy, Black Leaders Working to Improve Promotion, Recruitment," Best Buy, February 2, 2020, https://corporate.bestbuy.com/best-buy-black-leaders-working-to-improve-promotion-recruitment.

17. Katie Koranda, "Best Buy Makes 2020 DiversityInc Noteworthy List," May 6, 2020, https://corporate.bestbuy.com/best-buy-makes-2020-diversityinc-noteworthy-list/.

18. "The 2022 World's Most Ethical Companies Honoree List," 2022, https://worldsmostethicalcompanies.com/honorees/.

19. Best Buy, "Doing a World of Good: Fiscal Year 2020, Environmental, Social and Governance Report," accessed April 18, 2022, https://corporate.bestbuy.com/wp-content/uploads/2020/06/Best-Buy-Fiscal-2020-ESG-Report.pdf.

20. Becca Johnson, "Best Buy Recognized for Leading with Inclusion," Best Buy, August 19, 2020, https://corporate.bestbuy.com/best-buy-recognized-for-leading-with-inclusion.

21. Bianca Jones, "Best Buy Commits More Than $44 Million to Diversity, Inclusion and Community Efforts," Best Buy, December 9, 2020, https://corporate.bestbuy.com/best-buy-commits-more-than-44-million-to-diversity-inclusion-and-community-efforts/.

22. Ale Valeriano, "Best Buy Creates Scholarship Fund for HBCU Students," Best Buy, January 15, 2021, https://corporate.bestbuy.com/best-buy-creates-scholarship-fund-for-hbcu-students/.

23. Best Buy, "Doing a World of Good: Fiscal Year 2020."

24. Jones, "Best Buy Commits More Than $4 Million."

25. "Best Buy Commits to Spending $1.2B with BIPOC and Diverse Businesses by 2025," Best Buy, June 24, 2021, https://corporate.bestbuy.com/best-buy-commits-to-spending-1-2b-with-bipoc-and-diverse-businesses-by-2025/.

26. Best Buy Teen Tech Center Programs, https://www.bestbuy.com/site/misc/teen-tech-center/pcmcat1530212400327.c?id=pcmcat1530212400327.

## CHAPTER 8

1. Emsi Burning Glass, "Parsing the Unemployment Rate for Community College Graduates," Emsi, May 30, 2014, www.economicmodeling.com/2014/05/30/parsing-the-unemployment-rate-for-community-college-graduates/; Community College Research Center, "Community College FAQs," accessed April 18, 2022, https://ccrc.tc.columbia.edu/community-college-faqs.html.

2. For the racial makeup of community colleges, see Brittney Davidson, Tess Henthorne, Josh Wyner, and Linda Perlstein, "Aligning Talent and Opportunity: An Employer Guide to Effective Community College Partnership," Aspen Institute, Washington, DC, September 26, 2019, https://highered.aspeninstitute.org/wp-content/uploads/2019/09/The-Employer-Guide_20190926_Final-for-Approval.pdf. For the economic status of these students, see Christine Cruzvergara, "Companies Hiring from Community Colleges Have a Leg Up: Here's Why," *Forbes*, May 27, 2021, www.forbes.com/sites/gradsoflife/2021/05/27/companies-hiring-from-community-colleges-have-a-leg-up-heres-why/?sh=318fa4683354.

3. Jeff Kavanaugh and Lakshmi Prabha, "Infosys Talent Radar 2019: How the Best Companies Get the Skills They Need to Thrive in the Digital Era," Infosys Knowledge Institute, 2019, www.infosys.com/navigate-your-next/research/talent-radar.html.

4. For difficulty in finding enough candidates, see Kavanaugh and Prabha, "Infosys Talent Radar 2019." For capabilities of people with associate's degrees, see Todd Deutsch, Deirdre Blackwood, Toi Eshun, and Zoia Alexanian, "New Report: Degree Inflation

Hurting Bottom Line of U.S. Firms, Closing Off Economic Opportunity for Millions of Americans," press release, Harvard Business School Newsroom, October 25, 2017, www .hbs.edu/news/releases/Pages/degree-inflation-us-competetiveness.aspx; Joseph B. Fuller and Manjari Raman, "Dismissed by Degrees: How Degree Inflation Is Undermining U.S. Competitiveness and Hurting America's Middle Class," Harvard Business School, October 2017, www.hbs.edu/managing-the-future-of-work/Documents/dismissed -by-degrees.pdf; and Sue Ellspermann and Jeff Kavanaugh, "Your Next Great Hire Is Graduating from a Community College," *EdSurge*, April 26, 2021, www.edsurge.com/ news/2021-04-26-your-next-great-hire-is-graduating-from-a-community-college.

5. Crystal L. Hoyt, et al., "I Can Do That: The Impact of Implicit Theories on Leadership Role Model Effectiveness," *Personality and Social Psychology Bulletin* 38, no. 2 (2012): 257–268; Thekla Morgenroth, et al., "The Motivational Theory of Role Modeling: How Role Models Influence Role Aspirants' Goals," *Review of General Psychology* 19, no. 4 (2015): 465–483.

6. Infosys, "Partners," accessed April 18, 2022, www.infosys.org/infosys-foundation -usa/grants.html.

7. Infosys, "Partners."

8. Infosys, "History: Infosys Is a Global Leader in Next-Generation Digital Services and Consulting," accessed April 19, 2022, www.infosys.com/about/history.html.

9. "Awards," Infosys, https://www.infosys.com/about/awards. html#:~:text=Infosys%20ranked%20No.,for%202002%20by%20Forbes%20Global.

10. Yoshita Singh, "HUL, TCS & Sun Pharma among most innovative companies in the world: Forbes," Business Today (India), August 20, 2015, https://www.businesstoday .in/latest/corporate/story/forbes-says-hul-tcs-and-sun-pharma-among-most-innovative -comapnies-in-the-wolrd-52636-2015-08-20.

11. Infosys, "Diversity and Inclusion," accessed April 19, 2022, www.infosys.com/ content/dam/infosys-web/en/about/corporate-responsibility/esg-vision-2030/diversity -and-inclusion.html.

12. JobsForHer, "DivHERsity Awards, 2020," accessed April 18, 2022, www.jobsforher .com/accelherate-2020/divhersity-showcase.

13. "Infosys Ranked Number 3 on 2019 Forbes 'World's Best Regarded Companies' List," September 25, 2019, https://www.infosys.com/newsroom/press-releases/2019/ worlds-best-regarded-companies2019.html.

14. "Infosys has been recognized by the Top Employer Institutes as a 2020 'Top Employer' in Australia and Singapore. We are among the top three employers in Japan," https://www.infosys.com/about/awards/top-employer-institutes2020.html.

15. "Infosys featured in the Top 10 Best Company for Women in India in 2021 Working Mother and Avtar Best Companies for Women in India (BCWI) and 'Exemplar of Inclusion' in the Working Mother & Avtar Most Inclusive Companies in India (MICI)," https://www .infosys.com/newsroom/features/2021/top-ten-best-company-women-india2021.html.

16. "Great Place to Work and Fortune Name Infosys One of the 2021 Best Big Companies to Work For," https://www.infosys.com/newsroom/features/2021/best-big -companies-work-for-2021.html.

17. Macrotrends, "Infosys Revenue 2010–2021," accessed April 18, 2022, www .macrotrends.net/stocks/charts/INFY/infosys/revenue; Infosys, "Investor Presentation," Infosys Limited, Bengaluru, India, 2019 (updated 2021), www.infosys.com/investors/ investorpresentation/ir-presentation.pdf.

18. Infosys, "Diversity and Inclusion."

19. Ananya Bhattacharya, "A Former Executive Is Accusing Infosys of Racism That Favours Indians," *Quartz India*, June 21, 2017, https://qz.com/india/1010965/a-former-executive-is-accusing-infosys-of-racism-that-favours-indians.

20. Wigdor, "Wigdor LLP Files EEOC Charge Alleging Systemic Gender and Race Discrimination at Infosys," Wigdor Law, January 13, 2021, www.wigdorlaw.com/infosys-gender-race-discrimination-eeoc; "Shannon Doyle, [redacted], Carrie Subacs, and Sylvie Thompson, Claimants, v. Infosys Limited, and Infosys Americas, Respondents," case submitted to Equal Employment Opportunity Commission, New York District Office, accessed April 19, 2022, https://regmedia.co.uk/2021/01/13/eeoc-infosys.pdf.

21. Infosys Foundation, "Overview," accessed April 18, 2022, www.infosys.com/infosys-foundation/about.html.

22. Infosys, "Reskill and Restart," accessed April 18, 2022, www.infosys.com/reskill restart-america.html.

23. Elizabeth Freedman, "Why Corporate and Political Leaders Turn To Infosys President Ravi Kumar About The Future Of Work," Forbes, June 9, 2021. https://www.forbes.com/sites/elizabethfreedman/2021/06/09/why-corporate-and-political-leaders-turn-to-infosys-president-ravi-kumar-about-the-future-of-work/?sh=6cf771c9dce0.

## CHAPTER 9

1. John C. Miller, et al., "Inside Denny's Decades-Long DEI Journey," hbr.org, September 13, 2021, https://hbr.org/2021/09/inside-dennys-decades-long-dei-journey.

2. Jim Adamson, *The Denny's Story: How a Company in Crisis Resurrected Its Good Name* (New York: Wiley, 2000), 9.

3. Stephen McGuire, et al., "Denny's Learns to Manage Diversity," *i-Manager's Journal on Management* 9, no. 4 (2015): 48–72, doi:10.26634/jmgt.9.4.3364.

4. Denny Chin and Jodi Golinsky, "Employment Discrimination: Moving Beyond *McDonnell Douglas*; A Simplified Method for Assessing Evidence in Discrimination Cases," *Brooklyn Law Review* 64, no. 2 (1998): 659–679.

5. Zachary W. Brewster and Sarah N. Rusche, "Quantitative Evidence of the Continuing Significance of Race: Tableside Racism in Full-Service Restaurants," *Journal of Black Studies* 43, no. 4 (2012): 359–384.

6. R. Rousseau, "New Denny's Ads Welcome Blacks," *Restaurants & Institutions* 107 (April 1997): 22, www.ou.edu/deptcomm/dodjcc/groups/02C2/reference%20list.htm. Vic Harris, et al., "Crisis Communication Strategies, Case Study: Denny's Class Action Lawsuit," US Department of Defense, accessed April 19, 2022, www.ou.edu/deptcomm/dodjcc/groups/02C2/Denny's.htm.

7. McGuire, et al., "Denny's Learns to Manage Diversity."

8. Anne Faircloth, "Denny's Changes Its Spots Not So Long Ago," *CNN Money*, May 13, 1996, https://money.cnn.com/magazines/fortune/fortune_archive/1996/05/13/212386/.

9. Howard Kohn, "Service with a Sneer," *New York Times Magazine*, November 6, 1994, www.nytimes.com/1994/11/06/magazine/service-with-a-sneer.html.

10. Faircloth, "Denny's Changes Its Spots."

11. U.S. v. TW Services, Inc. (U.S. District Court for the Northern District of California) 1993, U.S.Dist.LEXIS 7882, consent decree, April 1, 1993. For full text, see Civil Rights Litigation Clearinghouse, accessed April 19, 2022, www.clearinghouse.net/chDocs/public/DR-CA-0001-0009.pdf.

12. Denny's, *2020 Annual Report*, Denny's Corporation, Spartanburg, SC, accessed April 19, 2022, https://s29.q4cdn.com/169433746/files/doc_financials/2020/ar/2020 AnnualReport_IndexedPDF_V2.pdf.

13. Miller, et al., "Denny's Decades-Long DEI Journey."

14. Zachary W. Brewster and Gerald R. Nowak III, "Racial Prejudices, Racialized Workplaces, and Restaurant Servers' Hyperbolic Perceptions of Black–White Tipping Differences," *Cornell Hospitality Quarterly* 60, no. 2 (2019): 159–173.

15. Faircloth, "Denny's Changes Its Spots."

16. Zachary W. Brewster and Sarah N. Rusche, (2017). "The Effects of Racialized Workplace Discourse on Race-Based Service in Full-Service Restaurants," *Journal of Hospitality & Tourism Research* 41, no. 4 (2017): 398–414.

17. Michàlle E. Mor Barak, *Managing Diversity: Toward a Globally Inclusive Workplace* (Los Angeles: Sage, 2016), 246–256.

18. Mor Barak, *Managing Diversity*, 246–256.

19. Mor Barak, 246–256.

20. Faircloth, "Denny's Changes Its Spots."

21. "Denny's Participates in 2016 Corporate Equality Index," GlobeNewswire website, November 20, 2015, https://www.globenewswire.com/fr/news-release/ 2015/11/20/789339/0/en/Denny-s-Participates-in-2016-Corporate-Equality-Index .html.

22. Miller et al., "Denny's Decades-Long DEI Journey."

23. "Hungry to Win! 2020-2021 Diversity Report," Denny's, January 14, 2022, www .dennys.com/news/2020-2021-diversity-report.

24. "Hungry to Win! 2020–2021 Diversity Report," Denny's, http://dennysdiversity report.com/.

25. Denny's, https://www.dennys.com/sites/default/files/2021-09/Dennys-Social -Impact-Report.pdf.

26. Information provided by April Kelly-Drummond. Denny's, "We Love to Feed People: The Principles That Guide Us," Denny's web page, accessed April 18, 2022, www .dennys.com/company.

27. Brené Brown, "The Power of Vulnerability," video transcript, TEDxHouston, June 2010, www.ted.com/talks/brene_brown_the_power_of_vulnerability/transcript.

28. Miller et al., "Denny's Decades-Long DEI Journey."

29. Earl Fitzhugh et al., "It's Time for a New Approach to Racial Equity," McKinsey & Company, December 2, 2020, www.mckinsey.com/featured-insights/diversity-and- inclusion/its-time-for-a-new-approach-to-racial-equity.

30. VB Staff, "Report: 40% of Diverse Employees Say Their Companies Haven't Improved DEI Practices," *VentureBeat*, October 19, 2021, https://venturebeat.com/2021/ 10/19/report-40-of-diverse-employees-say-their-companies-havent-improved-dei -practices/.

31. Juliet Bourke and Bernadette Dillon, "The Diversity and Inclusion Revolution: Eight Powerful Truths," *Deloitte Review*, January 2018, www2.deloitte.com/content/dam/ insights/us/articles/4209_Diversity-and-inclusion-revolution/DI_Diversity-and-inclusion -revolution.pdf.

32. Amy C. Edmondson and Josephine P. Mogelof, "Explaining Psychological Safety in Innovation Teams: Organizational Culture, Team Dynamics, or Personality?," in

*Creativity and Innovation in Organizational Teams*, ed. Leigh L. Thompson and Hoon-Seok Choi, 129–156 (Psychology Press, 2006).

## CONCLUSION

1. Rachel Lobdell, "Introducing Measure Up, our partnership with Refinitiv to measure racial diversity," *Fortune*, November 17, 2020, https://fortune.com/2020/11/17/measure-up-fortune-refinitiv-racial-diversity/.

2. "FORTUNE and Refinitiv encourage unprecedented corporate diversity disclosure and accountability through new Measure Up partnership," PR Newswire, October 26, 2020, https://www.prnewswire.com/news-releases/fortune-and-refinitiv-encourage-unprecedented-corporate-diversity-disclosure-and-accountability-through-new-measure-up-partnership-301159688.html.

3. David Craig, "Companies will need courage to keep their promises on race," *Fortune*, June 2, 2021, https://fortune.com/2021/06/02/racial-equity-diversity-inclusion-data-fortune-500-measure-up/.

4. Grace Donnelly, "Only 3% of Fortune 500 Companies Share Full Diversity Data," *Fortune*, June 7, 2017, https://fortune.com/2017/06/07/fortune-500-diversity/.

5. Maro Carrasco, "Gen Z: Brands Need to Prioritize DEI and Gender Liberation," *Forbes*, March 1, 2022, www.forbes.com/sites/forbesagencycouncil/2022/03/01/gen-z-brands-need-to-prioritize-dei-and-gender-liberation.

## APPENDIX

1. Crunchbase, "Iora Health," accessed February 9, 2022, https://www.crunchbase.com/organization/iora-health/company_financials.

2. PitchBook, "Iora Health," accessed February 9, 2022, https://pitchbook.com/profiles/company/54034-21#overview.

3. Life Healthcare Inc., "At Iora Health, We Work to Restore Humanity to Healthcare," One Medical, accessed February 9, 2022.

4. The numbers differ according to source (Craft.co, Crunchbase, or PitchBook).

5. Megan P. McGrath, "Iora Health and Human Expand Relationship to Provide More Humana Medicare Advantage Plan Members Access to Additional Coordinated Care in Arizona, Georgia and Texas," *BusinessWire*, September 4, 2019, www.businesswire.com/news/home/20190904005339/en/Iora-Health-and-Humana-Expand-Relationship-to-Provide-More-Humana-Medicare-Advantage-Plan-Members-Access-to-Additional-Coordinated-Care-in-Arizona-Georgia-and-Texas.

6. Life Healthcare Inc., "At Iora Health, We Work to Restore Humanity to Healthcare."

7. Team at Slack, "Diversity at Slack, an Update, April 2020," Slack, April 28, 2021, https://slack.com/blog/news/diversity-at-slack-2020.

8. PwC, "Building on a Culture of Belonging," accessed April 19, 2022, www.pwc.com/us/en/about-us/purpose-and-values/purpose-report/diversity-equity-inclusion.html.

9. PwC, "Welcome to PwC Products, the Evolution of Problem Solving," accessed March 30, 2022, www.pwc.com/us/en/products.html.

10. Mike Davies, "PwC Global: How We Are Structured," PwC, accessed January 11, 2021, www.pwc.com/gx/en/about/corporate-governance/network-structure.html.

11. Davies, "PwC Global."

12. PwC, "Global Annual Review 2021: The New Equation; Building Trust, Delivering Sustained Outcomes," PwC, 2021, accessed January 11, 2022, www.pwc.com/gx/en/about-pwc/global-annual-review-2021/downloads/pwc-global-annual-review-2021.pdf.

13. Varya Davidson and Martijn Schouten, "Organisational Culture and Purpose: Harnessing Culture to Deliver Results," PwC, accessed January 11, 2021, www.pwc.com/gx/en/services/people-organisation/organisational-culture-and-purpose.html.

14. Mike Davies, "Our Clients."

15. Mike Davies, "Our Clients," in Global Annual Review 2021: Our Clients: The New Equation; Building Trust, Delivering Sustained Outcomes, by PwC, accessed January 11, 2021, www.pwc.com/gx/en/about/global-annual-review-2021/clients.html.

16. CEO Action for Diversity & Inclusion, "CEO Action for Diversity & Inclusion Is the Largest CEO-Driven Business Commitment to Advance Diversity and Inclusion in the Workplace," 2017, accessed January 11, 2021, www.ceoaction.com.

17. Laura Taylor, "Global Public Policy Committee: Role and Objective," accessed January 11, 2021, www.pwc.com/gx/en/about/global-regulatory-affairs/gppc-role-and-objective.html.

18. Mike Davies, "PwC Global: About Us," PwC, accessed January 11, 2021, https://www.pwc.com/gx/en/about.html.

19. Shannon Schuyler, "Responsible Business Leadership: What We Do Matters; Why We Do It Matters More," PwC, 2017, accessed January 11, 2021, www.pwc.com/us/en/about-us/corporate-responsibility.html.

20. PwC, "Stakeholder Engagement: How We Engage PwC Global Corporate Responsibility 2016," accessed January 11, 2021, www.pwc.com/gx/en/corporate-responsibility/assets/stakeholder-engagement.pdf.

21. Uncle Nearest, "More about Our Founder and CEO, Fawn Weaver," accessed April 19, 2022, https://unclenearest.com/fawnweaver/.

22. Uncle Nearest, "Distributors," accessed April 19, 2022, https://unclenearest.com/distributors.

23. Uncle Nearest, "Uncle Nearest Venture Fund," accessed April 19, 2022, https://unclenearest.com/unvf/.

24. Moss Adams, "Inclusion and Diversity: 2019 Annual Report," accessed April 18, 2022, www.mossadams.com/getmedia/efca1604-247f-4f1d-8158-5c8b69ee4554/inclusion___diversity_2019_annual_report.pdf.

25. Craft, "Moss Adams Competitors," accessed April 19, 2022, https://craft.co/moss-adams/competitors.

26. Sodexo, "A Better Tomorrow 2021: Sustainability & Corporate Social Responsibility Report," accessed May 5, 2022, https://us.sodexo.com/files/live/sites/com-us/files/our-impact/ABetterTomorrow2025Report.pdf.

27. SodexoMagic, "Serving Equality for Communities," accessed May 5, 2022, www.sodexomagic.com/sodexo-magic.html.

28. Sodexo Stop Hunger Foundation, "Our Vision," accessed May 5, 2022, http://us.stop-hunger.org/home/about-us/our-vision.html.

29.  "U.S. Political Activity & Public Policy Report 2021," Best Buy, https://corporate
.bestbuy.com/wp-content/uploads/2022/03/2021-Political-Activity-Public-Policy-Report
.pdf.

30.  Infosys, "About Us: Subsidiaries," accessed April 19, 2022, www.infosys.com/
about/subsidiaries.html.

31.  Infosys, "Gender Pay Report 2019," Infosys Limited, France Branch, accessed
April 19, 2022, www.infosys.com/careers/discover/culture/documents/infosys-gender
-pay-gap-report-eng-france2019.pdf.

32.  Shakeel Hashim, "Infosys Is Hiring 12,000 People—and Not from the Ivy League,"
*Protocol*, September 8, 2020, www.protocol.com/infosys-hiring-us-community-colleges.

33.  Yahoo! Finance, "Denny's Corporation (DENN)," accessed April 19, 2022, https://
finance.yahoo.com/quote/DENN/financials?p=DENN&guccounter=1.

34.  Denny's, "Investor Relations," accessed April 19, 2022, https://investor.dennys
.com/overview/default.aspx.

# INDEX

# Index

# Index

# Index

# ABOUT THE AUTHOR

**DR. ELLA F. WASHINGTON** is an organizational psychologist who finds inspiration through the intersection of business, diversity, and leadership. Her life's work has centered on elevating humanity in the workplace through the work of Diversity, Equity, and Inclusion. Dr. Washington has a wealth of experience through her involvement as the founder and CEO of Ellavate Solutions, a DEI strategy firm. She is a professor of practice at Georgetown University's McDonough School of Business, and is the co-host of Gallup's *Center of Black Voices Cultural Competence* podcast.

Dr. Washington has global consulting experience in the human capital space, which has allowed her to impact clients across myriad industries including financial services, sports and entertainment, oil and gas, higher education, and government. Previously, Dr. Washington worked at Gallup and led the Diversity and Inclusion practice where she provided insight to clients on issues of inclusion, culture, strategic diversity, and engagement. Her research and client work focuses on women in the workplace and barriers to inclusion for diverse groups, and working with organizations to build inclusive cultures.

Before joining Gallup, Dr. Washington was a talent management consultant at Ernst & Young and a DEI consultant at the Federal Reserve

Bank of Chicago. She earned her PhD in organizational behavior from the Kellogg School of Management at Northwestern University and her BA in psychology from Spelman College.

Growing up in Durham, North Carolina with a tight-knit family gave Dr. Washington her roots. Today she lives in Washington, DC and values balancing her work and personal life by remaining active in her church, giving back to her local community, traveling the world and staying closely connected with loved ones.

You can find Dr. Ella F. Washington at ellafwashington.com and on Twitter @ellafwashington.